The Cinema of John Huston

GERALD PRATLEY

Normally, John Huston lets his work speak for itself, shunning press conferences, public appearances and discussions. However, the well-known and respected Canadian broadcaster Gerald Pratley has persuaded this master filmmaker to tell the story of his early life and entire film career.

In this book—which has been distilled from some fourteen hours of tape-recorded reminiscing—Huston recalls how as a small boy he was privately entertained by Chaplin, how he progressed to writing scripts in Britain and Hollywood, and finally gained a directing break with *The Maltese Falcon.* On later pages, he describes his progress to location shooting with *The Treasure of the Sierra Madre* in Mexico, and how he became a regular traveller to far-flung locations in his efforts to provide audiences with original and challenging motion pictures. Huston talks of his experiments in style, of the great players and writers he has known, and also of his occasional failures.

This is a book that is both immensely enjoyable and highly instructive. Its value is further enhanced by detailed credits for all the films Huston has directed and a careful selection of over 70 photographs.

GERALD PRATLEY has been a film critic and commentator for CBC in Toronto since 1948. He is also director of the Ontario Film Institute and Theatre at the Ontario Science Centre in Toronto and chairman of the International Jury of the annual Canadian Film Awards Festival. He is a member of the Society for Cinema Studies (U.S.A.) and teaches film appreciation at various universities. He has written extensively about the Canadian cinema and has published three previous books with the Tantivy Press and A. S. Barnes: *The Cinema of John Frankenheimer, The Cinema of Otto Preminger.* and *The Cinema of David Lean.*

The Cinema of

JOHN HUSTON

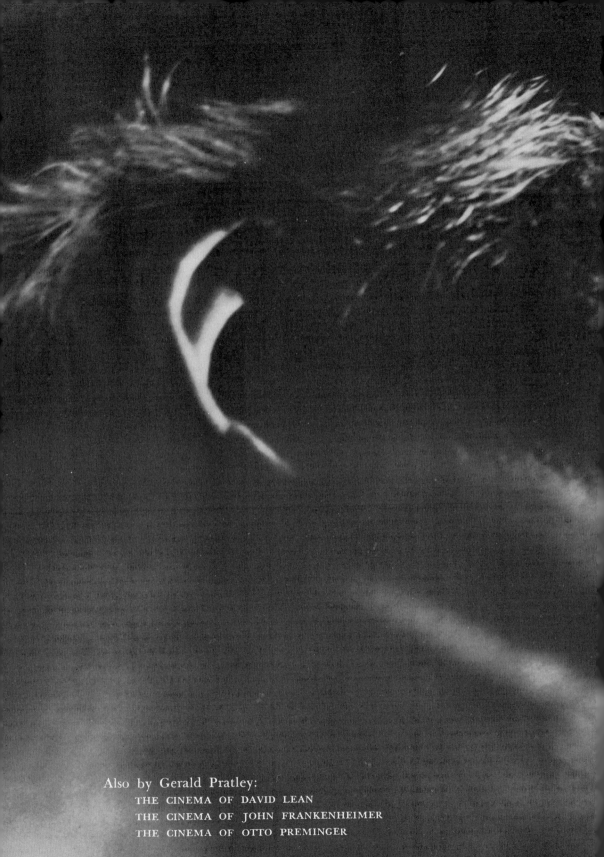

Also by Gerald Pratley:

THE CINEMA OF JOHN HUSTON

Gerald Pratley

SOUTH BRUNSWICK AND NEW YORK:
A. S. BARNES AND COMPANY
LONDON: THE TANTIVY PRESS

A. S. Barnes and Co., Inc.
Cranbury, New Jersey 08512

The Tantivy Press
Magdalen House
136–148 Tooley Street
London SE1 2TT

Library of Congress Cataloging in Publication Data

Pratley, Gerald.
    The cinema of John Huston.

    Includes index.
    1. Huston, John, 1906–   I. Title.
PN1998.A3H84   791.43′0233′0924   73-13192
ISBN 0-498-01443-6

PRINTED IN THE UNITED STATES OF AMERICA

Contents

Acknowledgements

The author and publishers wish to thank John Huston for the time he gave us in the preparation of this volume. Our thanks are also due to Gladys Hill, the British Film Institute (the source of most of the illustrations via the National Film Archive Stills Library), Joe Ritter (the illustrations from *Independence*), the Ontario Film Institute, and the Canadian Broadcasting Corporation (Robert Weaver), Toronto.

Prologue

AT THE BEST OF TIMES, studios never did look the way they were, and sometimes still are, presented on the screen. Moviegoers are familiar with films which either have a studio background, or in which the main characters visit a studio, and where, in either case, exterior shots would have us believe that hordes of extras dressed up as Red Indians, beefeaters, African natives, Arabs, cowboys and slave girls were at any given time making their way leisurely from one sound stage to another. On the set, all activity was frantic and high-pitched, with shouted commands, the noisy commencement of a take, and its termination by cries of "cut" from an irritated director. In actual fact, exotically dressed extras were rarely encountered on studio streets, the stars seldom lunched in the commissary, and activity on the sound stages was usually quiet, disciplined and unspectacular. The buildings themselves, so large outside, so big and empty inside, tend to overwhelm people, and seem to call for quietness and respect.

At the worst of times, studios tend to be depressing when productions have come to a stop due to the perennial crises which afflict companies, studios and countries with monotonous and cyclical regularity. The visitor walks into a graveyard of memories of personalities who came and worked there from around the world, departing and leaving discarded pieces of scenery to show that once famous films had been made. Names can still be found on office and dressing-room doors of people who created their world of make-believe, only to disappear for ever into the real world outside once their time was over.

In May 1973, the British cinema was in trouble once again. Financing by the Americans had been reduced, due largely to their country's balance of payments deficit, and unfavourable economic conditions in the U.K. contributed to a lack of money being made available to support production. Twickenham's stages were empty. A small studio with a long and interesting history, not at all like the big, better-known studios with their rows of stages and massive backlots, it is set in a quiet, tree-lined residential district and never comes into sight until the car turns into the narrow gates and stops in the cramped forecourt. A few workers drift by, others sit over indifferent food in the cafeteria. Everything seems to be in the process of decay and dampness clings to paint-damaged walls and well-used furniture.

John Huston climbs out from the front seat of the medium-sized car which has brought him from central London. He is very tall and hasn't much room for his legs, yet he is nimble and quick. He is smoking a long cigar; throughout the days, from the time he awakes until the time he retires, he is never without a cigar and never stops smoking them. The only reason he would show displeasure with his driver would be the latter's failure to keep a large and well-stocked box of Havanas always in the car.

Huston walks quickly toward the door of the nearest building. He stoops slightly, and always appears to be thinking about what he's going to do, what he's just finished; certainly, he always conveys the impression that he is somewhere else. This is not to say that his mind is not on his work. That somewhere else is probably in the world of the film he is making, or the one he is thinking of doing next. Yet he is unfailingly courteous, attentive and friendly. With his trimmed version of Noah's beard, he is a distinguished figure in well-cut casual clothes, an extremely kind and thoughtful man with an amused look, a keen sense of humour, an infectious laugh, and a constant cough from his non-stop smoking. More than this, he is an exceptionally modest man who tends not to know quite what to say when he is complimented on his work. He is on easier grounds when asked direct questions about certain aspects of his films, both technically and artistically; but he shuns press conferences, public appearances and discussions. He much prefers to let his films speak for themselves on the screen, and to start planning the next film once the previous work is finished. He willingly concedes that some movies succeed and others do not for reasons which are frequently inexplicable and part of what the fascination and unpredictability of film-making is all about.

He goes to the dubbing, or re-recording, studio where a small group of technicians are quietly waiting for him behind a huge mixing console. After an exchange of greetings followed by conversations in low tones about what has been done with sound and editing effects since the viewing session of the day before, the lights dim and reel four of *The Mackintosh Man* comes on the screen. A meter counts off the footage. The work print, rough, jumpy and grainy, with lines passing from side to side in certain spots, flashes on the screen something like a primitive silent picture.

The Mackintosh Man was filmed entirely on location in London, Ireland and Malta. There are no studio shots. But a studio is required for post-production work—the sound and picture editing, and re-recording—for which the players are not needed unless dialogue has to be redone—and Twickenham was available.

After this reel has finished, the lights go on and Huston moves over to the technicians and goes into another quiet discussion. He suggests certain changes in the sound levels, a balance between sound and music, the briefest trims in the editing in some scenes. There is a wait of about half-an-hour as the magic is performed by the technicians, and once again the reel comes on the screen. The difference does not appear to be noticeable, but what has happened does make a difference to the whole, and Huston is satisfied. Another reel follows. Huston has seen them all a hundred times. He sits, his long legs apart, one arm resting on his knee, puffing constantly on his cigar. His eyes seem unseeing, yet he is listening to every word and nothing escapes his attention. This is Monday, and by Friday he will have completed almost ten weeks of this post-production work and will leave with a finished print for the heads of the Warner Bros. studio in Los Angeles. He has sold his great home and estate in Ireland and, while negotiating for a smaller one, will live in Los Angeles. For the man who was once described as having left *The Red Badge of Courage* for others to complete, he is certainly seeing this film through in a thorough and conscientious manner.

As it turns out, he follows the same procedure with all his films, and has always done so. It is painstaking, sometimes dreary and repetitious, but this is where the actual shooting is perfected, where the images are brought into the shape envisioned in the imagination, and where other effects may be realised that were not in the original concept.

Huston is joined by Russell Lloyd, his editor of many years. He discusses the scene where James Mason's yacht sails out of the harbour on its way to Malta, with Paul Newman and Dominique Sanda watching it leave. "We can shorten this," he says. "Cut down the part showing the ship going out to sea. With the footage we have, the audience might think they could catch up with it." The film is stopped from time to time, it is run backwards, with and without sound or music. Some reels are in black and white, others in colour. Huston knows every word of the dialogue, every movement of the players, every cut and fade, sound effect and note of music.

By the time the week is over, he says it is finished. He doesn't say it is perfect, but he cannot see that anything more can be done to make the picture any more satisfying to him than it is. "A director sees his footage so often it becomes difficult to see it with a fresh eye and a sense of discovery," he observes. "Other people's advice can only be confusing at times. The discovery will now be made by the audience. If they don't like it, there is no way of knowing what I should have done to make them like it."

He shakes hands with all the technicians and thanks them for their contribution to the film. He walks out and climbs into the waiting car. He may never see them again, yet some may work on his next picture, or the picture he might make five years from now. Everything is very quiet, very still, very lonely. A charlady goes by with a tray of teacups. The car drives slowly through the gates. There seems to be no life here any more; only the sense of the presence of hundreds of actors and film-makers who have been here before, their films perhaps living on, perhaps forgotten. Huston's visit now becomes a memory. The world's most travelled film-maker, he will possibly never be here again.

The Cinema of
JOHN HUSTON

On Childhood, Youth and Discovering Life and Art

I WAS BORN in Nevada, Missouri, in 1906, on August 5th. The Water and Power company had been won by my grandfather in a poker game. My father was on the road with my mother—they'd been married at the St. Louis World's Fair. My father was playing with a touring company in "Convict's Stripes," and it went bust in Arizona, so my grandfather brought them back to Nevada and made my father the chief engineer of the Water and Power. He took a correspondence course in engineering and things went reasonably well until there was a fire, as a result of which I gather we weren't altogether popular in Nevada. The fire department, such as it was, kept calling for more pressure, and my father, who was a congenial man but didn't know too much about light and water, gave it to the firemen and something happened to the machinery. The valves broke, resulting in half the town burning down. My father left that same night and went to Weatherford, Texas, where he went on being an engineer at their Water and Power utility. After a term there, he decided that he was really not cut out to be an engineer and he went back to the stage. He returned to New York and played in other stock companies that toured, and then went into vaudeville.

Presently, he and my mother separated and I would only see him on occasions. My mother became a newspaperwoman. We lived mostly around the middle West, travelling, on and off. She wrote under the name of Rhea Gore, later changing it to Ray Jory. I was about four years old when all this happened, and my mother went to work for "The St. Louis Post-Despatch" and "St. Louis Star." She also worked in Indianapolis, Dallas, Fort Worth, and Cincinnati. My mother and father were divorced in 1914 and she re-married, to a man who was an official in the Northern Pacific Railroad. We went to live in St. Paul, Minnesota. After a couple of years in St. Paul, I was considered to be very ill. I don't think I was, but I was pronounced so—mistakenly by the doctors. They thought I had Bright's disease and a heart condition. They said an enlargement of the heart. It was a mistake that couldn't be made today—it was just a big heart for what was to become a big man. I never felt ill, but they put me to bed, and at one time I was immobilized for over a period of months. I was taken first to California and then advised to go to Arizona. This was when I was about twelve years old. During this time my mother gave up writing to be with me, and taught me herself as I was never much longer than a year or so in a school in the many places we stayed.

I cannot remember having any desire to write or act then, but I remember when I was very young, a baby practically (I have photographs of me as a child prodigy), my mother and my grandmother, who were very close, used to read to me. There was one book containing forty-eight verses about the Revolution, a book of poems, she particularly enjoyed. One day she couldn't find her glasses, so I read the book to her. I was three years old. The next thing I knew I was in an Uncle Sam suit on a stage reciting these verses and that went on for about a year. Then, thank God, she had sense enough to stop that. Nevertheless, we wandered around the middle West when my mother was working on papers, and I was never in one place very long. My first realisation that there was a war going on was in St. Paul, when my mother was re-married. I was in Arizona, I remember, when Armistice was declared.

Today I'm noted for being a traveller, I'm always moving around, and when I look back on my childhood and youth I imagine that moving around as I did when I was young influenced me in later life. I became restive after a certain time in one place, and yet something that I never had I appreciate very much now, and that is a home, a permanent place to go back to and be able to lick my wounds. By the time I left school I knew America pretty well, except for the Deep South. Visiting my father in New York was an adventure, full of excitement. Three days by train. By the "Chief" to Chicago, and change to the "Twentieth Century." Finally, I went to school in Arizona after this long period. We lived in Arizona for the most part, and Los Angeles.

Being supposedly ill, however, was dreadful, a dreadful experience. I remember it very distinctly. I remember one day I was whistling and the doctors were having a conference in the other room. One doctor came into the room and said, "You shouldn't whistle, you shouldn't exercise in any way," and stopped me whistling. Finally I rebelled against this. We'd go to the doctor's office, sometimes in a car, and I would see people swimming in the canal which was only a couple of blocks from where we lived. One night, in the middle of the night, I got an idea. I went down to the canal and went swimming. I used to do this when everyone was asleep. I wasn't caught. There used to be an irrigation canal there, to raise the locks and make a waterfall, and one night I got too close to this waterfall and was swept over it. I was perfectly all right. Those were hot Arizona nights on the outskirts of Phoenix. After going over the waterfall once I used to go over for sport. Finally, another doctor, who came as a godsend, said, "He's dying of malnutrition." I was. My hair had fallen out, I had been put in sweat baths. Christ, it was dreadful! So I was allowed to walk a block, then around the block, and finally I was allowed "to go swimming" and when I went swimming, why, I went over the waterfall in the daylight and everybody saw this, and then the other swimmers began to do it. Then I went to school in Phoenix and got back to normal. I think I was eleven when I was taken to Phoenix, and this "illness" lasted until I was about thirteen. These were terrible years. It's a wonder they didn't mark me for life, really.

Then I was brought to Los Angeles with my mother and grandmother, and went to high school. There something very important, so far as my development is concerned, took place. My grandmother read a great deal to me, as I said, and it was largely indiscriminate reading—Dickens, Tolstoy and Marie Corelli among others. Do you remember the "Hearst Sunday Supplement"? Well, first I would read the funny paper and then the "Sunday Supplement"—we went backward at that age—and I remember turning its pages and here was an article on abstract art, making fun of modern artists and of what they called "Futurism." But it was indeed about Cubism. I could always draw a little, and I liked these drawings and paintings. They were very interesting to me, mysterious and haunting. I went down to the library and got a book on "Futurism" and that led me to another book, "Cubism and Post-Impressionism," and I thought it was fascinating. Then I marked time until I could see some real paintings, but I devoured all the books on the period, all the articles I could find. I think my interest in art began there.

Presently I left high school—I never finished—and went to an art school. I was also boxing at the time. The art school I went to was academic and not very interesting. After a few weeks of it I realised this didn't have much to do with Cubism or Post-Impressionism! This was drawing from casts and models who sat in frozen positions. I heard about a place called the "Art Students' League," after the famous "New York Art Students' League." It was just a group of painters who fell together, hired a model and a little room down on Main Street, which was a slum area of Los Angeles. I made it my business to meet one of them, and eventually I joined them. They were very good, very interesting painters, some of them, and they were the predecessors of the now California School, which has made something of a mark in American art history today.

I used to go and draw three nights a week. There I met a painter who came from California, but who had spent most of his life in Paris, who is in the art history books, named S. MacDonald Wright. He and a man named Morgan Russell followed a school called "Synchronism." That was in the days when, to be any kind of a painter, it was necessary to be a member of a school. If one hadn't started a school, one at least had to be a member! They were doing abstract painting right after the First World War. Along with DeLannay and Kandinsky they took another tangent, but at the same time they were contemporaries of those painters. They prevailed upon Wright to recognise the seriousness of some of these painters, to come and give his advice and instruction at this school. He was an enormous influence on me, I realise now. He opened many doors. He introduced me to Balzac, which required me to learn French, and although I had been exposed to music, opera and ballet, he introduced me to another aspect of music, the works of Scriabin and Anton Berg and other experimentalists. He was more than just a painter, although he was a very good painter indeed and a magnificent draughtsman. At this school—forgive me if I ramble—there was a man named Val Costello. I looked upon him at that time as an elderly man, although he was probably in his middle forties. He was a sign painter and worked for a sign painting company in Los Angeles. He drew and painted beautifully, with a feeling of poetry, and made pastels. I used to try to arrange to sit next to him in these classes, and I'd look at the way he was drawing. Long after I left the school I remembered Val Costello's drawings. Many times, on returning to Los Angeles, I tried to find him. But Val Costello died, and his wife died, and God knows what happened to the body of his work. I remember it quite vividly, and only recently I came across one of the original painters, Nick Bragante, in L.A., who had a couple of Costello pastels and they were as beautiful as I thought they had been. He gave them to me because of my affection for Val Costello. To discover that his works were every bit as good as I thought they had been was delightful, an affirmation, a reassurance, because so much we revere when young turns out to be not all that good in later years. One day, too, only a few years ago, I was in New York and the television was on, as usual, in my hotel room. A programme came on, a philosophical discussion on life and art, between a professor in the Department of Philosophy of Harvard or Princeton and his guest. I listened to this discussion and it was very interesting. Slowly I perceived that it was MacDonald Wright who was at the other end of this discussion. I went to the telephone and called the broadcasting company, but the programme was taped and he was in Japan. Whenever I had been in California he wasn't there, so I knew he had gone to Japan to live. The last time I was in California I enquired if anyone had heard recently from Wright and he was there, I saw him, and I've seen him several times since. Here again was excellence personified. a man of great taste and of great knowledge. He is still painting. He occasionally gives a lecture. His wife died a long time ago and he is re-married to a young and very attractive woman. He has the same knife-edge quality of perception and understanding that he ever did. He is in his eighties and, to quote that *cliché,* younger than most young people I know. A joy to be with. He paid very little attention to my career as a film-maker, and was rather disappointed I hadn't gone on as a painter. I gave him a book about myself, a picture book more than anything else, and I inscribed it to "my old master." He knew, by the way, more about Italian oil painting and more about Oriental art than anyone I've ever met, including Behrenson. I gave him the book and he said, "Huston showing off, as usual."

The other interest in my life at the time I studied painting was boxing. When I stopped being "an invalid," why, physical things attracted me very much and I discovered that I had a kind of talent for boxing. I naturally threw a straight blow. I didn't swing, I didn't telegraph my punches. I began boxing in high school, and then I went to a school called Lincoln Heights. There were two future world's champions going to the school at that time. It was in a seedy part of Los Angeles, and it used to take me more than an hour to get there by streetcar. There I went into amateur boxing. The two future world champions were Jackie Fields and Fidel LaBarba. A number of men there later became challengers and main event fighters. I could reel off a whole list of them. I had a wonderful time boxing there. Then there were little clubs around the city and boxing at them was all an adventure for me. I enjoyed the atmosphere, there were great chums and good friends.

I remember there was a place down on Central Avenue, the coloured district of Los Angeles, which called itself "Madison Square Gardens." We used to go down there. The organisers would make up the names and weights and put bills up, then we would go down on the night of the fight and be introduced as we came into the ring by these names. We would be matched more or less according to our weights! I fought twice at "Madison Square Gardens" and each time under a different name. When I put on the gloves, I felt easy and I hit straight. I was so damned skinny I'd feel a beating for several days afterwards. I had in mind to become middleweight champion of the world! I had a few more fights. I was very lucky and pretty good. It wasn't a lonely life, it was a very full life, very full, crammed full.

When my father left my mother, it made no conscious impression on me. Certainly, I thought a lot about my father, and I went back and forth between the two of them. They didn't get along together so it was best for them to part. My stepfather was a very kind and good man, and he had two children of his own, he was a widower, and they were living in the house with us. They were both younger. He was very well disposed towards me, and he had a beautifully fitted private railway car with his own chef. He would take me with him on trips to the north-west, and to Seattle. My life as a boy, except for those dreadful, isolated years, was really something of an adventure, not that of ordinary children going to school.

Los Angeles in those days was rapidly becoming the centre of film-making, but I was not greatly conscious of that going on. I never went to studios then, but my mother and I did stay when we were in Los Angeles at the Alexandria Hotel. It was the social centre of Los Angeles, not Hollywood. The Hollywood people came because they didn't have a place in Hollywood which was out in the sticks, a place where there were some studios. There wasn't even an Ambassador Hotel in those days. The Alexandria was on Spring Street, the great hotel of the time. It wasn't a *big* hotel, but it was the best hotel in Los Angeles and all the stars used to come to the Alexandria, and would throw big parties or balls. This was during that period when I was ill, and I'd become known in the hotel as "the kid who was upstairs ill in bed." I was usually in Los Angeles to see specialists, and my mother took me there to see them. One day the telephone rang. It was Charlie Chaplin. Charlie asked: "May I come up and see the little boy?" And he did. He said to my mother, "If you'd like to go out, perhaps you have something to do, I can spend an hour with him." I can't tell you how entertaining and wonderful he was. I asked him questions about how they made the film slow down, for instance, and he explained it to me. Then he did little tricks and, for a few moments now and then, was Charlie the tramp. He was delightful. I never saw him again until many years later, when I was grown and making pictures. We became friends, not close friends, but friends, and I would see him at parties. Always, of course, I treasured this memory of him and his kindness on that occasion. One evening at a party I said, "Charlie, I must remind you of something" and I told him of his visit. He immediately became very shy and reserved, as though he didn't want to be reminded of it. So we never spoke of it again. I think he didn't want to be reminded of a very good deed! An essential modesty.

I used to see my father periodically and spend holidays with him. Then I went to New York to visit him and my life changed again.

On this occasion he was rehearsing for an O'Neill play, "Desire Under the Elms." I saw this several times and met O'Neill. I sat through the rehearsals and discovered how he wrote scenes, I mean what comprised scenes and how he made dialogue work.

I had always been, like so many others of my generation, infatuated with motion pictures. Charlie Chaplin was a god, and William S. Hart. I would go to see the films of Valentino, Wallace Reid, Theda Bara. These people dwelt on Parnassus. I remember the enormous impact the UFA films had on me, those of Emil Jannings, and *The Cabinet of Dr. Caligari*. I saw this many times, rather like a film buff of today, because it seemed to me to be art. I didn't think then of working for films. That didn't occur to me until much later and it seemed to be, in a way, too much to aspire to. That was another world, it was a pantheon of the Gods as it were, having no connection with real life. Even when I go to Los Angeles I can never believe that that is actually where it started. I still think that it must be somewhere else, some higher place! Quite!

Well, there I was in New York and I went very briefly on the stage as an actor. My father had done "Desire Under the Elms" and there was a man named Kenneth Macgowan, and Robert Edmund Jones—names that you are perhaps familiar with—and Robert Edmund Jones eventually married my father's sister, Margaret Carrington. Kenneth Macgowan said, "Why doesn't John come down and read for a part?" Well, I did. I forget what I read, though. There was a group called the Provincetown Players. They had a reading and they gave me some lines to read, which I did. Then I got a call one day from Kenneth Macgowan to come down and see him. I was living with my father then, so he said, "See if you'd like to do this." Well, it was a great part—in Sherwood Anderson's "Triumph of the Egg"—and it was one-half of a two-play bill put on by the Provincetown Theatre. It was a big part, *the* part, the star part. I did it, and to tremendous kudos, great kudos. I was nineteen, I think, and it was 1925. Then I did a play by Hatcher Hughes called "Ruint". But, even then, I thought this isn't for me, not to be an actor. The Provincetown Theatre still exists on McDougall Street. It was a very famous little theatre. It was the only off-Broadway theatre at that time and it had quite a following. O'Neill first wrote for the Provincetown Theatre. All his early plays were done by the Provincetown Players. Then the producers, Macgowan and Jones, took the plays uptown, and that's how my father did "Desire Under the Elms."

By the way, I forgot to mention one thing. I was always a horseman. My first dim memory is of my mother putting me in front of her on the saddle. She used to ride at night in Texas, and I can remember being in front of her on the saddle and hearing the horse's hooves on the cobbles, a galloping horse going over cobbles—which is now just an echo. I always had this love of horses and rode during most of the time in St. Paul. Before I was ill I had a horse and then after my recovery in Arizona, why, I had a horse, and ever since I have loved horses and riding. I'd even hunted with my aunt in Porchester, Conn. When I was living in New York I used to go up there and hunt. She had a house there. In New York I had a mastoid, which was a serious thing in those days, so I went down to Mexico to recover and there I met a great teacher of dressage. This was after my brief appearance on the stage in New York. I'd never been down to Mexico and the place always attracted me. The colour and the legends of Mexico and its history. I was eighteen years old then, and in Chapultepec I met a general, a teacher of dressage, a famous horseman, and he again stimulated my interest in horses and riding. I took lessons from the general in dressage, a kind of riding I'd never done. Finally, I was getting short of money. I was there just a little more than a year. I kept staying, it was ever so interesting. I love the place and I had a wonderful time. I told the general my lessons would have to come to an end presently and he said, "How about taking an honorary commission? I can arrange this and you can ride with the Mexican Team." Well, I did that and again it was such an enjoyable experience. I became a member of their equestrian team. I was made an honorary lieutenant and wore the uniform. I saw no army life whatsoever. I was a long string-bean of a kid and they treated me as a kind of mascot and were wonderful to me.

Eventually, I came back to the States and then got homesick for Mexico again. I went down the first time by boat to Vera Cruz, and then took the train to Mexico City, but this time I came down the coast on a tramp steamer. I felt a great curiosity and great desire to see everything, to do everything, and experience everything, these different modes of transport, different ways to reach a destination. I was avid after life, as most young people are, although the opportunity is denied to many. I went back and again spent about six months in Mexico. I didn't go into the army this time, but pushed around through the country. I did ride with them, but not as a member.

I had earned some more money back in New York to make this trip possible by writing some short stories. I just sat down and wrote them. It was a way of making money and they were published. The first ones weren't exactly short stories. I wrote about O'Neill. That was the first article I had published. Then there was a magazine, I've forgotten its name, a California magazine, which paid me for more of these. Then I went back down to Mexico, I was there for a few months, and then came back to the States and got married to a girl

I'd known in high school. Her name was Dorothy Harvey. Then I sat down and wrote some short stories. I sent them to my father who was performing in a play by Ring Lardner. He showed the short stories to Lardner, and he sent them to H. L. Mencken. They were published in "The Mercury." This, I suppose, was the high moment of my life because "The American Mercury" was a kind of gospel to people of my time and when I got a letter of acceptance—a complete surprise because I didn't even know they'd been sent to Mencken— signed "H. L. Mencken," why, I suppose that was the biggest moment I've ever experienced. They were published in "The Mercury" and then I went to New York and wrote some more, with my young wife. There are copies of these stories left, and one of them has been in an anthology. I was really writing to make money and the idea of them being published in "The Mercury" was so remote as to be inconceivable. That's why I had no aspirations. The inspiration came to me from my short life. I wrote about boxing. I drew on my experience of people I had met.

Those short stories led, then, to me being brought to the coast by Sam Goldwyn to write for pictures. A man named Herman Shumlin, whom I'd met in New York, was working as a producer for Sam Goldwyn and he showed the stories to him. I am sure he never read "The American Mercury" on his own! He invited me out. When I was a kid in Los Angeles, it was a very sleepy town. It had no industry. I think it probably had the sweepings of the country: people who came there for the climate, to retire, and invalids, semi-invalids, to get well. It wasn't a very attractive place. Downtown Los Angeles was a pretty hideous proposition, architecturally speaking. The old and infirm tottered around Pershing Square.

Hollywood, of course, was another world entirely. All I knew of that was what I saw in the Alexandria Hotel. No one ever expected Los Angeles to come up to San Francisco so far as a business place was concerned. They never anticipated its metropolitan aspect of today, to say nothing of oil then. Shortly after that, Signal Hill came in—but the aircraft industry and other forms of manufacturing were very much, much later. It was a peculiarly unattractive part of the world. I think people were lured there by abalone shells! Up in the mountains, of course, it was interesting. I used to go back as a kid to stay, when I was in high school, in Los Angeles. I used to go by myself up into the San Gabriel Mountains and spend a couple of weeks. I used to always come out reluctantly, as a rule. My mother would have to send strangers in after me. The school life was very interesting. The artistic life I enjoyed in the Art Students League. But the physical attributes of L.A., as I said, were deplorable.

On the other hand, when I went to New York, I was utterly

fascinated and I used to walk the streets in wonder. All the things that the rest of America seemed to lack (except wilderness areas, which were always wonderful), New York contained. The very book stores off Madison Avenue were fascinating. I patrolled the city, fell in love, and presently, after I was married, I went to live there. Well, I had lived there briefly before, for more than a year down in the Village. Sam Jaffe, the actor, and I were in the same building and I had a two-room flat above him and I used to be burgled regularly. I had a wonderful life there. It was on McDougall Street, a few doors from the Provincetown Theatre, and a bootlegger made use of a hall cupboard to store his synthetic gin. I wrote a puppet play with music, around the legendary characters of Frankie and Johnny. It was produced under that title by Ruth Squires, and Sam Jaffe wrote the score. All this was the Prohibition period and I had a marvellous time. Then I went down to Mexico, as I told you, came back up and eventually came back to New York again. There were so many levels of existence in New York. There was the social level, to which I was introduced by my aunt, Margaret Carrington, and the sporting, the literary, the artistic, and the theatre. Each one had its own followers and own group of people who kept rather to themselves, but I drifted from one to the other and so my life was never wanting in variety. We used to go to Harlem, Madison Square Garden, and fight arenas, the St. Nicholas Rink, and the six-day bicycle races. Those were the days before wrestling was *pure* showmanship. There were the great American playwrights: Anderson, O'Neill, George Kelly—a man whose name is more or less forgotten but, I think, one of the most extraordinary playwriters that America had. And the novelists whom I met, including Dreiser, Fitzgerald, Sinclair Lewis; and a great friend of mine was Paul De Krief, who wrote on science. Karl Van Vekten was another interesting figure.

I worked briefly on a paper in New York—the worst possible scandal sheet, a model for all bad newspapers—it was the first illustrated newspaper, "The New York Daily Graphic." Books have been written about it. They were the authors of the composite picture, where actors pose in the situation, usually a bedroom situation, and then the faces of the real people are placed on the actors' shoulders. Oh, they were guilty of anything! When I say I worked briefly, I worked for a period of months, but on and off. I had no talent as a journalist whatever, and I was fired oftener than any reporter ever has been within such a limited period of time. There was a kind-hearted city editor, who kept hiring me back. Finally I did something quite irreparable. I went to cover a story of a killing in New Jersey in a tobacco factory which made cigars. A worker had struck another

At left, with his father, Walter Huston. Taken in 1930s.

one with a knife. It was a minor incident, so far as New York crime was concerned, or they wouldn't have sent me! I got my notes mixed, and I had the owner of the factory down as the worker, and that ended my newspaper career for ever! It was printed, and there was all hell to pay. In the meantime, however, I was writing stories and at the end of that time I was brought out to Hollywood.

About my Aunt Margaret. She was a contralto and she sang in Europe. She was the first woman to sing Debussy in the United States, a concert contralto. I've a memory as a child, a very early memory, of walking with my aunt and another woman. Each had a hand of mine, and the other woman sang, and I thought her singing was beautiful. This woman said, "That's perfect singing," and Margaret said, "Yes, Melba." Margaret lost her voice, lost the middle register, which ended her career as a singer. She then coached my father and a number of people, including Jack Barrymore. When I say a number of people, oh, probably eight altogether, the people she thought had great talent. She played an enormous role in their lives. Talk to Orson Welles about her! Probably in Orson's book there is something about Margaret. Her name was, of course, Margaret Huston, and she became Margaret Carrington when she married. Her apartment on Park Avenue was her salon. We never got along very well until finally towards the end of Margaret's life, and then we became close. She was a rather dictatorial person and ruled her surroundings and whoever came into that circle. Eventually, after her husband Billy Carrington died, she married Robert Edmund Jones, who was the great figure in the American theatre at that time, the great designer—an American equivalent of Gordon Craig in England. She fostered my father's career and it was through her that he did his first play, "Mister Pitt," and went on from there.

My father and I were great chums, great friends. We saw each other frequently and I watched his plays. I think at times he held up his hands in dismay at what I was doing. It was repeated to me by someone who was very close to him that my father said: "John will either come into something extraordinary, or he'll be no good. He's a Red Indian. God knows what will happen to him. We can only hope for the best." He was always extremely sympathetic to me.

These thoughts about the differences between New York and Los Angeles came to mind as I went out to California on the train after receiving Herman Shumlin's invitation to the Goldwyn Studio. I think this was in 1929 and I was twenty-three. Working at Sam Goldwyn's studio, however, came to absolutely nothing.

Film-Making in Hollywood: Goldwyn and Universal, 1929-32

A House Divided (1931, William Wyler)
Murders in the Rue Morgue (1932, Robert Florey)
Law and Order (1932, Edward Cahn)
Laughing Boy

I STILL REMEMBER the first meeting with Goldwyn. He sat behind his desk. I don't think he rose or moved when I came in. He spoke in this familiar accent that we all know. He wished me very well, he wasn't very friendly. I remember, Sam wore a spike collar. He and Shumlin didn't get along. I don't think Sam got along well with anybody, that wasn't his approach to life. He went at everything as though he was the antagonist. He was contemplating doing a story about German submarines, and I worked for a while on it and it came to nothing. I was given an office but didn't meet many writers. Sidney Howard came to work there. I think he wrote a script finally, or a treatment, but it was abandoned.

Goldwyn did pay me $150 a week, something like that, which was an enormous sum at that time, untold wealth. After three or four months I went to Universal. There I wrote three or four films. I experienced a very modest success. I think Junior Laemmle was running the studio. His father, Carl Laemmle, had just retired and put the studio in Junior's hands.

Willie Wyler was doing westerns. I met him then, for the first time, and he did his first feature film for my father, *A House Divided*. I wrote that picture with Willie. It wasn't a very good script, but a fair picture. My father was now in Hollywood working at Universal. Then I got them to make a picture for my father, *Law and Order*.

Walter Huston in LAW AND ORDER (1932), above with Andy Devine (kneeling), Raymond Hatton, Harry Carey and Russell Hopton.

That was a pretty good script, but not all that good a picture. It could have been, I feel. I read it again not so long ago and it isn't bad, pretty good for the time. I also wrote dialogue for Robert Florey's *Murders in the Rue Morgue*.

Continuing to learn about screenwriting, I then wrote what I consider now is a good script—*Laughing Boy*, the Oliver Lafarge book about the Navahos. I was talking to Willie Wyler just the other day recalling the wondrous location trip we took into Monument Valley, long before Ford made it his territory so to speak. Why, we could have made a superb picture then. Not one of those foolish melodramas of Indians riding in circles around the wagon train. It was never filmed by Universal . . . they sold the whole property to Metro, and they didn't use my script. They did a very vulgar version of the story—Metro still own it—and it was an unsuccessful picture.

A Hollywood treatment of what the public largely, at that time, thought should have been done with the Navahos! Robert Flaherty or Murnau should have made it. I would still like to film it except I'm not so sure that Metro-Goldwyn-Mayer is inclined in such directions today with their leadership. It would be tremendously costly, and they'd rather sit on those assets than sell them, or make them. After this experience with Universal I came to England under contract to Gaumont British and had no success whatever—none.

London 1932

Death Drives Through

THIS WAS my first visit overseas. I wanted to come to Europe and here, I thought, was an opportunity. I'd met Mark Ostrer in California, the head of Gaumont-British Studios, and I wrote to him saying I'd like to work in London. He said, "Come on," and I came over. I've rather the impression, perhaps unfounded—I may be doing him an injustice—that my presence at the studios wasn't all that welcome, that I had been foisted upon them by the boss, as it were. In any case, the atmosphere at Shepherds Bush wasn't all that sympathetic or conducive to bringing out my best efforts. Then, through a series of circumstances—my wife came over, she fell ill—I was broke, very broke indeed. I believe instinctively, not with any logic whatever, in that old gambler's credo that one can't evade a bad streak. You have to pull your way through it. There's no such thing as asking for help. I could have asked—my father would have been instantly forthcoming—but I just thought there was no use. I was here, broke. I pulled a bluff on the powers-that-were at Gaumont-British, and said that, unless certain requirements on my part were met with, I wished to quit. I'll be damned if they didn't call it! Much to my surprise, they availed themselves of my offer instantly and here I was in London without a sou. I remember the day that the answer sent by registered post came to my door. I was living in Glebe Place in Chelsea, and I sat on the sofa, and I think the sweat came out because of the situation I was in. I owed money, my wife was here, she was ill, we had separated, she'd been in hospital, I'd brought her back to my house, and she'd been living there alone. I thought, "What in God's name am I going to do?" There came another ring at the door. I went, and here was a messenger boy with a telegram which said, "Congratulations, you've won £100 in the Irish Sweep, consolation prize." The £100 was enough to get Dorothy, my wife, back to California on a boat. Then it was steps going down for a while. I didn't have enough to get back myself and I had no money to live on. I then left this house and went to a small room.

A friend of mine came over, Edward Cahn, who was a director who'd worked at Universal and did *Law and Order*. He joined me. This was at a time when there were even more fly-by-night companies than there are today. They would give themselves a name and set about making a motion picture. Sometimes they'd last a few months, sometimes a few weeks, sometimes a few days! Well, Eddie had been brought over by one of these companies to direct a film, and by the time he got here it was non-existent. He found himself in exactly the same spot as I was in, so at least we were together, I had a chum. What might have been a very bitter experience turned out to be a lark. There was a girl who worked at Universal as a secretary, who had met a man in California and married him, and I bumped into her by sheer accident on the street. She'd married a man named Gordon Wellesley who was head of the Scenario Department for Basil Dean when he had a studio, and she was now Kay Wellesley. She knew both Eddie Cahn and me, and so through her husband we got an offer to write a script "on spec" while we were sleeping on the Embankment and living in Hyde Park. To earn money we even sang cowboy songs on the street! I can play the harmonica! Eddie sang "Bury Me Not" for coppers (*laughter* . . .). We weren't allowed to work and ever since then I've thought there should be a fifth freedom: anybody should be allowed to work anywhere! We survived and I wrote a script. It was one of these stories about automobile racing. I knew nothing about it and wrote the script out of complete ignorance, but got a few points from some men we met who were by the merest chance in the automobile business. I wrote the script on pages of magazines, just over the print. Occasionally the Wellesleys were very kind to us, we'd go to their home and avail ourselves of their bathroom and get a shirt laundered.

I remember my father became anxious he hadn't heard from me. There was no use writing to him and telling him lies about how everything was fine, I didn't want to do that. I just hadn't written. He wanted me to see a doctor just to see what state I was in. This word came down to me through a grapevine, so I went and saw a doctor. Later on I saw the letter he had written to my father, in which he said that I seemed to be in wonderful condition, a very fine state of health, but was I perhaps eccentric because all I was wearing was a pullover sweater, trousers and tennis shoes? Everything else was in a suitcase being held by a landlord! I had a number of experiences at this time, and it's extraordinary seeing London from that side. Quite another world from the one I'm privy to today.

Anyway, Gordon Wellesley, our saviour and mentor, took my handwritten script and had it put into manuscript form. I'll never forget that day. I waited at the Wellesleys, at their apartment, while Eddie Cahn went out to have a meeting with members of the production company. He'd had a previous meeting which was rather wonderful, too—he was the front man, the big director from the

States! He'd spent an evening with them and I think he had probably one shilling. He put that shilling into a one-armed bandit, pulled the lever and hit the jackpot, so he was able to buy drinks with it! This was, however, a final meeting where decisions would be arrived at, and he came into the apartment and stood with his hat on—he'd stage-managed this beautifully. He took his hat off presently, and it was full of pound notes and they fluttered to the floor. Then he took his handkerchief out of his breast pocket (he'd been got-up for the occasion, believe me) and five-pound notes came out with his handkerchief! Well, he had five-pound notes all over him, and we promptly moved into the Dorchester! They actually made the film and Eddie directed it, though I never saw it. I have no recollection of who was in it. I made a quick trip to Paris, and then I went back to the States.

Writing for Warner Bros., 1937-41

Jezebel (1938, William Wyler)
The Amazing Dr. Clitterhouse (1938, Anatole Litvak)
Juarez (1939, William Dieterle)
Dr. Ehrlich's Magic Bullet (1940, William Dieterle)
Sergeant York (1941, Howard Hawks)
High Sierra (1941, Raoul Walsh)
Three Strangers (1946, Jean Negulesco)

I MET Robert Milton, the theatre director, in London. I'd known Bob in the States before I met him here, and I saw him a couple of times. Back in the States again, I received a telephone call from Bob Milton in New York and he said, "A very talented young man has written a play called 'The Lonely Man' and I'd like you to read it. Would you consider acting in a play?" He said it would be staged in Chicago and all the arrangements had been set up. I said, "Well, let me see the play." I had no strong inclinations to become an actor, but the writer was Howard Koch and the story was of young Lincoln, a kind of reincarnation story. Lincoln was a professor in a university in the coal country, and his name was not Lincoln. It had a spiritual aura—if not a mist—around the whole thing. But it had moments as a piece of play-writing. I played him without any of the usual Lincoln trade-marks. There was no make-up, it wasn't called for. I just fell into the role as it was written. I didn't exercise any penetrating insights or analysis, I just got up there and did it (*laughter*). My father came to see it and he approved, he liked it. He'd played Lincoln in D. W. Griffith's film just three years earlier. I didn't take myself seriously as an actor at any time. It wasn't what I wanted to do. I thought my father had distinguished himself in that field so far as our family was concerned. But I did form a lasting friendship with Howard Koch, and eventually after I'd become established at Warner Bros. I recommended they bring him out. He made a very fine career as a writer in California—*Casablanca* and so on. He wrote the Orson Welles' "War of the Worlds." In the meantime, I married again, to Leslie Black, wrote two unproduced

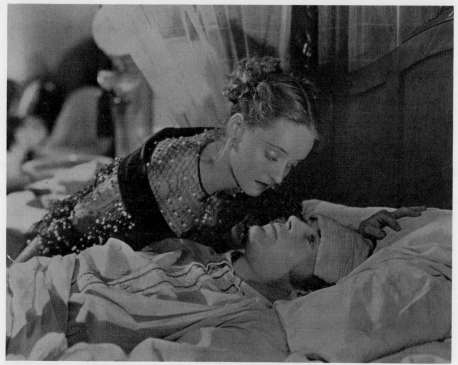

Bette Davis and Henry Fonda in JEZEBEL (1938).

plays, "Shadows Pursuing" from a Hugh Walpole story, and "Storm Child."

The play was very well received in Chicago, and the intention was to bring it to New York. While that was hanging fire, I wrote a story and went to California. Warner Bros. bought the story, which was later filmed as *Three Strangers,* and that was the beginning of my association there. In California, the first picture I worked on was *Jezebel.* Willie Wyler was now at Warner Bros. and this was just a coincidence. He was having trouble with the script and so I worked on it with him. From then on things went very smoothly. The auspices there were very good, and something had happened to Hollywood in the meantime. The level of taste had risen—two or three pictures and two or three innovators had made their mark. One might not think of them as criterions of taste today, but they had at least imagination, and Warners reflected this. Zanuck had just come to the studio, and Hal Wallis, a man of fine taste and of excellent judgement, was there. They had a producer who was probably the finest producer I ever worked with, Henry Blanke. He produced *Jezebel,* that's how I met him. We became very close, and he championed me as a writer. It was a very sympathetic atmosphere, and Warners had talented people in the writing department, and as directors. I got along famously with William Wyler. We were great friends, and are to this day.

I forget the details of his problems with *Jezebel,* but I think it happens oftener than it doesn't happen. In studying a script to make it work, the director comes on snags and areas that aren't sufficiently developed or are mistaken, and scenes that don't jell. My son made an observation one day recently that seemed to have a good deal of sense—he said, "Motion picture writing is not like play-writing, it's not like novel-writing, it's more like poetry. The scenes scan as it were." All too often, mistakes are not found until the film is on the floor. Then it's often too late. You know, by reading the script, what is working. There are so many things, of course, that can

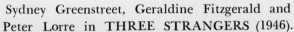

Sydney Greenstreet, Geraldine Fitzgerald and Peter Lorre in THREE STRANGERS (1946).

happen to make a film good or bad after the script has been written. I've seen beautiful scripts perverted and ruined in their direction, in their casting. A script is a very fallible thing indeed. But essentially the picture to be projected is contained in the script. Oftener today than in the time we have been talking about, scripts go into production which are really half-baked and the directors and writers work on the script as the picture is being made. Well, this never happened at that time at Warner Bros. When a script was written, that was it. Writers of that time, perhaps because they were on salary and not doing just a script to be sold, to be delivered, and to be paid for, wanted to stay on a script as long as possible, to perfect it, to make it as good as they possibly could. Certainly the front office wanted this. They would harass and harry and prod and pursue the writer to do it as quickly as possible. Nevertheless, they wanted the finished screenplay before going into production, and they wanted it to be right. In any case, I worked on this picture for Willie and then passed from it to whatever came next. I wrote a series of pictures at Warner Bros. Maybe *Dr. Clitterhouse* was first—I forget. There was *Juarez* and *Dr. Ehrlich's Magic Bullet* by William Dieterle. *High Sierra* by Raoul Walsh. *Sergeant York* with Howard Hawks and *Three Strangers* by Jean Negulesco. Some were written by myself, some with others. They were brought to us by the story department. *Three Strangers* was the script that I had written for them while I was playing Lincoln, and they bought; but the studio didn't film it until 1946, when I was in the army. I didn't think very much of it. They made some changes and they rather sentimentalised it. I did get back to the stage briefly in 1940 to direct my father in "A Passenger to Bali," a three-act play by Ellis St. Joseph. I thought it was very good, but the critics didn't.

Directing at Warner Bros., 1941-43

The Maltese Falcon (1941)
In This Our Life (1942)
Across the Pacific (1942)

THEN I ASKED that I be allowed to direct. They indulged me rather. They liked my work as a writer and they wanted to keep me on. If I wanted to direct, why, they'd give me a shot at it and, if it didn't come off all that well, they wouldn't be too disappointed as it was to be a very small picture. They acted out of friendship towards me, out of good will. This was Jack Warner, but largely Hal Wallis and Henry Blanke. They were the producers. Jack Warner was the overall head of the studio, but Hal Wallis was the Executive Producer and Henry Blanke one of the producers.

We took ourselves very seriously as writers. There was a good deal of talent in the writers' building there. The writer seldom visited the set. That was a great honour to be invited out to the set. Only on a few occasions did I ever get on the sound stage, actually towards the end of my time as a writer, before the time I became a director. My prestige as a writer had risen to those heights where I was consulted by the director on occasion.

When I asked to do a film, they said, "What would you like to do?" I said there was a book by Dashiell Hammett, "The Maltese Falcon," that had been filmed twice before, never very successfully. It would be a re-make of a story they owned and could be done for a very limited budget. I think the picture came to be made for under $300,000, which was much more than $300,000 is today, of course. Nevertheless, it was a small budget for a Warner Bros. picture. They helped me marvellously with the casting. When a director came on a picture at Warners he was given a good deal of authority and the fact that I was the director allowed me to call the shots so far as the actors were concerned. That is, if they were available. Now I more or less took up permanent residence in Los Angeles. I built a house in the valley and I had horses. I've always gone back to horses one way or another. That was my life, and I played little or no part in the social life, the Hollywood party. I never went in for that very much.

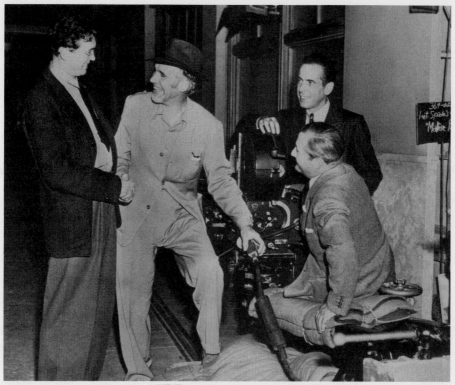

Father greets son on the set of THE MALTESE FALCON (1941) watched
by Humphrey Bogart and Arthur Edeson.

There was a small group of friends: Lewis Milestone, Willy Wyler,
Billy Wilder. I saw a good deal of Wolfgang Reinhardt who had
worked with me as an associate producer on *Juarez*. I used to see
Hal Wallis and Henry Blanke. I saw little of actresses and actors
away from the studio. Bogart and I became friends. Having written
High Sierra, I came to know him well. I knew all the actors on the
lot, but Bogart I probably knew better than anyone else.

When I went to make *The Maltese Falcon,* why, they had a
commitment with George Raft, who was a big star at that time, and
he was famous for being difficult. This will be the first time
George has ever heard about this. He was surrounded by a little
coterie of acolytes and I said to myself, "Well, I've heard about the
trouble that people had with George and with his henchmen,"
so I secretly made up my mind to put a sap in my pocket! If worst
came to worst, I knew how I had to deal with George. Well, he

turned down the picture because he didn't want to do it with an unknown, inexperienced director, which I can't blame him for at all. So I thanked God when I got Bogart—a blessing! Raft fancied himself as an actor, but he was not really a good actor. Howard Hawks made him. In later years when I met George and got to know him—I'd never known him well—I found him perfectly charming and I have great sympathy for him. To a certain extent, he lived the way he thought he was expected to live. It was part of a show, but you know, he'd come to blows with people. I think it was about that time that he hit Eddie Robinson because he thought Eddie Robinson was upstaging him, or something like that. Poor George wouldn't have known if he was being upstaged or not. Somebody told him, one of his henchmen!

Anyway, I got Bogart and Sydney Greenstreet and Mary Astor. I've never had a better cast. I still remember going on the floor for the first day when I started to direct. As I hadn't been on the set very often when I was a writer, directing was something that came instinctively. I knew almost exactly what I was going to do. I made drawings of every set-up, through the whole picture from beginning to end. I made the drawings myself. I showed the pictures and the drawings to Willy Wyler and he criticised them, and whatever ideas he had I incorporated if they seemed to be good. Before going on the set, Henry Blanke gave me the best advice I ever had, that any young director could have in my opinion. That was: "Each scene, as you go to make it, is the best scene in the picture. You should think of it as the best scene in the picture, the most important." There is no such thing, simply, as a man getting out of a car door and going into a building. It's got to be made into a scene; it's got to be photographed to create this interest in it. Nothing is just "to be got through." "Each scene as you make it is the most important scene in the film": whenever I've forgotten that, I've had reason to regret it.

So I went on the floor and everyone was giving me their support. The script was a very good script, and I followed what I had blocked out. In working with the actors I drew on what I had seen in the theatre, and this is something I've done all through my life as a director: to let the actors show me first, just to give it over to them. About half the time they would themselves fall into the set-ups that I'd designed, and about a quarter of the time I'd have to bring them into those set-ups. The remaining quarter of the time, what they showed me was better than what I had drawn; something better than what I had thought out beforehand would be forthcoming. It was a thoroughly delightful experience. I only do these drawings

Elisha Cook Jr., Peter Lorre, Sydney Greenstreet and Humphrey Bogart
in THE MALTESE FALCON (1941).

today when it's an action sequence, when the Art Department needs
to know certain things. For instance, in *Moby Dick* with the whale,
where there is a mechanical element, where they had to build
sections of whales for a shot, I'd draw those things.

The Maltese Falcon was produced twice before I did it, not with
very much success. I decided to follow the book rather than depart
from it, which was considered to be somewhat radical! This was
almost an unheard of method with any picture taken from a book.
I attempted to transpose Hammett's highly individual style into
camera terms with sharp photography, geographically exact camera
movements, and striking but not shocking set-ups. The book was
told entirely from the standpoint of Sam Spade, and so too, is the
picture, with Spade in every scene except the murder of his partner.
The audience knows no more and no less than he does. All the
other characters are introduced only as they meet Spade, and upon
their appearance I attempted to photograph them through his eyes.

This too, was something of an innovation at that time. Since then, the camera as protagonist has become a familiar technique.

Most of the stars in my second film, *In This Our Life,* were the Warners stock company. I felt rather ashamed afterwards of the way I got into that. Remember Bryan Foy? Well, Bryannie Foy paid me a very left-handed compliment indeed when he said, talking about the success of *The Maltese Falcon,* "You don't really rate as a director until you've worked with the stars and show how you make out with them!" None of these people in *The Maltese Falcon* had been stars when I directed them. Bogart was. He had two or three careers and one of them was just about ending, until he did *The Maltese Falcon* which started him again. I always had the highest regard for him as an actor, but they tried to make a leading man out of him, a conventional leading man. That wouldn't work, he didn't have the countenance or the physique for that, to be a competitor with Errol Flynn. By the same token, Mary Astor, who had been in silent films, reached a high point with this picture. It re-established a number of people. So the next film, for which Howard Koch had written the script by the way, was *In This Our Life,* and there was one aspect of it that was interesting to me, which I'll come to in a moment. I'm afraid I was guilty of being persuaded. Ambition stepped in there slightly, I suppose. I said, "Let's see how I can get along with the stars." I didn't think all that well of the material, but here was a chance to work in "the big time," an all-star cast, and it was an unprecedented honour for a brand-new director, somebody with one picture under his belt, to be given such an opportunity. I'm afraid I fell for it. It was not a bad script, by the way—it just had terrible sentimental overtones. There was one aspect of it that was interesting: it was the first time, I'm certain, that a black man had ever been treated other than as comedy relief, or a faithful servant or an underling. He was a man who played a part in the story, a character in his own right. He was victimised, a human being like the rest of us except for his colour. That was the distinction the picture made, which inclined me towards it.

Anyway, I did the film and one amusing situation occurred. There was a feeling on the part of the studio that the star, Bette Davis, if given her head, was perhaps inclined to over-act. I never felt this about Bette, and she got everything, God knows, that was to be had out of a scene. I went the whole way with her and Hal Wallis saw the rushes and said, "My God, John, hold Bette Davis down." I said, "How? She's doing what I want her to do." He said, "Well, I think you're wrong, dead wrong. She's just going wild with this picture." I replied, "Well, I think that's the way it should be."

He went along with me, but I had a couple of encounters with Hal, and I could see he was vastly concerned with the way the picture was going so far as her performance was concerned. Jack Warner had been away. He came back and they ran all the material together, and Jack Warner was even more convinced than Hal Wallis that Bette Davis was over-acting, tearing the picture to pieces. I had a meeting with them and I said, "Look, this is the way I see it." Well, they talked to Bette and she said, "John is my director and John approves what I'm doing." So they said to me, "My God, it's wrong, it's bad, it's not right!" I said, "This is the only way I see to do it. If you don't agree with it, you'd better get another director." They didn't want to do that and finally I think they just threw up their hands, tossed their cards into the pot, a way of saying to hell with it!

One day, Hal Wallis called me. I'd filmed a scene with Olivia de Havilland and Hal called me and said, "John, that's a very bad scene you've done. It's not good." Once more, I said, "Hal, look, I'm sure it's good. I know it's a good scene. If I can be sure of anything,

George Brent, Ernest Anderson and
Bette Davis in IN THIS OUR LIFE (1942).

it's this." "Oh, Jesus," he said, "let's run it tomorrow morning, the two of us together." Before starting the next morning, I ran over the scene with Hal Wallis and it was thoroughly bad. He was dead right, it was terrible! I said, "Oh, God, it's awful!" I think, in a sense, this threw him even more off balance, that I agreed that this was bad and said the rest was right.

Anyway, I finished the picture, they put it together, and Bette got a nomination from the Academy. She didn't win that year. That's what happens. Of course I was concerned, but I was more certain than I was concerned, and when I saw it on the screen I felt, I knew, that it was good. You have to have a certain amount of confidence in yourself, with all these people expressing their opinions. Those assaults occur occasionally, and you've got to be sufficiently detached also to be sufficiently critical of yourself, to know if they are right or if they are wrong.

The Maltese Falcon was a short schedule, about eight weeks, I think. We shot on Saturdays in those days. *In This Our Life* was a longer, bigger picture, with more sets. From the beginning I've always shot the picture, edited the picture in the camera. Sometimes, to my regret, I do very little covering of material, I don't do any covering material. I'll shoot the same scene over several times but I don't protect myself, as they say. So, to a certain extent, the editors have to put it together the way it's shot. At that time, few other directors did this. Sometimes I've not taken a close-up when I should have, and after the picture is finished I've made the close-up, or something like that occurred. There is a certain danger involved in this, but I shoot so that the picture can be edited as we go along and last week's work has been pretty well finished by the time I'm in the present week. It also means that I have to be very sure of myself, and what material I'm going to have and what the picture's going to look like. I've always done this. I have been told I shoot probably less film than almost any director. Less film goes through the camera. Sometimes I cut out a whole sequence or a whole scene, but rarely in shooting the scene are not all the shots used, every shot.

The United States was now in the war, and I enlisted. Awaiting directions, I started *Across the Pacific*. The cast included many players who were in *The Maltese Falcon*. That's why we all did it. It was a thriller, of sorts, and I worked on the screenplay. When I was up to the last sequence in the picture, with a few more days required to finish, I got a call. I'd enlisted about ten weeks before and I was waiting to hear, to be called-up. The call came to me on the set, and the voice from Washington asked to speak to Lieutenant Huston. Lieutenant Huston came to the phone and he was instructed

ACROSS THE PACIFIC (1942). Above, shipboard banter: Sydney Greenstreet, Humphrey Bogart and Mary Astor. Below, the climax: Victor Sen Yung, Monte Blue, Mary Astor and Humphrey Bogart.

to embark for Washington immediately. I went back to the set, and first I called Jack Warner and Hal Wallis and told them. Jack Warner said, "Maybe we can delay your departure and finish the picture," and I said, "No, don't." I didn't want to embark on my future in the Army with anything like that behind me. So I went back to the set and Bogart was at this moment being held by the Japanese in the conspiracy to bomb the Panama Canal, very much as they had Pearl Harbour. He had gone down to stop this perfidy, and arranged to have himself made a prisoner. Now he was surrounded by his enemies in a tropical bungalow, all done on the back lot and on the stage. Bogart was sitting in a chair. When I came back to the set I had Bogart bound to the chair, and then I put automatic weapons into everybody's hands. I made the ring of captors into three rings, and put people outside the windows with guns pointing at him. It had been decided that Vincent Sherman would take over for me. It would now be up to Vincent to get him out of this! I spent the rest of the day making it utterly impossible for Bogart to make a false move without getting shot. Well, I saw the picture some time after the war and it lost credibility from that moment on!

It was during this time I first met Otto Preminger. I had written a play with Howard Koch called "In Time to Come," about Woodrow Wilson and the League of Nations. Otto directed it. This was a critical but not a popular success, and ran for two months at the Mansfield Theatre. I never saw it, never went to New York. Otto came to the Coast to discuss it. Howard went back to New York to watch the production.

THE MALTESE FALCON. 1941. *A* Warner Bros.-First National *Picture.*
Director: John Huston. *Executive Producer:* Hal B. Wallis.
Associate Producer: Henry Blanke. *Screenplay:* John Huston.
Based on the novel by: Dashiell Hammett. *Director of Photography:* Arthur Edeson. *Music:* Adolph Deutsch. *Film Editor:* Thomas Richards. *Dialogue Director:* Robert Foulk. *Assistant Director:* Claude Archer. *Art Director:* Robert Haas. *Gowns by:* Orry-Kelly. *Makeup Artist:* Perc Westmore. *Sound Recorder:* Oliver S. Garretson. *Orchestrations by:* Arthur Lange.
Running time: 100 minutes.
Players: Humphrey Bogart (*Sam Spade*), Mary Astor (*Brigid O'Shaughnessy*), Gladys George (*Iva Archer*), Peter Lorre (*Joel Cairo*), Barton MacLane (*Lieutenant Dundy*), Lee Patrick (*Effie Perine*), Sydney Greenstreet (*Casper Gutman*), Ward Bond (*Detective Tom Polhaus*), Jerome Cowan (*Miles Archer*), Elisha Cook Jr. (*Wilmer Cook*), James Burke (*Luke*), Murray Alper

Walter Huston, Lee Patrick and Humphrey Bogart
in THE MALTESE FALCON (1941).

(*Frank*), John Hamilton (*District Attorney Bryan*), Emory Parnell
(*Mate of the La Paloma*), Walter Huston (*Captain Jacobi*).

Story

  Sam Spade and Miles Archer, partners in a private detective
agency, are hired by a Miss Wonderly to shadow Floyd Thursby.
Miles is killed while on the assignment, and Thursby is killed later
the same night. Miss Wonderly, confessing that her real name is
Brigid O'Shaughnessy, tells Spade that she is in danger and implores
him to help her. He agrees to keep her name out of the case, his
doubts mitigated by her beauty and her money.

  Spade is visited by Joel Cairo, who offers him $5,000 to find a
black statuette of a falcon. Spade reports the offer to Brigid, who
asks for a meeting with Cairo. Here Spade learns of a third person,
"the fat man," who also is interested in the falcon and whose gunsel,
Wilmer, has been trailing him. Wilmer takes Spade to the fat man,

Casper Gutman, and Spade professes to know the falcon's where-abouts. But beyond scoffing at Cairo's offer, Gutman refuses to reveal any information about the black bird, and Spade storms out.

Brigid vanishes, and Wilmer summons Spade to a second meeting with Gutman. This time Gutman tells Spade the falcon's history and value but puts a drug in his drink, knocking him out. Recovering, Spade finds a clue which leads him to the ship "La Paloma," but it is on fire when he arrives. Returning to his office, he is interrupted by the arrival of Captain Jacobi of the "La Paloma," shot several times, who gives him the falcon and dies. Placing the falcon in a deposit box, Spade goes to his apartment to find Brigid waiting outside and Gutman, Cairo and Wilmer inside.

He learns from Gutman that Wilmer killed Thursby and Jacobi and proposes that Wilmer be the "fall guy," to which Gutman consents. After negotiating a price for the falcon, Spade has his secretary, Effie Perine, bring it to the apartment. Upon examination the statuette proves to be a fake, and during the excitement Wilmer escapes. Recovering from his disappointment, Gutman proposes to Cairo that they continue their search. Brigid remains with Spade who telephones the police to pick up Gutman, Cairo and Wilmer. Then, faced with the question of Miles's half-forgotten death, Spade deduces that it was Brigid herself who killed him. She confesses, but, citing their love, implores Spade not to send her over. But Spade won't "play the sap" for her; and he grimly hands her over to the police.

Comment

Huston's first film as writer-director is still considered as a master-piece, a text-book movie in terms of economy, pace and direction. In the narrative and essence of Hammett's complicated thriller is found the first statement of Huston's art and philosophy about the individual and his search for a better life through the acquisition of wealth, and of the attainment which turns victory into ashes. He used the conventions of the private detective tales to make a perceptive commentary on the greed of men, and moved the events and characters along with style, tension and a laconic sense of humour.

IN THIS OUR LIFE. 1942. *A* Warner Bros.-First National *Picture*. *Director:* John Huston. *Produced by* Hal B. Wallis *in association with* David Lewis. *Screenplay:* Howard Koch. *Based on the novel by:* Ellen Glasgow. *Photography:* Ernest Haller. *Musical Score:* Max Steiner. *Musical Direction:* Leo F. Forbstein. *Gowns by:* Orry-Kelly. *Art Direction:* Robert Haas. *Editor:* William Holmes. *Running time:* 97 minutes. *Players:* Bette Davis *(Stanley Timberlake)*, Olivia de Havilland

(Roy), George Brent (*Craig Fleming*), Dennis Morgan (*Peter Kingsmill*), Charles Coburn (*William Fitzroy*), Frank Craven (*Asa*), Billie Burke (*Lavinia*), Hattie McDaniel (*Parry's Mother*), Ernest Anderson (*Parry*), and Lee Patrick, Mary Servoss, William B. Davidson, Edward Fielding, John Hamilton, William Forest, Lee Phelps.

Story

Stanley Timberlake, the selfish and spoiled daughter of a genteel but impoverished Virginia family, is accustomed to having her wishes satisfied. Her mother Lavinia, a bedridden neurotic, encourages Stanley to get what she wants while constantly complaining that Asa, her husband, is ineffectual. Lavinia points with pride to her wealthy brother, William Fitzroy, a ruthless but successful bachelor who has an unnatural affection for his niece Stanley.

Three days before she is to marry handsome Craig Fleming, a successful attorney, Stanley runs off with her brother-in-law, Peter Kingsmill, a promising surgeon. Roy, her heartbroken sister, divorces Peter so he can marry Stanley. Roy turns to Craig in her grief and their mutual unhappiness culminates in a deep love. Stanley's marriage to Peter, who realises his mistakes too late, ends in tragedy; he commits suicide.

Returning home, a somewhat less than grieving widow, Stanley is forgiven by Roy and her family. When she learns Roy is in love with Craig, whom she threw over for Peter, Stanley cuts her mourning period short and makes an obvious attempt to win him back.

Firmly refusing to yield to Stanley's wiles, Craig fails to keep a date with her. Infuriated, Stanley drives away from the roadhouse at high speed and runs down a woman and child—killing the child—and drives away without stopping to investigate.

Witnesses identify her car but, when questioned by the police, she insists she had been home all evening on the night of the accident and had given her car to the cook's son, Parry, to wash. The boy is arrested but his mother swears he was at home at the time of the accident. Roy believes her and asks Craig to handle Parry's case.

Uncovering proof of Stanley's guilt, Craig confronts her and asks her to make a confession. She refuses and goes to her Uncle William, certain he will help her. Just informed that he has only weeks to live, Uncle William shows no interest in Stanley's dilemma but prevails upon her to stay with him during his last days. Realising he is suggesting an incestuous relationship, Stanley reviles him and rushes from the house.

She drives off at high speed and is pursued by a patrol car. Trying to outdistance her pursuers, she skids around a blind curve on the highway and crashes off the road. The car overturns and she is killed instantly.

Comment

Bette Davis is brilliantly unpleasant as a spoiled daughter of a wealthy family in small-town America. Contained within the impassioned melodrama are the seeds of Huston's social conscience, expressed in the sympathetic treatment of the Negro and the suggestion of incestuous feelings between the uncle and his niece, neither subjects being normally permissible at this time.

ACROSS THE PACIFIC. 1942. *A* Warner Bros.-First National *Picture.*
Director: John Huston [and Vincent Sherman]. *Produced by:* Jerry Wald and Jack Saper. *Screenplay:* Richard Macaulay. *Based on the "Saturday Evening Post" serial "Aloha Means Goodbye" by:* Robert Carson. *Director of Photography:* Arthur Edeson. *Music:* Adolph Deutsch. *Film Editor:* Frank Magee. *Dialogue Director:* Edward Blatt. *Assistant Director:* Lee Katz. *Art Directors:* Robert Haas and Hugh Reticker. *Gowns by:* Milo Anderson. *Make-up Artist:* Perc Westmore. *Special Effects:* Byron Haskin and Willard Van Enger. *Montages:* Don Siegel. *Sound Recorder:* Everett A. Brown. *Orchestrations:* Clifford Vaughan.
Running time: 97 minutes.
Players: Humphrey Bogart (*Rick Leland*), Mary Astor (*Alberta Marlow*), Sydney Greenstreet (*Dr. Lorenz*), Charles Halton (*A. P. Smith*), Victor Sen Yung (*Joe Totsuiko*), Roland Got (*Sugi*), Lee Tung Foo (*Sam Wing On*), Frank Wilcox (*Captain Morrison*), Paul Stanton (*Colonel Hart*), Lester Matthews (*Canadian Major*), John Hamilton (*Court-Martial President*), Tom Stevenson (*Tall Thin Man*), Roland Drew (*Captain Harkness*), Monte Blue (*Dan Morton*), Chester Gan (*Captain Higoto*), Richard Loo (*First Officer Miyuma*), Keye Luke (*Steamship Office Clerk*), Kam Tong (*T. Oki*), Spencer Chan (*Chief Engineer Mitsudo*), Rudy Robles (*Filipino Assassin*).

Story

Court-martialled out of the United States Army, Rick Leland attempts to enlist in the Canadian artillery but is rejected. At Halifax he takes passage on the "Genoa Maru," a Japanese ship bound for Yokohama via New York and Panama. On board he meets Alberta Marlow, on her way to Panama, and Dr. Lorenz, an avowed admirer of the Japanese. He tells Lorenz of his dishonourable discharge and of his intention to sell his services to the highest bidder.

When the ship docks at New York, Rick reports to Army Intelligence headquarters, where he is revealed as a secret agent trailing

Lorenz. As the "Genoa Maru" proceeds toward Panama, Rick allows Lorenz to prod him into revealing details of the military installations guarding the Panama Canal. He also conducts a light-hearted romance with Alberta, and they fall in love.

In Panama, Alberta disappears and on a tip Rick goes to Dan Morton's Bountiful Plantation, where he is captured by guards. He finds Alberta and Morton, her father, held prisoners by Lorenz, who is using the plantation as a base from which to direct a bombing attack on the Canal. Overpowering his guard, Rick makes his way to a landing field where a Japanese plane is being prepared to bomb the Gatun Locks. He captures a machine-gun and shoots down the plane as it is about to take off. Returning to the plantation, he finds Lorenz preparing to commit hara-kiri, but the doctor has no stomach for the ritual and Rick takes him into custody.

Comment

Bogart, Astor and Greenstreet are re-united in similar roles involving them in a riotous spy story concerning the destruction of the Panama Canal. Huston treats familiar material with freshness and humour, and brisk, tight, direction. It turned out to be highly topical, as were so many Warner films of the time, no matter where the action took place.

The Army Films 1943-46

Alaska: **Report from the Aleutians** (1943)
Italy: **The Battle of San Pietro** (1944)
U.S.A.: **Let There Be Light** (1945)
and in England and Africa

I WENT to Washington for a few weeks and I was very anxious to get going. I can't sit around and wait. I get terribly impatient. I remember walking down the street one time with Anatole Litvak, who was also in the army, and I very nearly burst into tears at hanging around—my God, all these events were just beginning to happen and I wasn't there. Very shortly after I had made complaints, the bomb bay doors opened and I was looking down to Kiska. They sent me up to the Aleutians where I did a picture—*Report from the Aleutians,* a documentary. That was an extraordinary experience.

While I was there I learned how easy it was to make simple mistakes when working without a trained crew. We were shooting with Kodachrome cartridges, and the guns had cameras on the fighter planes, so I decided to put these cartridges of colour film into the cameras. I wasn't on this raid because it was just fighter planes with no room for passengers. Changes were made in the cameras and I had cartridges put in on six planes. It was an extraordinary raid. The pilots swept right in at water-level practically, came over a little saddle and swept across Kiska and then turned around and went over Kiska again with their guns going. They were firing on emplacements and it was a very daring raid and the results were extraordinary. I heard them described when they came 'back. I sent the films to Washington, and they came back blank; nothing was on the film, nothing whatever. I had neglected to run out the leader. The leader on all the cartridges had just been run out and that was all. The leader was four feet or something like that on each camera. Well, four feet of 16mm is a lot of film and that multiplied by six would have been an extraordinary thing. Nothing like it had ever been shot and never was shot. An opportunity for it never came again. I felt terrible, awful, that's what can happen.

In fact, my whole time in the Army was, I suppose, the most

compelling experience of my life. I was up in the Aleutians for some months, then came back and put that picture together, then worked briefly on the *Why We Fight* series. I met Ford, Capra and Zanuck— all were in the army at that time. Incidentally, it was understood when I went into the army it was to make films. They realised the importance of film, although it took them a little while to get going, which was quite understandable. My orders gave me a great deal of freedom. I didn't choose what I wanted to do, but whatever they wanted me to do was according to my choice.

I'm often asked how I turned from doing, you might say, the synthetic studio material with actors to shooting documentaries of actual life. It all seemed to me to be one. The composing, the script, of course, on a documentary such as *Report From The Aleutians* was written as work proceeded, as the director sees it and experiences it. I wrote at night by the light of a Coleman lantern up there, but by the time I got back to the States I knew exactly what would be used. Of course, in those instances one shoots everything, not according to the script. The script is written according to what is shot. But a design and shape emerged and at that time the only probably false note in it is one of optimism, which the country needed at that moment.

Then I worked briefly on a script for one of the *Why We Fight* series—I didn't do any actual photographing. Then, with the landings in North Africa, it was discovered that Tola [Anatole Litvak] went on that assignment and everything that Tola photographed sank in a boat that was bombed. All that material was lost, and there hadn't been any adequate coverage of that operation. An emergency call went out after the President asked to see the film material and there wasn't any. It was decided that we might "manufacture" something like it, and we shot some aerial footage. I went down to Orlando, Florida, and flew around in bombers that were attacked by other planes and so on. None of it was very convincing. What follows sounds like what happened in *The Americanization of Emily*! This was under Capra. Frank had been given the task—not a very happy one, either. It was then projected that, as the Americans and the British had done this jointly, it should be made into a combined film, as it had been a combined operation. Frank and I came over here with Anthony Veiller to negotiate this, and to be part of making a film about the combined operation. The British had a good deal of very fine material. I must say I didn't have much heart for any of this. They had a picture quite ready to show, and it was delayed for us. They were polite and congenial as they could be, but I felt that an injustice was being done in delaying their film to make a picture that we didn't have the material to supply. That went staggering along, still trying to reconstruct, trying to put together most of the fictitious material that we had, and to come up with the kind of film that they had in mind, with this very good material the British had. I think, finally, a very lame article did appear but it was a couple of years later. Frank busied himself with it here. Then I got orders, for which I was duly thankful, to go to Italy where I made *The Battle of San Pietro*. London, on this my second visit, was a wonderful place at that time. It was during the "Little Blitz" and the whole spirit of the people and the place was extraordinary. I was staying at Claridges, just round the corner from here. Everytime I come here the place is full of memories.

However, I was excited finally to be off for Italy to film an actual battle, *The Battle of San Pietro*. I was there for some months, again writing the script, writing the lines as the situations occurred. Again, I had an invaluable experience as a result of the war, tragic though the conflict was. I was working with cameramen. I carried a camera, but I never made one successful shot. I never even made one successful still photograph shot of anything in my whole life. As I was the so-called leader, why, you know, I thought it better to carry a camera than a swagger stick. At least it was an excuse for being there. After it was done we took the footage back to the States, back to New York and California. There was an awful lot of film exposed, because we never knew what we were going to get. We just photographed. It took a while, and finally we finished putting the picture together in California.

Then I was asked to do a picture about battle neuroses, combat neuroses, at Mason General Hospital and, by the time I'd finished that, the war was practically over. This was *Let There Be Light,* and was the film the army didn't want to show, and they never have shown it. I was very moved to find the men like this, and the actual photographing of them was, by God, practically a religious experience. I felt there what some people feel in church. These men came in from the boats in batches of seventy-five and 100, mute, shaking, with amnesia, blind, with paralysis, as a result of warfare. Many were healed. The original idea was that the film be shown to those who would be able to give employment in industry, to reassure them that men discharged under this section were not insane, but were employable, as trustworthy as anyone. When the brass in the Pentagon saw the film, the reaction was strongly against releasing it for general viewing. Those decisions had to go through channels.

I'll never forget the showing of *San Pietro*. Oh, they all liked *Report From The Aleutians* enormously, but in *San Pietro*, why, I'll

Frame enlargement from THE BATTLE OF SAN PIETRO (1944).

never forget the room where it was shown: full of generals, three-star generals, two-star generals, and one-star generals, and their entourage. Each general with his staff. I forget which one it was, anyway, the highest ranking officer, after a period of silence, stood up and walked out with his staff. He must have been a three-star general, I don't think there were any four-stars there. Then the two-star general walked out, and it went down the line until I think the last to leave was a Lieutenant Colonel. The reaction was very strongly against the picture being shown, and I was called in to General Surrold's office. There were two or three others there, high-ranking officers, and this conversation ensued: one of them said, "Well, this could be interpreted as an anti-war film." I couldn't repress myself, and I said, "Gentlemen, if I ever make anything other than an anti-war film, I hope you take me out and shoot me, because I'll very well deserve it." This didn't go down well, either. The next thing was that the picture was not to be shown. Then General Marshall saw the picture and said, "Every soldier who knows he is going into combat must see this picture, and the country should see it in order that they know what a soldier is going through in battle." I agreed with the few deletions that were made, and it was used then as a training film, because as you know the first few days in combat is when an army encounters a number of emotional casualties and desertions, and the men must be prepared for what they are going to encounter. This was Marshall's point, that was taken up and generally agreed.

But there was no General Marshall with *Let There Be Light,* but in this instance it wasn't a military matter, you see. I wasn't present at that initial showing. Although the film had been made by the military, it was public relations people rather than soldiers who determined the outcome—although in making the film I was motivated by the same anxieties that affected the army's thinking on the other films. I don't think the true reasons for withholding the picture from the public at that time were ever expressed. They said it was an invasion of the men's privacy. The men would have welcomed this invasion of privacy. In fact, they were looking forward to it and, as a matter of course, they had all signed releases permitting the showing of the film. They did it out of their own feeling for the film. They were very proud of what was on the screen. The men saw it, most of them at least, so I'm inclined to doubt that was what was really behind it. At first they said they had no releases. Then they did have the releases and this was brought to their attention. Then the releases were lost. What I think was really behind it was that the authorities considered it to be more shocking, embarrassing perhaps, to them, for a man to suffer emotional distress than to lose a leg, or part of his body. Hardly masculine, I suppose they would say. It was, as I said before, an ever so compelling experience. I learned to have a great feeling for the American soldier and his behaviour was magnificent. I used to just stand back and wonder when they'd given us an assignment like a frontal assault on positions that were practicably unassailable, and they went forward without question, without a murmur. It was done with a spirit, with a high spirit of endeavour. The atmosphere of that was, I am sure, a very different one to Vietnam, very different indeed. Nobody wanted to go home until it was over. I admired all soldiers, of course, but it was the American forces I saw more of. Many times since the war I've been offered war stories to direct, but I can never bring myself to film any. That was "the production." If there was a war picture to be made about that war, that was the time to do it, rather than on a back lot or a fake location. I didn't go to war for adventure, but it all falls into the pattern of my life. I came to admire the Italians. Seeing farmers going out with their oxen and their ploughs into the fields, which they knew damn well were mined.

After we had taken an area, they'd be brought in because their legs were blown off, not because they were dead. That whole time was something unforgettable and lives with me. It gave me a sense of the reality of human behaviour as against the conventions that the Hollywood screen rather cannibalistically had come to accept as behaviour. It also inculcated in me a vast desire to work away from studios, not within the walls of a sound stage. I find a freedom and an inspiration from a location that the barren walls of the studio don't give me. It all depends on the material, of course. Certain pictures lend themselves to the more or less artificial and unrealistic backgrounds. The kind of stories which have appealed to me over the years since the war take place out of doors in remote regions.

REPORT FROM THE ALEUTIANS. 1943. *Director:* John Huston. *Produced by:* The Army Pictorial Service of the U.S. Signal Corps. *Distributed by:* The War Activities Committee through MGM. *Photographers:* Capt. Ray Scott, Lieut. Jules Buck, Sgt. Freeman C. Collins, Corp. Buzz Ellsworth, Corp. Herman Crabtrey. *Music by:* Dimitri Tiomkin. 45 mins. Technicolor. *Narration spoken by:* Walter Huston.

THE BATTLE OF SAN PIETRO (SAN PIETRO). 1944. *Director:* John Huston. *Produced by:* The Army Pictorial Service of the U.S. Signal Corps. *Script:* John Huston. *Photographers:* John Huston, Jules Buck and cameramen of the U.S. Signal Corps. 32 mins. Black and white. *Narration spoken by:* John Huston.

LET THERE BE LIGHT. 1945. *Director:* John Huston. *Produced by:* The Army Pictorial Service of the U.S. Signal Corps. *Script:* Charles Kaufman, John Huston. *Photographers:* Stanley Cortez, John Huston. *Music by:* Dimitri Tiomkin. 59 mins. Black and white. *Narration spoken by:* Walter Huston. (Never officially released or shown.)

Return to Warner Bros., 1947-48

The Treasure of the Sierra Madre (1948)
Key Largo (1948)

I DIDN'T immediately return to Los Angeles after leaving the Army. In 1946 I directed another play on Broadway, Jean-Paul Sartre's existentialist "No Exit," translated by Paul Bowles, at the Biltmore Theatre. Claude Dauphin, Annabella and Ruth Ford were the principals. It was well received by the critics, but hard to get audiences to respond. Those who saw it found it difficult to grasp. Then I went out to Los Angeles. Warners was almost exactly as I had left it, except Hal Wallis had gone. I did some work with Howard on the screenplay for *Three Strangers,* which I had written earlier with him. It had been put down as a directing assignment for Jean Negulesco. I had completed a script with Tony Veiller for a film of Hemingway's short story, "The Killers," which I hoped to direct. I didn't agree with Mark Hellinger's interpretation (he was the producer) so I withdrew. The picture was finally made at Universal, but I received no credit for it. One day I was with Hemingway and he said, "You know, the only picture made out of anything I've written that was any damn good was *The Killers."* I didn't tell him I wrote it. Then he found out and he said, "You bastard!" The screenplay was nominated for an Academy Award. Tony said if it got the Award he was going to make an announcement from the stage that I had written it with him. I said, "Don't you dare." He said he would anyway.

Then I worked on the screenplay, with Tony Veiller, of an original story by Victor Trivas called "The Stranger," about a Nazi war criminal who escaped to America, changed his identity, and became a school teacher in a small New England town. The producer was S. P. Eagle, who later changed his name to Sam Spiegel and became my partner. I was to direct with Orson playing the Nazi. Sam was afraid that he wouldn't get Orson to play the part if he couldn't direct it too, so I withdrew and went on to my first postwar picture at Warners, *The Treasure of the Sierra Madre,* which probably turned out to be the best of the possibilities at that time.

Of this film, I think almost everything has been said. I think it is probably the first American studio feature film to be made entirely on location outside the continental limits of the United States. The Flaherty and Murnau films had been made abroad, but they were documentaries and were brought to companies after they had been filmed. Before I ever went into the army I wanted to make this picture. If it hadn't been for the war, I would have made it earlier. Then, towards the end of my time in the army, I began to think about the screenplay, and I wrote it, finishing the writing after I'd been mustered out. I was in correspondence with the "mysterious" B. Traven [the author of the book] and a number of letters went back and forth. Paul Kohner played a role in this, he's my agent in California, and I was his first client some forty years ago! Paul was married, and still is, to Lopita Tovar, and she had been a Mexican star and had received fan letters from B. Traven. On one occasion she was supposed to meet him and he never showed up. She appeared, but he didn't. Then she received a letter from him describing all her actions. He was somewhere watching her. Altogether strange! He was supposed to meet me in Mexico City and I wanted him to work on the picture with me as I made the film. I went down to Mexico City to keep this appointment. No one, by the way, had ever met him. Alfred Knopf, the publisher, had tried on a number of occasions to arrange a meeting with him and Traven had never shown up. Letters were addressed to him at a Post Office Box in Acapulco.

Anyway, I was in my hotel room in Mexico City and I awoke early in the morning. I'm one of those people who never locks his door wherever he is. Standing at the foot of my bed was the shadowy figure of a man. He took a card out and gave it to me. I put on the light, it was still dark, and it said, "Hal Croves, Interpreter, Acapulco and San Antonio." I said, "How do you do, Mr. Croves." Then he said, "I have a letter for you from Mr. B. Traven," and he gave me the letter, which I read. It said that he himself was unable to appear but this man knew as much about his work as he himself did and knew as much about the circumstances and the country and he would represent Traven in every way. We had conversations, Croves and I, for the few days I was in Mexico City. I gave him the script, he read it, liked what he read and said he was sure Traven would like it very much.

Traven, in his letters, was apt to enlarge on a point; he was expansive, so to speak. He had written one extraordinary script for his own book "The Bridge in the Jungle," fascinating, not just for its treatment of the subject, but for the way that it would digress and go into the philosophy of the camera. The script was rather a point of many departures, and after the fashion of Melville and so on, it would go off into another area. In other words, Traven was not a man who reduced his material to the bare essentials, the bone structure, but he was always putting on flesh. Croves, on the other hand, spoke in short sentences and didn't have a great deal to say. Croves was a little man, had a long nose, white hair, grey-blue eyes, rather awkward in his clothes, I would say, like a country man, and wore a Mexican hat; not a sombrero, but a Mexican straw hat, and a flannel shirt. I don't think the coat and trousers matched.

I returned to Los Angeles. A few weeks later I went to Acapulco and again saw Croves, not Traven. Of course, by this time, the idea had occurred to me that this was Traven. In fact, the letter, in a sense, said he was Traven. I mean, "he will represent me" and "he knows as much about my work as I do," and it was a form of codal communication that led me to think that it was indeed Traven himself. When I came back to Acapulco I wasn't surprised to meet with Croves again. We went fishing and talked, then I returned to the States. We reached an understanding that Croves would be on the picture acting as technical adviser, which he did. I received letters from Croves and they weren't in the vein of Traven's letters. The style was different and I was confused, I didn't know what to believe, whether this was Traven or not. In the course of making the picture, I decided he wasn't Traven. I never asked him the question myself— but people with some boldness, I thought—it was embarrassing to me—would just come up and say, "Are you B. Traven?" to Hal Croves, and he would slide away from the question and the interrogator. I said—no, this can't be Traven. By the way, he was most retiring. That was one of the qualities which led me to think he was Traven. I felt he was a little bit over-retiring, that he made a point of retiring, and retired so that people's curiosity would be whetted. These were just private feelings that I had and it all added to the mystery. Yet he had none of that largeness of spirit and generosity with words that Traven evinced. Croves was another article entirely. I liked Hal Croves, but he wasn't my idea of the Traven who wrote with that sort of devil-may-care grandeur, let-the-chips-fall style that we know from his books.

After I'd made *Treasure* and time passed, I heard that Croves was living in Mexico Ciy and he was generally accepted as Traven, although he was still calling himself Croves. The sister of the then President Mateos of Mexico had worked with Traven as his secretary. With the advent of the picture, when his name became all the more famous, he had been followed by some reporters from Mexico City, who wanted to find out where he lived outside Acapulco, in the jungle to the south of the city. They went to his house where he had a little store, a little shop in the jungle. They rifled his desk and they found evidence that this was Traven. Then they pursued him in the marketplace in the village and they photographed him. There's a picture of him holding his hands up to hide his face from the camera. All this pointed to the fact that he was Traven, and then his ex-secretary died—I think she committed suicide. She was the only true link who could possibly identify Traven as Croves. Croves married, and his wife had a daughter already, before their marriage. He then began to be called, and permitted himself to be called, Traven. It was generally accepted that this was Traven. I could never believe it. To this day I have my doubts. I recall a conversation I had with his wife and daughter not so very long ago and the daughter was describing to me his behaviour in her house in Mexico City, how he always dressed for dinner, in a black tie, and how they weren't allowed to come to the table other than in formal clothes. It was a formality that was quite unknown to the man I'd met in Mexico City for the first time. It sounded strange to my ears, this turn in his character. I'm still, as I say, quite mystified by the whole thing. Croves died a few years ago.

I've known, however, other writers who were, in themselves, a contradiction to what they wrote. This is something that can happen. I've never known a man who is less like what he writes than Ray Bradbury, for instance. I can find no common ground between the man and his work. Some random things Traven had written before this time were collected and published—short stories and articles. But Traven-Croves during his whole time in Mexico City did not write or publish anything. "Bridge in the Jungle" was his last book, but it was written before "Treasure" was published. He was also supposed to have been a German, but I have never felt anything Germanic in the Traven books. Many of the *littérateurs* all thought he was German, that was the speculation. So in talking to Traven one day—or Croves—the names are interchangeable—I asked him where he was born. He said he was Scandinavian, which made much better sense to me as the Traven books don't have a Germanic ring to them. There's not that care and precision, there's a kind of *largesse,* even wastefulness about them. He spoke with a decided accent but it was not a German accent, it was Scandinavian. He told me he had gone to Chicago as a child and all of what Croves told me coincided with the Traven legend. Yet I still don't think he was really Traven, and I couldn't say that he wasn't. I'm mystified. Perhaps the question is the mystery of a personality rather than a fact. I didn't penetrate to its ultimate depth the personality of the man.

So far as going on location to another country to make the picture

THE TREASURE OF THE SIERRA MADRE (1948). Above, Walter
Huston and Humphrey Bogart in a scene. Below, John Huston with
Alfonso Bedoya and Bogart.

came about, I just said that the place to do most of the film was Mexico, it's required, and Warners went along with me. All the equipment went out and we were in the wilderness practically. Warners also agreed to let me use my father in the film. The studio was very much for it and I remember I talked to Dad—I had talked about him doing it long before—and I said, "Well, here we are, you are to look like an old man—an older man than you are, even," and so he took out his bridgework! I sent him records of what he had to say in Spanish, and he learned the Spanish so that it sounded colloquial. We made the picture in Tampico and San Jose de Perua, with a few shots in Durango. Then the interiors—the night material—were shot in the studio, because it makes no difference, if it's night, where you shoot.

At the time the film came out, it was successful. It wasn't a raging, wild success like a DeMille film, but it was a very successful picture both with the critics and at the box-office, and has been popular in all the years since. The ending was just as it was written—the gold blew away, the old man laughed, the young boy went back to the States, and the old man went back to the Indians, and the other man was dead. The studio didn't ask for any changes. The only anecdote connected with the picture, except for the things that happened in Mexico, is that I shot a lot of it in Spanish and there is a good deal of Spanish spoken throughout the film. I didn't want the Mexicans speaking Hollywood English. Jack Warner saw the rushes as they came up and said, "Christ, what's Huston doing? Has he lost his mind entirely? He's making a Spanish version!" Having been in Mexico during my youth increased my determination to make the film there, to capture the true colour that was required for the story. The film is exactly as I wanted it.

In *The Maltese Falcon*, Mary Astor goes to prison at the end. This was fairly uncharacteristic for the time, when the studios preferred to have happy endings because they thought that's what the audiences wanted. Warners never suggested anything different. It was Dashiell Hammett's ending. I've been congratulated from that time to this on the screenplay. It was simply a matter of editing Dashiell Hammett's book. It's his book on the screen and it took me all of three weeks to write that screenplay. On the other hand, all the elements in the film of *Treasure* are in the book but they are organised quite differently from the way that Traven wrote them. Gold Hat, for instance, goes right through the picture, whereas he was just an episode in the book.

Key Largo was again given to me by the studio. I liked to write away from the office, from the writers' building. Now I was a director and they would let me do things like that. Richard Brooks and I went down to Florida, to Key Largo, and wrote the script there. It was quite a departure from the play, which was not one of Anderson's best plays. We went into a hotel on the Key, a remote detached place. It had to be opened for us, and we brought our own cook. Presently there began to appear roulette wheels, a dice table and blackjack set up. We wrote the picture and gambled, alternately, and came back with the script, written I guess in six to eight weeks down there, and made the film. It was a joy working with Dick Brooks—he hadn't started as a director then. I scarcely remember the play now, but it was given, I think, a stronger dramatic line than it had. It was brought up-to-date, of course, to take place just after the Second World War. This man had returned and already disenchantment had set in—I mean the high hopes and aspirations of Roosevelt, the war-time era, were being dissipated and the dark shadow of the future was even then to be seen. That was taken as the theme, here with the return of the underworld. It was, of course, representative of the reaction that was even then enveloping the country. Although we wrote it at Key Largo, it was filmed entirely in the studio. There were some outside scenes, I recall, on the boat; these were done in a tank in the studio. I thought it was beautifully done, particularly by the players, Lionel Barrymore and Betty Bacall, of course, Eddie Robinson. I think the picture is best known probably for his introductory scene, in the bathtub. Whenever I hear it spoken of, this scene is always mentioned. But it was an easy film to make. I've never liked making pictures in studios, I like working on location always, and I don't like simulating a location. There are some pictures that should be made in studios in their entirety. They require the magic that can be practised on a set within a sound stage that can't possibly be done without the machinery of the studio. These pictures I believe in doing in a studio, otherwise I don't like doing Hong Kong on the back lot, which today is not acceptable.

While I was in New York, Teresa Helburn, one of the heads of the Theatre Guild, called me and asked me if I'd have lunch with her. My great hero—as a young man from the time I've already told you about when I visited my father and saw him in rehearsals doing "Desire Under the Elms" and "The Fountain"—was Eugene O'Neill, and Miss Helburn asked me if I would be interested in directing a Eugene O'Neill play for the Theatre Guild. I said I very much wanted to, and would be delighted. She said, "I'll send you a copy of the play." I replied, "I'd like nothing better than to read the play, but if it's by O'Neill, why, I want to do it." Whatever it would be, I would direct it in the spirit of a tribute or an *hommage* to O'Neill.

Lauren Bacall and
Humphrey Bogart
with Felipa Gomez in
simulated exterior for
KEY LARGO (1948).

It was a very interesting play, "The Moon of the Misbegotten."
Then I had a meeting with O'Neill and he remembered when I was
a younger man and had attended rehearsals, and he knew I was my
father's son, and had gone into films. When I went into the army
and when I came out I was still under contract to Warner Bros. In
those days they didn't like us to work for anybody else, and to do
anything for anybody else. So I'll be damned if they didn't refuse
me permission to do this play. I went back to the studio and took
it up with Jack Warner. No, I wasn't to be permitted. It was in
violation of my contract. I had to call Miss Helburn and say I couldn't
do it. I spoke first to her to tell her how much I regretted this, how
deeply my feelings were about it, and my indebtedness to O'Neill,
because he had done more to form my opinions than anyone I'd
ever met so far as writing was concerned. She said, "Wait a minute,
he's here, I wish you'd tell him these things." For once, perhaps
because it was over the telephone, I was able to speak straight from
the heart and he said, "Thank you, John, I can't begin to thank you

enough. You don't know what this means to me to hear these things. It means more than any approval of any play of mine or of what I've written could mean, to hear that I've had some effect on somebody's thought." He spoke with great clarity. He had Parkinson's Disease when I saw him, his hands trembled and he was very frail, but his voice was clear and sharp. I would probably have been with Warner Bros. until it stopped being Warner Bros. if it hadn't been for that incident. I waited quietly until my contract expired and made other plans. I went back and made *Treasure* and *Key Largo*. When *Key Largo* was finished, I left, that was my last film for Warners. Jack Warner didn't want me to leave. I told him why I would not remain. He said there had been a misunderstanding. I never got over that. Then O'Neill died, and there was no opportunity to make up for that. I hold no rancour now towards Jack Warner. I'm very fond of him, I like him enormously, I'm one of his admirers, in fact.*

TREASURE OF THE SIERRA MADRE. 1948. *A* Warner Bros.-First National *Picture. Director:* John Huston. *Producer:* Henry Blanke. *Screenplay:* John Huston. *Based on the novel by:* B. Traven. *Director of Photography:* Ted McCord. *Music by:* Max Steiner. *Film Editor:* Owen Marks. *Assistant Director:* Dick Mayberry. *Art Director:* John Hughes. *Set Decorations by:* Fred M. MacLean. *Make-up Artist:* Perc Westmore. *Special Effects:* William McGann and H. F. Koenekamp. *Sound Recorder:* Robert B. Lee. *Orchestrations by:* Murray Cutter.
Running time: 126 minutes.
Players: Humphrey Bogart (*Dobbs*), Walter Huston (*Howard*), Tim Holt (*Curtin*), Bruce Bennett (*Cody*), Barton MacLane (*McCormick*), Alfonso Bedoya (*Gold Hat*), A. Soto Rangel (*Presidente*), Manuel Donde (*El Jefe*), Jose Torvay (*Pablo*), Margarito Luna (*Pancho*), Jacqueline Dalya (*Flashy Girl*), Bobby Blake (*Mexican Boy*), John Huston (*White Suit*), Jack Holt (*Flophouse Bum*).

John Huston won two Academy Awards for directing and writing

---

* Released a month before *Key Largo* was a film called *On Our Merry Way* or *A Miracle Can Happen*. "In 1947," says Huston, "as a favour to Burgess Meredith, I directed an episode with James Stewart and Henry Fonda in *A Miracle Can Happen,* which Burgess produced. I never saw it, and I believe I and several other directors went uncredited, which we agreed to." Henry Fonda has recalled that he asked for Huston to direct the episode. When Huston was unavailable to complete it, George Stevens came in and also went uncredited for his work on the picture. King Vidor and Leslie Fenton were the credited directors.

The Treasure of the Sierra Madre, and Walter Huston won as best supporting actor for his remarkable performance as "Howard." The New York Film Critics Award went to *Treasure* for best picture of the year, and to John Huston for best direction.

Story

Dobbs and Curtin, two Americans on the loose in Mexico, meet in the plaza in Tampico. Surfeited with cadging handouts, they take jobs in a construction camp, but their contractor, McCormick, decamps without paying them. In a flophouse they meet Howard, an old-time prospector, whose tales of gold-mining fire their imaginations. Encountering McCormick, they overcome him in a barroom fight and recover their earnings. With this money, and that won by Dobbs in a lottery, they have enough to buy provisions for a gold-hunting expedition. They seek out Howard, who agrees to accompany them. but warns them of the perils ahead and of the greed, distrust, and hatred that gold can cause.

En route to Durango, their train is ambushed by bandits whose leader is distinguished by his gold-coloured hat. The attack is repelled by soldiers hidden aboard the train, and the three prospectors arrive in Durango to buy burros and equipment for their expedition. Their trek into the mountainous Sierra Madre begins, and old Howard proves to be the hardiest of the three. As the tortuous trip proceeds, the first manifestations of bitterness appear, with Dobbs leading the bickering. They arrive at a site chosen by Howard and begin digging, eventually striking gold. Their find brings them tentative unity, and they work side by side to increase their riches, but as the gold dust accumulates friction returns. Dobbs becomes increasingly fearful and suspicious of his partners, and must be repeatedly cooled by Howard and Curtin as he falsely accuses them of coveting his "goods."

While in town for supplies, Curtin meets a Texan, Cody, who follows him to the camp and proposes partnership with the three miners. Egged on by the avaricious Dobbs, the partners decide that the interloper must be killed, but the execution is interrupted by the arrival of bandits, commanded by the same gold-hatted chieftain who led the attack on the train. After unsuccessfully attempting to obtain the prospectors' guns by barter, the bandits attack the camp and during the battle Cody is killed. The bandits are routed by the sudden appearance of the *Federales.*

The three prospectors decide to call it a day and return to civilisation. On the way down the mountain they are approached by friendly Indians, who tell of a boy near death from drowning. Howard accompanies them and revives the boy, and the grateful

Indians make him a virtual prisoner as their village medicine man, leaving Dobbs and Curtin to go on alone, taking Howard's share of the gold with them. The trip becomes a nightmare, as Dobbs's paranoia increases until, ridden by fear and distrust, he shoots Curtin. Leaving Curtin for dead, Dobbs continues on alone with the burros and all the treasure in his possession. Curtin is found alive by Indians, who take him back to Howard.

As Dobbs pauses to drink from a waterhole, he is held up by three bandits, led by the familiar Gold Hat. When Dobbs resists them, they kill him and make off with his clothes and burros, dashing the gold dust to the ground in the belief that it is dirt that was hidden among the animal hides to make them weigh more and increase their value. In Durango the bandits attempt to sell the burros and hides but are apprehended when the townspeople recognise Dobbs's clothing and identify the burros by their brand-marks. The bandits are swiftly executed just as Howard and Curtin ride into town. They hear of Dobbs's fate and rush to the scene, only to find themselves the victims of a cruel jest of fate. The desert winds have blown away their treasure and they can only laugh at the sardonic end to their adventure.

Comment

This excellent story of three drifters who find gold in Mexico in the Twenties, leading to their eventual self-destruction, is told with simplicity, brilliant characterisation, a sense of frayed nerves, fear, and discomfort, and with a great feeling for and graphic use of settings. Exciting and profound in its study of human nature, it remains a masterpiece—much imitated, never bettered.

KEY LARGO. 1948. *A* Warner Bros.-First National *Picture.*
Director: John Huston. *Producer:* Jerry Wald. *Screenplay:* Richard Brooks and John Huston. *Based on the play by:* Maxwell Anderson. *Director of Photography:* Karl Freund. *Music by:* Max Steiner. *Film Editor:* Rudi Fehr. *Assistant Director:* Art Lueker. *Art Director:* Leo K. Kuter. *Set Decorations by:* Fred M. MacLean. *Wardrobe:* Leah Rhodes. *Make-up Artist:* Perc Westmore. *Special Effects:* William McGann and Robert Burks. *Sound Recorder:* Dolph Thomas. *Orchestrations by:* Murray Cutter. *Song, "Moanin' Low" by:* Ralph Rainger and Howard Dietz.
Running time: 101 minutes.
Players: Humphrey Bogart (*Frank McCloud*), Edward G. Robinson (*Johnny Rocco*), Lauren Bacall (*Nora Temple*), Lionel Barrymore (*James Temple*), Claire Trevor (*Gaye Dawn*), Thomas Gomez (*Curley Hoff*), Harry Lewis (*Toots Bass*), John Rodney (*Deputy Clyde Sawyer*), Marc Lawrence (*Ziggy*), Dan Seymour (*Angel*

KEY LARGO (1948). Above, Huston with Lionel Barrymore, Lauren Bacall and Humphrey Bogart. Below, same players in scene with Edward G. Robinson.

Garcia), Monte Blue (*Sheriff Ben Wade*), William Haade (*Ralph Feeney*), Jay Silverheels (*Tom Osceola*), Rodric Redwing (*John Osceola*).

Story

Ex-army major Frank McCloud, arriving on Key Largo, an island off the Florida coast, goes to a hotel run by James Temple and his daughter-in-law Nora, the father and widow of a wartime comrade. McCloud finds the hotel taken over by a "Mr. Brown," his alcoholic girl friend, Gaye Dawn, and four henchmen, Curley, Toots, Angel and Ralph. McCloud recognises "Brown" as Johnny Rocco, a notorious deported racketeer, whom he views distastefully but apathetically. He rejects a chance to kill Rocco at the cost of his own life; he is disillusioned by the war's aftermath and is reluctant to fight again for any cause.

The island is swept by a storm, and Rocco becomes terrified, refusing to let Temple admit a group of Indians requesting shelter in the hotel. He promises Gaye a drink if she will sing an old favourite for him, but she is not the singer she once was, and her pathetic performance embarrasses them all. When Rocco cruelly refuses her the drink, McCloud pours it for her, taking a slapping from Rocco for his trouble. Nora and Temple ask McCloud to stay on at Key Largo and to look on them as his family.

When the storm abates, Rocco receives a visit from Ziggy, an old gangland crony who has come to buy a shipment of counterfeit money. After Ziggy departs, Sheriff Ben Wade comes looking for his deputy, Clyde Sawyer, who was after the Osceola brothers, two Indians on a drunken spree. When Wade finds the body of Sawyer, whom Rocco has killed, Rocco implies that the fugitive Osceolas are guilty. Wade finds the Indians and, when they try to get away, kills them both. Sickened by Rocco's doings, McCloud realises anew that there can be no compromise with evil, and he unexpectedly agrees to pilot a boat taking the gang to Cuba. When Rocco tells Gaye that he is leaving her behind, she takes a gun from his pocket and passes it unseen to McCloud.

At sea, Rocco, Curley and Angel go below, leaving Toots and Ralph on deck. Gunning the boat, McCloud throws Ralph overboard, shoots the seasick Toots, and picks off Curley as he comes up the passageway. Below, Rocco orders Angel topside, killing him when he refuses. Alone now, Rocco bargains with McCloud, offering him all the money obtained from Ziggy, but McCloud waits patiently for Rocco to show himself and kills him when he does. Turning the boat around, McCloud heads back to Key Largo and the waiting Nora.

Comment

Essentially theatrical and confined to one set and few exteriors, this familiar gangster plot is given new meaning through its expression of liberal theories on freedom and responsibility and by its sense of post-war disenchantment on the part of its ill-assorted characters and their lack of ability to change with the times. Finely written, fluidly directed, and beautifully acted, with Robinson's first appearance in the bath chewing his cigar described by Huston as "the look of a crustacean with its shell off."

Final Films under the Studio System, 1949-51

We Were Strangers (1949)
The Asphalt Jungle (1950)
The Red Badge of Courage (1951)

WE WERE STRANGERS, which was set in Cuba, dealt with revolution. Years later, a revolution did come to Cuba and in a way it was somewhat prophetic. All the conditions in Cuba certainly indicated that a revolution was required, regardless of the form it took. It was, at that time, just about as corrupt a place as there was in my experience of the world. Everybody was corrupt in Cuba. It was damned near as bad as Egypt is at this moment. That's going pretty far! The only thing you could say for Cuba in those days was that the bars were good, but the Government, the police and the Secret Police and their practices made it a pretty wretched place. Liberals, I don't mean radicals, had done what they could to change the conditions in Cuba, to introduce democracy, and they received little or no help from the United States. I think that what happened in Cuba can be laid directly at the door of the United States, especially the industrialists, and sugar and fruit plantation owners.

I found the story in a novel written by a New York journalist, Robert Sylvester (he was on "The News"). It was one of a collection of stories in this book. This was the first time I worked with Peter Viertel, who collaborated on the screenplay. I'd known him since he was a boy. His mother was a very good friend of mine, Salka Viertel, whose house was a kind of salon in Hollywood where she entertained the intellectuals: Thomas Mann, Charles Chaplin, singers and musicians, and other writers and actors used to come. It was my first encounter with John Garfield. He was an enormously talented young actor who, I felt, would be right for this part. It also brought me into contact again with Sam Spiegel. I'd known him before the war. I'd met him first in London when I was over there and on my uppers, and as I said, I wrote *The Stranger* for him. He was one of

Jennifer Jones and John Garfield in WE WERE STRANGERS (1949).

those promoters trying to put a deal together. Then he came to Hollywood and again worked at various studios as an independent producer. He did a film called *Tales of Manhattan*. I knew Sam and recognised his abilities as a producer. He had a great talent. He wasn't just a promoter by any means, he's proven that over the years, but he had good judgment and imagination, and he knew where to spend the money. I bought the rights to the story, and with Sam formed a company, Horizon Films. As a matter of fact, I had read a review of the book and the reviewer remarked that it would be "material for a Huston picture." We got the book, and I thought, "Yes, it was."

It didn't turn out to be a very good picture. I thought it had a certain something, but it seemed to elude me. From the time I thought it would make a good picture to the time it was finished, something didn't come through. I just never felt it quite came off. One of the things that bothered me about the picture was that it was supposed to be in Spanish and the characters were Hollywood actors pretending to be what they weren't. It seemed to be counterfeit.

There was an air of falsity about it, I think. The idea was that a man was sacrificed for the cause, and it proved to be of no value. The sacrifice was quite in vain, so if there's any point, the end is not worth the means. That was the immediate point. However, the rebellion that eventually did occur through this, but indirectly, may have been worth the price in human lives. That isn't what was wrong with it. I think philosophically or ideologically, let's just say logically, the idea was good, and it was dramatically demonstrated in the writing, but there was an air of falsehood about it. John Garfield and Jennifer Jones were not Cubans, and nothing I or God Almighty could have done could have made them so.

I first met Hemingway in Cuba on this occasion. I went to Cuba before starting to write the script and we became quite good friends. He was very generous and had me out on his boat and we went on trips together, we fished, and it was a splendid encounter. I continued to see him through the years. Peter Viertel, by the way, had a great deal to do with that. He had been through the war himself, had been a Marine, an officer in the Marines, started in the ranks and became an officer, and had had a very fine war record. I had seen him grow up, and now he's a white-haired man! Peter had met Hemingway, and I think Peter knew him in a way, probably, much better than those who have written about him in their reminiscences, Hotchner and so on. Peter, not wishing to violate the privacy of the man and to exploit a friendship, has refrained from writing about him, and Peter knew him better than anyone else. He regarded Peter as a son. If anyone should write about Hemingway, it's Peter Viertel—except, of course, Hemingway's wife, Mary. She protested Hotchner's book. I protested it, too, because the man contradicts himself. He tells how Hemingway hated anyone to use him as material, as it were, while he had a tape recorder going in the back of the car. This is bugging, so far as I'm concerned.

Most of the exteriors were filmed in Cuba, and we did some interiors at the Columbia studios in Hollywood. This was just before the studio system began to disintegrate. Sam and I were possibly one of the first directing-producing partnerships which decided to become more or less independent and free of studios by forming our own company. It was the result of a feeling I had of not wanting to work in a studio, or in future years, for a studio company. However, while I was an associate partner with Sam Spiegel, I took a contract with M-G-M. My agent negotiated it, saying it was best for me, but I agreed only on the basis of one picture for them, and one with Sam. The first picture I did for M-G-M was *The Asphalt Jungle,* which wasn't all that well received and was only a small success. It always surprised me years later when it was put in the category of Hollywood classics.

One studio was very much like another. M-G-M, in contrast to Warners, was a little grander, that's all. Warners was a bit more down-to-earth. The way the M-G-M studio was run, policed even, was extraordinary. It was just about as efficient as a place could be, unless they were turning out some machine-made object, or automobiles! The discipline that was practised there was of the strictest order. Every department was highly professional. Preparing to start a picture after the script was finished would be like the night before D-Day. There would be a meeting of all the department heads and the director and the producer would sit side by side, and questions would be asked. This was after the picture had been cast. The writer would never be present [laughter]. It was out of the writer's hands, unless he was a writer-director. The questions would be: How big do you want the ballroom in the ballroom scene? How many people should be in it? You will have seen the locations, which is your choice of locations? All those items would be considered and that's the last meeting that would be held. If I wanted to go on location, I would say I want to go on location to San Francisco. They would ask, how many days will you need? Well, five days in San Francisco. Make it a week!

Then came the meeting with Louis B. Mayer—for final instructions. I had met him before, but only socially and casually, introduced briefly to him, that was all. Then I saw a good deal of him at M-G-M and found him to be most extraordinary. Here was this dynamic little man who, although his shoulders were heavy, was as strong as a little bull. He was the most dedicated, if not the worst, actor I've ever run into! [laughter]. Everything was the occasion for a performance. Sitting behind his desk, why, he was acting like a magnate. If he was standing up, why, it was another performance, depending on whatever the role was or whatever the occasion required. It was a constant performance and one watched it with a mingled sense of wonder and embarrassment [laughter], and as I say, I concede a liking for him. I mean, the power that could sustain this twenty-four-hour performance was something to be rather in awe of, and there was nothing he would not do to make a point, no limit to his endeavours. I can give you an immediate illustration. I was going to do Quo Vadis—for five minutes! Well, I didn't do it! I actually worked on a script, but in writing the script I neglected the more religious aspects of the picture which, it turned out, was what they really wanted to convey to Christians. A spiritual, uplifting experience for theatregoers, and I wasn't prepared to provide this. I was more interested in the evil in this very good book. No film has ever done justice to the book. Parts of it are amazing. But they are not the parts that have been on the screen. The delineation of Nero really plumbs into a depth of evil that's more in Jean-Paul Sartre's territory than it is religious writing. This was the part that interested me, so they were very disappointed when they saw what my approach to it was. L. B. asked me, having read it, to go up and see him at his house. I did, and he said that if I were able to accomplish what he saw as his vision of this picture—why, there was nothing he would not do for me. He would crawl and kiss my hands. He told me then about an experience he had had with Jeanette MacDonald and how he sang the Jewish "Kol Nidre" to her. Now he couldn't sing, but he wanted to show her how he expected her to sing some song in some musical, and he didn't hesitate to say that he had been a champion of Jeanette MacDonald's against universal adversaries who claimed that she only pissed ice-water! He sang this song to her, she wept, and then she sang her song the way he had hoped she would, and fulfilled all his expectations! If I could do this with *Quo Vadis* he would—and then he *did*—get down on the floor and crawl. I was standing well back [*laughter*] and he crawled across the floor and took my hands for a time and kissed them [*roars of laughter*]. And I thought, "This is not happening, and I'm not here" [*roars of laughter*]. Well, that's what I mean. I never had any other encounters with him to equal that. That was the height of our drama! Finally, the producer of *Quo Vadis,* Arthur Hornblow, decided that it was all too much for him, and that gave me a reason to be asked to be excused. That's all there was to it.

Fortunately, Mayer had very little to do with *The Asphalt Jungle,* practically nothing to do with it. Of course, everything that went through the studio at that time was with Mayer's approval, but he didn't become personally involved in that picture. However, having seen it, he called me and told me how much he liked it. It was not a typical M-G-M picture and was even criticised for being sympathetic to the criminal element, and my defence of that was that unless we understand the criminal—why, there's no way of coping with him. I don't know if that was a very good defence, but Mayer never interfered with it.

I had read the story by W. R. Burnett, who in my opinion was, for a time, one of the fine American writers, much under-estimated, as Americans underrate Dashiell Hammett. His reputation in France

With Marilyn Monroe on the set of THE ASPHALT JUNGLE (1950).

and in the world is much greater at this time than in the U.S. To me, Dash Hammett was the master—head and shoulders above Chandler and any of the followers. First Poe and then Dashiel Hammett! As I say, Burnett was of that calibre—approached it, anyway. It remains for some of his books to be re-made. "Iron Man" is an extraordinary story. He wrote from the inside and had a great power of truth and understanding. A story of a gambler, "Dark Hazard," this could well be told again. A number of them would make very good films. I don't think "Giant Swing" has ever been made—perhaps it has, I don't know.* "Little Caesar" was the least of the things he wrote.

I had met Marilyn Monroe when we were doing *We Were Strangers*. She was a stage-struck, motion-picture struck little girl, and she would come on to the set and watch the shooting. She was a lovely little thing, absolutely lovely, and it didn't occur to me to think about using her at the time. Afterwards, I remember my impression of her was that she was beautiful but dumb. Not strictly dumb, there was a kind of *naiveté*, a complete innocence that amounted to that. Then a little (and I mean that literally) agent from the William Morris office came to see me. He said, "John, I have a client who I think would be wonderful for *The Asphalt Jungle*. She's read the script." At that time it was the practice to send scripts to the various big agencies and they would make suggestions from the ranks of the people they represented. He said, "I think this girl could play this beautifully." He brought her to the studio, and I didn't remember her name. He told me who he was going to bring, but I didn't recall it was the same girl. As soon as I saw her, I remembered. Marilyn had the script and had studied the part, and she read for me. I remember she got down on the floor to read the scene. There was no sofa there, and the scene that she was to play was on a sofa, so she used the floor as the sofa. She was very good, very good indeed. There was no question about her doing it, she had just exactly the right quality. Little Johnny, the agent, I discovered, was very much in love with her. Anyway, she played the part. It was suggested to M-G-M that she be put under contract, but strangely she wasn't. Then Darryl Zanuck saw the picture and said, "Let's put that girl under contract," and somebody said, "She has already been under contract, but we fired her, we let her go." "For God's sake get her back!" That was the beginning of her career.

I don't remember much else about the film now. The sequence where they break open the safe, which was totally visual without any

---

* Filmed as *Dance Hall* (1941), directed by Irving Pichel.

dialogue whatsoever, has been imitated many times since. This was described in the book and it was according to the best safecracking techniques carried out on excellent advice from my old safe-cracking friends! [*laughter*] Since this film was made, 101, if not more, films have been made like it, now called "caper" films, where somebody carries out a spectacular robbery and they either get away with it at the end or they lose their loot or it blows away in the wind. Since *Sierra Madre* this has been repeated a thousand times, but it is indicative of the change of audience acceptance, of moral standards, that now they get away with it, now they get to the border in time! I would not have wanted the ending of *The Asphalt Jungle* to have been any different than what it was. I was not working against myself in order to conform to the censorship standards of the day. No, this was the book, and the picture goes along fairly close to the book and I had great respect, as I said, for the writing of W. R. Burnett.

THE ASPHALT JUNGLE (1950). Sterling Hayden at right.

I showed him the script, and asked his advice. The story of the good Doctor, who was the brains of the gang, unable to tear himself away from the sight of this little girl's wiggling ass and thereby causing his downfall, had a lovely classic shape to it! Of course, it was all done in the studio, with a few location shots.

For my next picture, I got away from the studio for the greater part of it. To some people, *The Red Badge of Courage* is remembered more by a book written about the making of the film than the film itself. This is largely due to the fact that—at the time Lillian Ross came and watched the filming and wrote the book—it was most unusual for any books at all to be written about film-making—apart from fan magazines, of course. The only press people on the set were usually fan magazine writers to interview stars. I must say that as a journalist I've never known anyone to be her equal. Her reporting is uncannily correct. Uncanny from this viewpoint. She would never take a note. There was no such thing as a tape recorder. When I say she would never take a note, she only made them for the spelling of a name or a figure, an amount. There was a complete recall, at least, of an entire conversation. Now I knew at night she would go home and make her notes and work, but reading about conversations that I either overheard when she was present, or took part in, and the incidents, I couldn't fault them. They were exactly as I remembered them. Now it may be that a time or two in the book she misinterpreted something, but it's about as good a piece of reporting as I know. It was right to the line and she also has that extraordinary power of being able to "get over" a personality. Savage is the word for it on occasions, although I don't think there's anything savage in her. I have a great admiration for Lilly, even love, and I've got to know her over the years. She's a devoted person, and she stands for all the things which to me that marvellous, wonderful, great and good magazine "The New Yorker" stands for. To me, it's one of the most important journals of our times, nothing compares with it. Its excellence, its high standard of writing, its commonsense approach, its realisation of what is unimportant and what is very important, and how it maintains a calm, collected manner throughout all the changing social conditions and points of view, is admirable.

However, it was not true, as she wrote, that I left the film. I had completed the editing. It was completely finished, with music and everything else, it was a finished picture. I turned it in, and I went away to do *The African Queen*, which was waiting for me in Africa. It was while I was gone that the studio proceeded to change it, which they would have probably done whether I had gone or not. The studio system again! I left it in the hands of Gottfried Reinhardt,

THE RED BADGE OF COURAGE (1951). Costumed for a small role in the film, Huston talks to Audie Murphy.

who was a champion, and who defended it to the last ditch, but he had eventually to retire from it. Let me also say, in extenuating the circumstances of the incident, that when I saw the finished picture—my cut of the picture—with an audience, the reaction of that audience was the most disheartening experience I have ever been through in a theatre with one of my works. At what I thought, and what I still think to be the best scene in the picture (it was later taken out), the audience got up, I would say, in scores, and left the theatre. They didn't like it. They liked nothing about it. It was too much for them. They didn't want it. I conjectured about this, why they reacted so strongly. It was at the time of the Korean War and I remember myself turning the pages of "Life" magazine and skipping over those pages that had pictures of the Korean War.

The scene that was cut concerned the Boy and the Tattered Soldier after watching the death of the Tall Soldier. It's a monumental death, something mysterious about it. He says, "Don't touch me. Let me be. Don't touch me." They stand watching him with some awe as he pulls himself up and seems almost to grow in height and power. Then he falls like a tree, dead. The two of them then walk down a hill following this. (This is in the picture. I mean the death of the Tall Soldier.) The two of them walk down the hill and the

Tattered Soldier says, "Well, I've never seen a man die like that before." He keeps on talking, begins to ramble, he becomes incoherent, and presently he's walking in a circle. The circle gets smaller, the boy stands by, and the Tattered Soldier falls down and he dies. He's been wounded and it's a kind of anti-climax. It's terrible, because it didn't build up to this, it let down to it, and it's unbearable. As I say, it's a fine drama, it was beautifully acted, but it was too much for the audience. They didn't like it. The studio thought to salvage the picture by taking out that scene, and by letting the audience know that the film was from a book that was considered to be a masterpiece. They put another introduction to the picture. They opened it with the book, narration was introduced, and it did the picture damage.

I quite understand M-G-M taking these steps, however mistaken. I'll demonstrate to you later that I'm not all that broad-minded in certain instances when pictures of mine have been really messed around with without purpose, and the only understanding of the exercise on my part would be that of the stupidity of a producer who is responsible, so I'm not saying this out of any spiritual largesse, or magnificence, or munificence! It was something which one might very well have accepted. At that time, a contest developed between L. B. Mayer and Dore Schary over who really was to run the studio, that's what it amounted to. Schary wanted to make the picture and L. B. was against the picture, and the final decision was up to New York, or rather who New York would side with, whether it was L. B. or Dore Schary. In New York it was Nicholas Schenck who held the power. This realisation of what was occurring only came belatedly to me, before we went into production. In the meantime, I had grown fond of L. B. Mayer and this story will tell you why. I had a sense of what the man was. I was bothered by the fact that he didn't want the film made, and that it had become a *cause célèbre,* a kind of football, so I went up to see L. B. and said, "L. B., if you are against me in this picture, why, I don't want to do it." He said, "Why don't you want to do it?" I said, "Becase I don't want to do anything against you. If you are opposed to it, why, we can find something else to do. I certainly don't want to see this forced down anyone's throat." He replied, *"That's* your only reason for not wanting to do this film?" I said, "That's my reason." He said, "John, you ought to be ashamed." Dramatising the moment, too! "If you like it, you fight for it. Don't do anything to please me. It's the picture that is important, and what you think of it that's important. Personalities have nothing to do with this. You fight for what you believe in, you fight to do it. I will fight against its being done, not against you doing it, but against it being done. You must fight to see that it is made if you believe in it." Well, you have to take your hat off to that! So I did fight, and the film was made.

I took as the style for the picture the photographs of the Civil War photographer, Matthew Brady. I tried to reproduce the feel of the photographs with a kind of bleached effect, because originally they were made by wet plate photography. I wanted the blonde fields, the blonde, bright skies and foregrounds, contrasted with the explosive quality of the black-and-white. This was the first time in my film career that I had been able to actually bring into filming my interest in photography and art, the work of photographers and painters. In years to come, in other films, I was able to draw directly on my love of painting, drawing, photography. The organisation of subject and people within the frame is something which I learned to feel from looking at paintings within their frames. I don't believe there's been another film about the Civil War which looked like *The Red Badge of Courage*. I read it when I was quite young and read it again. It's one of the masterpieces of American literature and Stephen Crane was one of the first modern writers. I had played around with it and one day I said, "My God, this could be a very interesting film," and I saw the picture in my mind's eye. Having seen it, having conceived as to how it could be done as a motion picture, I wrote it in a few days. Although it's faithful to the spirit of the novel, there's very little spoken in the picture that is in the novel. I had to write all the dialogue in the style of the piece. Again I knew that style. My mother's family were Civil War. My grandmother was the daughter of a Civil War general, and I was raised in that style. My grandmother said "wownded" instead of "wounded." They were "ep-u-lets" and so on! I knew the way the people talked, so it was not hard for me to write this way.

Casting presented some troubles—to the studio, not to me. I championed Audie Murphy, who was known as the "most decorated soldier." The studio indulged the director. If they gave him the go-ahead, then he was responsible, it was in his hands. The rest of the cast were friends of mine who had never acted. John Dierkes I first met during the war in London. I first met Bill Mauldin in Italy when he was a cartoonist in the Army newspaper. Right through, the players were people I had known, and only a few others were professional actors; they had the quality of the characters which is more important to me. If someone has the quality, it comes over, and comes over better than if it is someone imitating the quality. The camera sees through a performance. Great actors sometimes don't ever quite come across on the screen. What we see is a fine performance rather than a spiritual thing, it's only a mystery of the personality.

WE WERE STRANGERS. 1949. *An* Horizon *Production released by Columbia.*
Director: John Huston. *Producer:* S. P. Eagle [Sam Spiegel].
Screenplay: Peter Viertel and John Huston. *From an episode in the novel "Rough Sketch" by:* Robert Sylvester. *Photography:* Russell Metty. *Editor:* Al Clark. *Art director:* Cary Odell. *Music:* George Antheil.
Running time: 106 minutes.
Players: Jennifer Jones (*China Valdes*), John Garfield (*Tony Fenner*), Pedro Armendariz (*Armando Ariete*), Gilbert Roland (*Guillermo*), Ramon Novarro (*Chief*), Wally Cassell (*Miguel*), David Bond (*Ramon*), Jose Perez (*Toto*), Morris Ankrum (*Bank Manager*), Tito Rinaldo (*Manolo*), Pal Monte (*Roberto*), Leonard Strong (*Bombmaker*), Robert Tafur (*Rubio*).

Story

In the early Thirties, Cuba is dominated by a tyrannical, brutally repressive government; a girl working in a bank, China Valdes, sees her brother murdered by Ariete, the chief of the secret police, and joins the underground movement to avenge his death. She arranges false credentials at the bank for Tony Fenner, an American revolutionary posing as a theatrical agent. Fenner conceives an extraordinary plan to rid Cuba of its oppressors: to plant a dynamite bomb under the family tomb of an important politician, by tunnelling from China's house to the cemetery. The politician will be assassinated when the tunnel is complete, and the bomb will be exploded when the cabinet attend his funeral at the tomb. After days and nights of exhaustive digging, during which one of the five men goes mad after shovelling through poor people's graves, they reach the tomb. The politician is assassinated, the bomb is laid, and at the last moment the funeral is held elsewhere, by a sudden decision of the dead man's family. The plot has collapsed, the work has been in vain. Fenner has to escape, but the plan misfires, and after a savage battle with the police he dies in China's arms. Outside, the first sounds and revels of a victorious uprising can be heard.

Comment

The question asked has been posed many times, in life and on film, but seldom as intelligently as in this picture: can non-violent people justify the use of violence to bring about a new and just order? In fighting ruthless dictatorship, which uses violence to remain in power, is violence, with its killing of the innocent as well as the guilty, the only way to end it? The situation is such that the question is never really faced, but the exploration of the theme makes this a vivid and compelling film, a gripping, thoughtful adventure of extraordinary realism and ruthlessness and, too, an unexpected glimpse into future events in Cuba.

THE ASPHALT JUNGLE. 1950. *An* M-G-M *Picture.*
Director: John Huston. *Producer:* Arthur Hornblow Jr. *Screenplay:* Ben Maddow and John Huston. *From the novel by:* W. R. Burnett. *Photography:* Harold Rosson. *Editor:* George Boemler. *Art Directors:* Cedric Gibbons and Randall Duell. *Music:* Miklos Rosza.
Running time: 105 minutes.
Players: Sterling Hayden (*Dix Handley*), Louis Calhern (*Alonzo D. Emmerich*), Jean Hagen (*Doll Conovan*), James Whitmore (*Gus Minissi*), Sam Jaffe (*Reimenschneider*), John McIntire (*Police Commissioner Hardy*), Marc Lawrence (*Cobby*), Barry Kelley (*Lt. Dietrich*), Anthony Caruso (*Louis Ciavelli*), Teresa Celli (*Maria Ciavelli*).

Story
    A brilliant criminal, Doc Reimenschneider, is released from prison, where he has perfected the plan for a million dollar jewel store robbery. His requisites, as for any business operation, are backing, manpower, and a market, and he looks for them in a bleak, ugly mid-western city. The backing is provided by a highly respectable lawyer who has taken to crime, and although Reimenschneider originally intends to approach an ordinary "fence," he is betrayed by greed when the lawyer, Emmerich, suggests that he can himself dispose of the jewels at a higher profit. The gang—a hunchback barkeeper, an expert safe-breaker who works to support his wife and child, and a hard-bitten killer—are assembled, and the crime successfully carried out. Emmerich, who is in fact bankrupt, desperately plans to doublecross his associates, and, with a confederate, he attempts to take the jewels from them. Dix, the killer, shoots Emmerich's partner and he and Reimenschneider go into hiding with the now valueless jewels. Meanwhile, the police close in; the bookie whose office has been the gang headquarters is arrested and betrays the others, Emmerich shoots himself when the police arrive, Reimenschneider is arrested trying to escape from the city. Dix, with his girl, sets off for his old home in the country; he reaches it, but he has been wounded in the fight and dies of loss of blood.

Comment
    This is an entirely convincing picture of the tension and isolation of the criminal world, in which men are destroyed by their greed and weaknesses. Immediate, direct, chilling and unsensational, this au-

THE RED BADGE OF COURAGE (1951).

thentic film, set against the harsh tempo of urban life, is also brilliantly acted by a superb cast.

THE RED BADGE OF COURAGE. 1951. *An* M-G-M *Picture.*
Director: John Huston. *A* John Huston *Production.*
Producer: Gottfried Reinhardt. *Screenplay:* John Huston. *From the novel by:* Stephen Crane. *Adapted by:* Albert Band. *Photography:* Harold Rosson. *Editor:* Ben Lewis. *Art Directors:* Cedric Gibbons and Hans Peters. *Music:* Bronislau Kaper.
Running time: 69 minutes (originally 100 minutes approx.)
Players: Audie Murphy (*The Youth*), Bill Mauldin (*The Loud Soldier*), Royal Dano (*The Tattered Soldier*), John Dierkes (*The Tall Soldier*), Douglas Dick (*The Lieutenant*), Andy Devine (*The Talkative Soldier*). *Narration spoken by:* James Whitmore.

Story
   Set in the last days of the American Civil War, *The Red Badge of Courage* chronicles a young Northern recruit's first experience of active combat—his early fears and flight from the battlefield, his baptism of fire and final emergence as a hero. The boy's second experience of battle dramatically confirms his fears of his own cowardice and he runs away. Behind the lines he joins a ragged line of retreating wounded soldiers and strikes up a quick, intimate friendship with the Tattered Soldier. Together, they stand helpless over the agonising death of the once courageous Tall Soldier, who had been the boy's friend and confidant. (In the novel, the Tattered Soldier, too, dies, but this scene has been cut from the film.) Making his way back to his unit, the boy comes into a brief but violent fight with a soldier hurrying from the front, who in the fever of battle strikes him with the butt of his rifle. The boy's wound—his red badge of courage—suddenly crystallises and resolves his personal doubts. Having tasted the approach of death and come to terms with it, he rejoins his unit and leads his comrades in a heroic and victorious charge.

Comment
   A classic movie of a great book courageously attempting to convey the confusion and complexities of war, this is a truthful, compassionate work, going deeply into the state of fear, exhilaration and resignation which soldiers experience. It is also memorable for the bold, visual style of its magnificently created battle scenes.

The First International Film-Maker

Africa (The Congo): **The African Queen** (1951)

WHILE THE VARIOUS mechanical things were being done to *The Red Badge of Courage*, I went to work with Jim Agee on the screenplay for *The African Queen*. Then, having finished the screenplay, Jim had a heart attack. A few years later he died from another heart attack. He would have come to Europe with me except for this. I came to London where there were brief consultations regarding the unit and then went off to Africa to look for locations. I had known of Forester's novel when I was at Warner Bros. and I thought it would make a very good film. As a result of this, Sam and I bought the rights from Warner Bros. and of course the idea of doing it with Katie and Bogie made it seem very attractive indeed. Jim had been a critic for "Time" magazine and he was a great champion of mine. He was, I think, probably the best reviewer that America ever had. He was one of the best writers—his books have become well-known, of course. Jim came out to California to write an article on me for "Life" magazine and there I got to know him. I used to go to Idaho to shoot a gun and fish, and Jim came with me. Jim wanted to stop reviewing, he wanted to get out of that, and I suggested that he work on the script with me. He fell in with that instantly. He was extraordinary, a beautiful writer, intelligent and creative. I enjoyed every moment I spent with Jim.

Then, as I say, I came to England and met Sam and set up a deal with the Woolf brothers, their Romulus company. After various occasions with them, mostly at Les Ambassadeurs, why, I shoved off to Africa. I didn't realise it at the time, but, looking back, this was an important turn in my career, because this was the first time I had come to Europe, and to Africa, to make a pre-arranged feature film. I came back to London which I had left years before and, while this was very much an American film, I used British technicians and British actors. This turned out to be my first step into the international field, the beginning of my constant travels in the making of motion pictures. The crew we finally took out to Africa was one of the best crews I ever had and the whole African experience was just, oh, a magnificent one. I went out with the art director, Wilfred Shingleton, and the adventure of Africa was utterly fascinating. There was a pilot there, Alec Newne, he owned the airline, and another pilot John Hangmans, and they had emergency strips across Africa where planes had never sat down on. They were built during the war when the British were transporting planes across Africa. We'd get permission to sit down on these strips and we saw a life that was completely untouched, that civilisation hadn't yet reached at all. We'd take trips in an aeroplane, which would take us to somewhere else, where we'd get into a pirogue and go a day or two up or down a river. It was looking for locations in the grandest way one could imagine. Africa was like a revelation. The whole trip was just an earth-shaking experience. I was looking at another world, of great animals and strange people. As they say, you never get into an automobile in Africa that it isn't an adventure. Something was always happening, something fascinating. It might just be a storm. The things that happened would make a book in itself.

On this one long trip, we finally found the ideal place to start the picture, on the Roui Key River in the Congo. We could bring supplies into the place. We then set about building a camp for the company and of course, the "scene" for the picture, the boat "The African Queen." I had an idea, so far as the shooting was concerned, of having flat-topped barges, rafts as it were, and putting a mock-up of "The African Queen" on one of these so that we could surround it, move around it, for the intimate scenes. The "Queen" herself was so small we couldn't do anything in the way of moving a camera. Then we could mount the lights, camera and sound equipment on that raft. Then a second raft would carry more equipment, and then another raft would carry the generator, and finally, all of this would be pulled by "The African Queen" herself, which furnished the power. And it worked! This river caravanserai would go chugging upstream. Turning around was a little complicated, but we learned how to do it. It was completely self-contained, and then we would go down the river photographing as we went. We had a marvellous cameraman in Jack Cardiff. There was one particularly good stretch that we navigated frequently with this procession of barges, which I compared to a caravan.

The straw that broke the camel's back was another raft that Katie added with a privy on it! Her private toilet! The "Queen" was incapable of carrying that. She had the raft with her little dressing room and a full-length mirror that managed not to get broken in getting there, but it was broken almost immediately after it arrived. The mirror dwindled continuously from its original full length! First it was broken in half, then in quarters, and then the quarters got smaller and smaller until she had a lot of little hand-mirrors! The bush served as her dressing room too! It worked so far as shooting the picture was concerned, it worked very well.

The entire adventure was rather enchanting. We'd tie up the rafts to shoot a sequence right on the river bank, and one afternoon we saw some shadows moving in the forest. We were very quiet and they came forward, and out of the trees emerged a family of baboons, a whole tribe. The little fellows went up into the trees, there must have been thirty or forty of them, and there was one old elderly gentleman who sat on a fallen tree and crossed his legs, just like a *bon vivant* at the French opera! Then every evening as long as we were there, they would come and watch until the light faded in the afternoon and we'd have to leave and go back to our ship (we were at Murchison). We'd leave the rafts tied up to the shore and when we went, why, the baboons would come and imitate what we'd been doing! They themselves became actors, and kissed like Bogart and Hepburn! [*laughter*].

Oh, we had a wonderful time! Katie was extraordinary. She has great energy and dedication and we had to finish within a certain length of time in the Congo location, not because of pressure from the front office, but because of pressure from the soldier ants! The place we'd built was very romantic, and it was beautiful. We went to sleep to the beating of the drums. There was native dancing every night and these affairs were controlled by a local king, King Paul. He wore a leopard skin. Our place, which had a bar, a restaurant and bungalows, was beautiful to look at and wonderful to live in, but made out of the materials of the forest: palm fronds, and leaves, and raffia, so it was vegetable matter, and as it decayed, why, then it became attractive to these soldier ants. We built little ditches, little shallow trenches, in case the soldier ants came. They were a very real danger, like fire. We poured paraffin into these trenches and set them alight. I slept through all this, but one night it was a foray rather than a real attack. Some forward patrols of the soldier ants came into the camp and the alarm was spread. Katie, who had been asleep, woke up and thought it was some sort of a revel going on, and she appeared on the porch of her bungalow and denounced these riotous men. Didn't they realise that there was work to be done tomorrow? When she was told what was happening and that it wasn't a drunken orgy, she led the fight against the soldier ants. It really sounds like something out of a film itself. As for Bogie, well, thank heavens Betty [Lauren Bacall] was with him. Betty was always with him when he filmed. Bogie liked the comforts of Beverly Hills. Actually, he didn't think it was any great shakes as an adventure!

I used to go out with a rifle in the morning before working on the picture, and Bogie never accompanied me. Katie did. Katie at first denounced me—I'd shoot meat for the pot—and the idea of my killing these beautiful animals was revolting and how could anyone with a sensitive nature lend himself to this act of murder, practically! Finally I got fed up with talk and said, "Katie, you don't know what the hell you're talking about and you couldn't possibly unless you witnessed it yourself, unless you saw what happened." She rose to this challenge and said, "I'll come with you." From then on she was Diane of the hunt! She would come in to my bungalow (they were little one-room places that's all, very pretty) or into my stateroom when we were aboard the paddleboat "The Isle of Murchison," and she'd wake me up before dawn, hours before, and I would have to go out. "Let's go, John." She loved to go! [*laughter*]. Her idea of hunting changed considerably. Bogart was not the outdoors man at all, not at all! Bogie would much rather have been on the Champs Elysées, or preferable to that even, in his house in Beverly Hills.

I had met Robert Morley before when I was at M-G-M contemplating doing *Quo Vadis*. Morley had just been doing Oscar Wilde and I saw him in the play in New York. I thought of him as Nero, but he couldn't do it because of the play. Then we shot a few interiors back in London for *The African Queen* and when the film was finished I was quite satisfied with it. It turned out the way I wanted it to be. The humour in the relationship between Bogart and Hepburn was implicit from the start. That relationship is very strongly put forward in Forester's book. As for the finish, well, Forester had two finishes for his novel, one for the English edition, and another in the American novel. He was never satisfied with either. The film had a third finish of Agee's and my own devising, and Forester agreed to it.

Each subject as it came along, each idea, was independent of everything that had gone before. I never had any doubts. I was always, you used the word, "confident." It never entered my mind to be anything else. I knew what I wanted and usually got it!

THE AFRICAN QUEEN. 1951. *A* Romulus-Horizon *Production.*
Director: John Huston. *Producer:* S. P. Eagle. *Script:* James Agee and John Huston. *From the novel by:* C. S. Forester. *Photography:* Jack Cardiff. *Second Unit:* Ted Scaife. *Colour Process:* Technicolor. *Art*

Director: Wilfred Shingleton. *Editor:* Ralph Kemplen. *Katharine Hepburn's costumes:* Doris Langley Moore. *Music:* Allan Gray. *Running time:* 103 minutes.
Players: Katharine Hepburn (*Rose Sayer*), Humphrey Bogart (*Charlie Allnutt*), Robert Morley (*Brother Samuel Sayer*), Peter Bull (*German Captain*), Theodore Bikel (*German 1st. Officer*), Walter Gotell (*German 2nd. Officer*), Gerald Onn (*Petty Officer*), Peter Swanwick (*Shona Fort Officer*), Richard Marner (*2nd. Shona Fort Officer*).

Story

Brother Samuel Sayer and his sister Rose, a prim but spirited spinster, run a mission in a German East African settlement. The time is 1914. News of the outbreak of war is brought by Charlie Allnutt, the scruffy, gin-drinking Canadian captain of "The African Queen," a small river trading steamer. German soldiers arrive to occupy the village, Brother Samuel resists, is knocked on the head,

Humphrey Bogart and Katharine Hepburn in THE AFRICAN QUEEN

loses his mind and dies. Allnutt returns the next day, buries Brother Samuel, and persuades Rose to escape with him on "The African Queen." Once aboard, Rose's patriotic instincts are stirred by the cargo: oxygen and hydrogen cylinders, blasting gelatin. She suggests to Allnutt that he make a torpedo to blow up a German gunboat, "The Louisa," patrolling the lake at the end of the river. As "The African Queen" goes down the river, navigating dangerous rapids, Allnutt slowly capitulates in the face of Rose's indomitable spirit; and she is beginning to have tender feelings for him. The plan to blow up "The Louisa" is formulated, Rose and Allnutt discover with surprise that they have fallen in love with each other, and after many rigours and adventures "The African Queen" reaches the lake. That night, steaming out towards "The Louisa" to torpedo her, they are shipwrecked in a heavy storm. They are captured by the Germans and sentenced to death as spies. The German captain accedes to Allnutt's last request, to marry them before they hang; hardly has he

. . . and relaxing with their director.

done so when the gunboat hits the shipwrecked "African Queen," still torpedo-laden, and blows up. Allnutt and Rose swim to safety on the British shore.

Comment

The first of many departures for John Huston was this tale of a gently humorous relationship between a gallant, determined spinster and a hard-bitten captain who loses his heart to her. Their relationship, at first a polite acceptance of each other, then a duel, and finally a love match, is one of the most endearing ever created by the director. The emphasis is on character, the adventure is incidental. Entirely delightful, warm and sympathetic, free of coyness, this is one of Huston's most popular and enduring works.

France (Paris) : **Moulin Rouge** (1952)

No one can ever say I make the same film twice! From *The African Queen* I went to *Moulin Rouge*, which was shot mainly in Paris. Here, all of my interest in art, which I discovered before I became a film-maker, served me well when it came to recreating the world of Toulouse-Lautrec. The picture, looking at it now, is physically, I think, very beautiful. The movement of the picture is excellent. So far as the character of Lautrec is concerned, well, Jose Ferrer played him admirably, I thought, though we weren't able to do the artist justice. We wouldn't tell that story now. It wouldn't be the same Toulouse-Lautrec today, as we did then, because of censorship. There was a sentimental turn to the film that, if anything, I think would have offended the painter himself, who was clinically detached. Within its own limitations, I think it was a good film. Those limitations, however, were unfortunate. I felt even at the time it's a shame we can't make the true story of Lautrec. We had to understand and accept what we could and could not show. Not only instinctively, it was laid down in the Code. We went as far as we could. When I contemplate the censorship at that time and the absurdities of it, it is hard to believe. I remember there was one scene where the girls raise their dresses and show their pantaloons, and in some places this was deleted.

Anthony Veiller again worked on the screenplay. I'd known him before the war, and then we were together, very briefly, when I was engaged on the *Why We Fight* series with Frank Capra. We wrote a bit on that series, and for this Combined Operations film we worked on the writing together. As a result of collaborating so well together we went on and wrote *The Stranger* and *The Killers*. Then, after the war, why, we did *Moulin Rouge,* again working from London. *The African Queen* was finished before we started on it.

I was saddened to read the other day of the death of Elliot Elisophen. Elliot was a very fine colour photographer with still cameras. I wanted to get a new colour technique to reproduce the style of Toulouse-Lautrec for *Moulin Rouge.* As Elliot knew more about colour perhaps than any other photographer in the world, we brought him over and he collaborated with us. We made various tests, and he made still photographic tests and effects. Then we came up with Oswald Morris, who was a very creative and experimental man who could work with this method. It was a result of putting our heads together. Instead of letting the colour be fragmented as it usually is in straight colour photography, we tried to give an effect of local colour, in other words to flatten it out, and this was done with the use of filters. We used a fog filter, something that up until then had only been used on the outside to simulate fog. We would burn the set-up with light, and then photograph it with a fog filter, then with colour filters, and using smoke, so that the whole thing would have a monochrome quality.

We found Ossie Morris when we were looking for an English photographer. I had shot tests with various photographers, watching them, how they worked, not hiring anybody but just shooting tests from day to day of actors as a rule. Not for the photography but the photographing of actors. We tried little stunts, however, with the photography and I'd see how the cameramen worked. None of them were what I was looking for. They all had their old-time methods, procedures. Then I met Ossie, and it was just a kind of chemistry that occurred. There was that realisation, that instinctive realisation, that Ossie Morris was a seeker. He hadn't found what he was looking for, and that was what I was doing and so we fell together and it was a fine collaboration. I also had Jack Clayton as our production assistant. He went on to become a very gifted director. The film was a collaboration between Romulus and United Artists, initiated by me. It was easier in those days than it is today!

Then we went off to France. Actually, the material just required the Paris scene, and we worked mostly on the real locations. All the exteriors were, of course, in Paris, with some studio work there—not a great deal—and some studio work here in London.

For Jose Ferrer, it was a muscular effort on his part, as well as being an artistic triumph. We had various devices. In the distance a small man would appear walking, and it would be a dwarf, someone made up to look like Joe. Then he would disappear behind a wagon and walk out from the wagon in a closer shot. Then he would

Colette Marchand and Jose Ferrer in MOULIN ROUGE (1952).

disappear behind another wagon and another small man would pick up from there and go on. These little tricks paid off very well. We had to think all these things out beforehand, but they are not all that difficult. They did work. I was delighted with the performances, Suzanne Flon, Colette Marchand, and the other players.

We used the hand-held camera. I think it was one of the first times a scene in a feature film was ever shot with a hand-held camera. The dance scene at the Bal Tabarin was hand-held and we thought we were being very daring when we did that!

To go back to this business of what we couldn't show because of censorship, the fact is I don't think we did really tell the essence of the man, because what we couldn't show was so much a part of him. He was completely detached, remote, uninvolved, a spectator, with a heart like an ice-box. He put down what he saw; he was a man of great truth, precision, and untinged with romanticism or sentimentality, and given to a cruel humour. Everything about the man demonstrated this detachment. This is one of the few instances in my work where I had to make a serious compromise, but in doing this I don't feel completely negative about the result. As I said before, within its limitations it works. Physically I'm delighted with the picture. Ossie Morris was on the television the other day and they showed some scenes from *Moulin Rouge,* and, my God, they're lovely!

MOULIN ROUGE. 1952. *A* Romulus-John Huston *Production. Director:* John Huston. *Associate Producer:* Jack Clayton. *Script:* Anthony Veiller and John Huston. *From the book by:* Pierre La Mure. *Photography:* Oswald Morris. *Colour Process:* Technicolor. *Editor:* Ralph Kemplen. *Art Director:* Paul Sheriff. *Costumes:* Marcel Vertes. *Music:* Georges Auric.
Running time: 120 minutes.
Players: Jose Ferrer *(Toulouse-Lautrec/his father)* , Colette Marchand *(Marie)* , Suzanne Flon *(Myriamme)* , Zsa Zsa Gabor *(Jane Avril)* , Katherine Kath *(La Goulue)* , Claude Nollier *(Comtesse de Toulouse-Lautrec)* , Muriel Smith *(Aicha)* , Georges Lannes *(Patou)* , Walter Crisham *(Valentin Dessosse)* , Mary Clare *(Mme. Loubet)* , Lee Montague *(Maurice)* , Harold Gasket *(Zidler)* , Jill Bennett *(Sarah)* , Jim Gerald *(Père Cotelle)* , Rupert John *(Chocolat)* , Tutti Lemkow *(Aicha's partner)* .

Story
   A fictionalised impression of the life of Toulouse-Lautrec, centered on his activities at the Moulin Rouge. We are introduced to some of the famous figures there—Jane Avril, La Goulue, Valentin Dessosse— and watch Lautrec sketching them. Lautrec's personal life is dramatised in two episodes: his infatuation with a grasping and debauched girl of the streets, Marie, who after many quarrels and reconciliations he finally abandons; and his friendship with Myriamme, a lonely model interested in culture, with whom, through pride and fear of being hurt again, he refuses to let himself fall in love. Myriamme is obliged to give him up and marry an admirer of long standing. Lautrec declines; he drinks more and more, becomes increasingly bitter. The inevitable collapse follows, and he is taken home to die in the family chateau.

Comment
   Huston, like all artists who seek to expand, search and create new worlds, here leaves behind his unadorned and utilitarian methods of work to experiment with colour and painting. With superb colour photography (his first collaboration with Oswald Morris) , imaginative sets and costumes and a lively cast, he brings extravagantly to life the

world of Toulouse-Lautrec as the society of the time was free to see it. The romanticised narrative is vivid, appealing and full of atmosphere, and the artist and his work are presented, where frankness was not permitted, with intelligence and understanding.

Italy (Ravella) : Beat the Devil (1953)

Peter Viertel and Tony Veiller did a script for *Beat the Devil* and it wasn't a very successful script. They are very fine writers, but it just didn't pan out. When I met with Bogart in Italy, why, I was pretty discouraged about our chances of getting any kind of a picture, and I even proposed that we abandon the whole thing. Bogey, who was a very provident man with a buck in small things, said, "Why, John, I'm surprised at you. It's only money!" That stiffened my back.

Jennifer Jones and Humphrey Bogart in BEAT THE DEVIL (1953).

Truman Capote just happened to be in Rome so I enlisted Truman and we went to work on the script shortly before we were supposed to begin shooting—very soon.

It was a joke from the start. Bogey and I were driving down to Ravella, via Rome. Ravella was to be the scene of our picture. The driver wasn't all that good and he drove faster than he drove well. We were speeding along through the night and the road divided. There was an island ahead and the driver couldn't make up his mind which road to take, whether to go right or left. He went into the island, into a stone wall! Bogey was asleep in the back seat. I was in the front so I had a chance to brace myself. Bogey rolls out of his sleep, blood pouring out of his mouth [*roars of laughter*] and I couldn't help but laugh. He'd bitten through his tongue, and there was a trap-door in the middle of his tongue! [*roars of laughter*]. I said, "Stick your tongue out and hold it!" He'd knocked some teeth out, too! [*roars of laughter*]. I saw he wasn't seriously hurt, though. I shouldn't laugh, but he looked so aggrieved. His comments were all obscene! [*laughter*]. So he went into hospital and had his tongue stitched up, and he had to get new teeth from Los Angeles. That gave us another week to ten days' relief to work on the script! That's what we did. We re-wrote the whole of the script entirely, and sometimes we were just trying to keep ahead of the production. Sometimes the shooting would catch up to us.

I remember one occasion, because I didn't want the company to know how bankrupt we were in so far as pages were concerned, when I staged an elaborate scene that would take them some time to prepare. They had to knock out a wall, and it was very difficult, the way I staged the scene. Then I went upstairs and joined Truman and we did our writing. We were able to work for two hours and write another scene—the one we shot! [*laughter*].

Truman was a little bulldog. He was an extraordinarily rare bird, Truman. Quite distinctive from his looks, he's a little powerhouse of pluck. Truman had an impacted wisdom tooth and his face was swollen to just hideous proportions, twice the size it was, way out, inches out! I was afraid of meningitis. He was desperately ill, and Jack Clayton and I carried him down to the ambulance to take him to the hospital (this was all in Ravella) and he had to go to the hospital in Naples, or in Amalfi. That night ten pages came from the hospital! Truman had written these on his hospital bed. That's the sort of spirit little Truman has.

We enjoyed the entire experience. It was, you know, a challenge, but we met it with gaiety and the script really took off and wrote itself after a while. We followed its writing of itself with considerable admiration! [*laughter*]. I didn't know how good it was, or how bad, or anything like that, we all knew that it was something. We just went with it.

Then the picture came out and, oh, the reviews were awful! Nobody found anything to recommend, including Bogart, and he hated it! [*laughter*]. He said, "Maybe I should have listened to you in Rome" [*laughter*]. I remember Bogey sent me a copy of an advertisement an

BEAT THE DEVIL (1953). Robert Morley, Marco Tulli, Peter Lorre and Humphrey Bogart.

exhibitor had taken out in a newspaper saying that this was the worst picture he had ever had in his theatre. It was generally conceded to be a minor disaster, frivolous, self-indulgent and all the rest of it, at a time when such qualities were not accepted. Then presently people began to talk about it and say, "You know, I liked it" [*laughter*], "I don't care what they say, I think it's good." More and more of these voices were raised, and then I discovered that it had a following even, particularly in university towns. It was one of the first "underground" films in the sense of appreciation rather than production. Then people would come up to me and say, "I've seen *Beat the Devil* eleven times." One said he had seen it a grand total of thirty-eight times, or something like that! There were those who actually went after a record for how often they'd seen it. It had its cult following, and the audiences actually knew the dialogue, and would say the lines along with the actors [*laughter*]. So it just grew and grew until it has its present status.

I assembled a mixed and fascinating cast. Gina at that time was very popular, a sex symbol almost. I'd worked with Jennifer and liked her very much. David Selznick was a very good friend of mine, and he always wanted me to use Jennifer whenever I could. I thought she'd be ideal for this. I remember David took a very active interest in anything that involved Jennifer and used to send me cables—those long cables, recommendations so far as the script was concerned, and what she should wear, how her hair was to be done, and so on. He'd seen the original script. These cables came, pages long sometimes. In retaliation we composed a cable to send to David, and the first page of the cable made pretty good sense. David used to number his cables, so we started with Page One, and then I said "Page Three" and we skipped Page Two, and referred constantly to points that had been made in Page Two! [*laughter*]. This kept David busy for weeks! Whenever he sent a query, we'd say "Refer Page Two" [*laughter*].

Bogey was as always ever so obedient. He would try to get what I wanted. He wasn't really against the film as we were making it. Only after he'd seen it did he decide not to like it! [*laughter*]. It was a very different type of film and character for him and he was going against what the public expected him to be. Again I had Oswald Morris, Wilfred Shingleton, Jack Clayton, Ralph Kemplen, people I had worked with before, which gives a director a certain assurance, too.

In essence *Beat the Devil* was more a lark than a satirical story. Bob Morley had this gallery of rogues and they were absurd to see and humorous to watch. James Helvick wrote the original novel and there's a spirit in him and his writing and in the novel that was lacking in the first script. The first script was rather conventional, sedately following the prescribed form of mystery writing, the thriller, so we just turned it inside out, and enjoyed ourselves doing it! [*laughter*]. It made no points about anything in particular, we just had a very good time. It was a description of the rogue, Petersen. Scenes that I thought were very amusing in themselves, when the three wicked men plot their bad moves while they are trying to close a suitcase, sitting on it, moments of that kind gave a certain joyousness to crime, to the pursuit of evil.

The formula is that everyone is slightly absurd. The crooks, ostensibly heroic people, the romance, even virtue, become absurd. Adventurers are rather out of date, hence the suggestion of satire, although the film itself cannot be described as satirical.

At times, I'm attracted to rogues and unusual men. As I said, when I was working on *Quo Vadis* I was more interested in the evil of Nero, which, of course, Louis B. Mayer wasn't. I think that conventional morality is a deadly bore. At least Satan is attractive because he is inventive, he's an innovator. The rogue by dint of his profession is almost required to be amusing, to be entertaining, and the better the rogue, the greater the fascination he exerts. Wholly good people, except for the very rare saint and he's usually a reformed rogue, are pretty thoroughly tiresome, wouldn't you say? So to a certain extent it has been in many cases frustrating to be bound by conventional morality in the censorship code, which dictated concepts of right or wrong. I respect the individual who has his own code and abides by it, who doesn't just swallow whole the prescribed morality, but behaves out of his own conscience. He can often have the appearance of a rogue and not be one, and have a more profound morality than the one who is simply imitating.

BEAT THE DEVIL. 1953. *A* Romulus-Santana *Production.*
Director: John Huston. *Associate Producer:* Jack Clayton. *Screenplay:* Truman Capote and John Huston. *From a novel by:* James Helvick. *Photography:* Oswald Morris. *Editor:* Ralph Kemplen. *Art Director:* Wilfred Shingleton. *Music:* Franco Mannino.
Running time: 100 minutes.
Players: Humphrey Bogart (*Billy Dannreuther*), Jennifer Jones (*Gwendolen Chelm*), Gina Lollobrigida (*Maria Dannreuther*), Robert Morley (*Petersen*), Peter Lorre (*O'Hara*), Edward Underdown (*Harry Chelm*), Ivor Barnard (*Major Ross*), Bernard Lee (*C.I.D. Inspector*), Marco Tulli (*Ravello*), Mario Perroni (*Purser*), Aldo Silvani (*Charles*), Saro Urzi (*Captain*).

Story
At a small Mediterranean port, a group of people are waiting for repairs to be made to the tramp steamer which will take them to Africa. They are the Chelms, an English couple going out to a coffee

plantation; Petersen, O'Hara, Ross and Ravello, who plan to acquire vast uranium deposits; Dannreuther, an American associate of Petersen's, and his wife, Maria. While they wait, Maria becomes interested in Harry Chelm and Dannreuther in his wife, Gwendolen; the latter, who is given to inventing romantic stories, tells Dannreuther that her husband has interests in uranium. Dannreuther discounts this story, but Petersen believes it and, afraid that Dannreuther will double-cross him, insists that they leave at once by air; their car is seen to go over a cliff; they are believed to be dead; and their associates reveal something of their plans to Chelm. When Dannreuther and Petersen return, on foot, the party at last puts to sea. Chelm announces that he means to tell the whole story to the authorities and Ross, the gang's assassin, is detailed to murder him: Dannreuther, however, comes to the rescue. Later, the passengers have to abandon ship; Chelm vanishes, and Gwendolen imagines him to be drowned. They reach North Africa, have a brush with the Arabs and make their way back to their starting point. Here, a C.I.D. man arrests Petersen and his gang for a murder committed in London. Gwendolen receives a cable from Chelm announcing that he has swum ashore safely and has bought up the land containing the uranium deposits.

Comment

Here, Huston is years before the times. The fragmented, erratic, incidental type of black comedy, now frequently praised, was entirely unexpected when this film was first shown, resulting in considerable bewilderment on the part of audiences and critics. It gave those who had praised him often the chance to lament his lapse. The jolly and wicked cast, the absurdity of human behaviour, Huston's detached view, the in-jokes, have established the film as an outrageous parody of the crime *genre*.

Ireland and Wales: Moby Dick (1954–1956)

Despite its excursions, to me "Moby Dick" is perhaps the great American novel, the greatest American novel along with "Huckleberry Finn." I wrote the script with Ray Bradbury. During the time I was making it, why, after it was first presented, people would tell me they'd read "Moby Dick" as a child. Well, they only *thought* they'd read "Moby Dick" as a child. I've yet to encounter a twelve-year-old in the middle of "Moby Dick"! He doesn't exist. More people think they've read "Moby Dick" and haven't. They've read about Moby Dick, and they think they know it more perhaps than with any other book I know, with the possible exception of the Bible. Part of their opinion of

"Moby Dick" was formed by the first picture that was made, John Barrymore's version, which had little or nothing to do with Melville's work. There was the general idea that Ahab was a ranting madman, wild and distraught and fanatical, whereas Melville would have him as a kind of Anti-Christ, noble in his blasphemy. It is the story of a blasphemy, of course, it's an assault on God.

It was Gregory Peck's performance that came in chiefly for criticism on the part of people, critics included, who didn't know the book. They wanted a character and a picture in keeping with some previous notion that had been formed out of a misunderstanding. Gregory Peck gave the part a dignity, an O'Neillesque silhouette and shape, that I thought was very impressive. Another interpretation would have been out of keeping with the requirements. It failed, so far as a number of critics were concerned, because it didn't coincide with their conception of Ahab, their false conception, and, they decided, it was completely out of character for Gregory Peck. I thought it was a very fine script. When I was working at Metro, Ray Bradbury wrote me a letter and said he would like to work with me. I'd read his books and I thought there was a poetic quality in them that would make him a good man to write this screenplay. There was a flight in what he wrote, a kind of soaring spirit that made him a very good candidate for writing on Melville. Now once again, I found myself filming on a ship, but this was much bigger than *The African Queen*.

This was probably the most difficult picture I've ever done. The imponderables were so great. A lot of mistakes were made, short cuts were taken that we paid for. Some of them that had been made I wasn't even aware of. There was a series of errors that compounded, and made even more difficult, the filming of the picture. For instance, the "Pequod," the ship itself. Instead of putting the generator where it should have been, so that it wouldn't interfere with the sound recording, why, it was put where it was cheapest. They would have had to build a whole section in the hull, and that would have paid off later on, when the recording made it all very difficult indeed. Some material we had to re-record, but we had to make revisions all the time to get round this difficulty. I didn't want to re-record after. Where we used the little harbour at Yawl in County Cork for New Bedford, the harbour wasn't dug out deeply enough, so that instead of having several hours a day shooting we could only shoot at high tide. These things affected the picture.

They are more or less minor compared to the big antagonist—the

Gregory Peck as Captain Ahab in MOBY DICK (1956).

MOBY DICK (1956). Huston discusses sketches watched by Oswald Morris
and Ralph Brinton.

weather. It was one of the stormiest seasons in the history of those seas.
Lifeboats were capsized. I don't mean our boats, but the coastal
lifeboats that went out to vessels in distress. Ships were blown on the
rocks. We were dismasted three times. Once there was no question in
my mind we were heading for the bottom and were just saved by a
miracle of seamanship. The captain was extraordinary and saved the
boat by his cool behaviour. The weather was unbelievable and the fact
that we didn't lose anybody was in itself remarkable. We did lose
whales, however! [laughter]. The reason we'd lose whales was that there
would come that moment of choice: should we save the people in the
long boats or should we save the whales we made. Being humans ourselves, why, our sympathy went towards these men rather than these
plastic fabrications [laughter]. Then we'd have to build another
whale. These whales were some ninety feet long, constructions of steel,
wood and latex—big, expensive articles. It would sometimes take
weeks, and we would have to shoot something else while we were
waiting for another whale to be made. We'd pull the whale through
the water and they were designed so that at a certain speed they'd
submerge and rise, and submerge again. In these seas the two-inch

thick nylon cable would separate. I knew if we lost our third and last whale we'd never recover. The whales were hollow and fairly sea-worthy, so I went down into the whale knowing they wouldn't let me sink, and they wouldn't lose me. I stayed in the whale with a bottle of whiskey, and they made heroic efforts and recovered the whale [*roars of laughter*] and me! Well, my gosh, it was a hardship and mine was the least part of it.

I remember one day we were on a tug alongside the "Pequod," bitterly cold, and the mastheads were manned. Three lookouts were on the masthead photographing the whole ship. My script girl was sitting beside me on the tug and said, "They've been up for quite a while, these men, in the crow's nests and they must be freezing up there." I said, "Yes, get them down." We called on the loud-hailer for them to come down. The seas were mountainous and sleet came down heavily. As the last man reached the deck, the three masts snapped. It's never just one mast because of the way they are rigged. All three always go, and all three masts went. Those men wouldn't have had a chance. If they had hit the deck, they would have been killed. If they'd hit the water, they would have surely been drowned. No recovery was possible. So we were very lucky, very lucky. We shot in that sea around Fish-guard, Wales, and then we shot a little bit in the studio, at Pinewood I think it was. Then we went down to Las Palmas, and shot down there. Even there the seas were running high. The seas were full all over the world that year. I've heard it described as the worst weather in European maritime history.

My word, Gregory Peck's behaviour during the film was extra-ordinary. We had discussed the character and its interpretation at great length. Anything that was required, not by me but according to his idea of what he should do, why, he saw fit to expose himself. For instance, there was a shot that I'd kept until the very last shot of the picture and with anyone else it would have been up to the stuntman, but I didn't want a stuntman, nor did Greg. It was of him lashed to the body of "Moby Dick" by the harpoon lines, dead, and his arm loose and beckoning the others to follow. We did this in the ocean. We had this part of the whale and the scene called for the whale to be rocking and revolving and wrapping him round and round. Anything could go wrong with a piece of machinery, as it were. We did it, and we got it, and I said, "Thank God!", and Greg said, "Let's do it again," and I said, "No, we don't have to do it again, Greg, we've got it." Greg said, "Let's do it again, anyway, I insist." We did it again. We were tempting fate, but that was Greg, and remember he was playing the part with a supposedly physical deformity—the loss of a leg.

There were many days when we never even turned the cameras.

Many days we just hung on to the mast or went below for refuge from the blasts. We were all living on the ship, from necessity rather than choice. On top of all this, we were again experimenting with colour with Oswald Morris. We devised, before we started shooting, our formula. Theoretically, it was a wedding of black and white to the colour, to fortify and give a strength to the colour, to make the figures have a strong outline and a shape, more forceful than just again regular colour treatment and, with that, something ominous and sinister. I thought it was very effective in the film. This was one thing they couldn't change, the prints. This was done in the lab, mind you, not in the cameras. Once the prints were made they couldn't issue different ones.

Now this picture was being made for my old studio, Warners, which eventually released the film. Elliot Hyman was the backer of the film, and we were, God, ever so slow. As I've said, there were days when we'd get nothing, nothing at all. It was very disheartening. We had a visit from Elliot Hyman and the Mirisch brothers and the others who were involved in the financing of the film. We were out at sea, and they appeared in a boat [*laughter*], and they picked a very good day—the seas were huge! [*roars of laughter*]. I think one young man succeeded in coming aboard. It's very dangerous to even try and transfer, and to bring the other boat alongside was endangering it, not the "Pequod," but endangering the other boat which could have been knocked to pieces on our sides. The others were very sick indeed, lying green in the bottom of the boat [*roars of laughter*]. Of course, we hung over the sides, you know, calling to them, "Try again!" and making gay exchanges with these poor devils lying in their vomit! [*roars of laughter*]. We had no criticism of our progress [*laughter*] from then on. There was a suggestion that we shift the operation to Africa, a little calmer! To build the "Pequod" we had a hull and a shipbuilder fitted it, but the art of building those old ships is a lost one. Mistakes were made in that. After the picture was finished it was used as a place for tourists to come aboard for a while here in England, I think. I don't know where it is now.

I had seen Orson on and off, and I wanted him to do Father Mapple, so this was a studio shot. You know the set: he stands in the bow, the preacher does, and gives his sermon of about five pages in length, at least five minutes. The congregation was there on the set, and Orson got up into the pulpit and rattled through the pages, I mean turning them. Finally he said to me, "John, I'm nervous. I'm terribly nervous. I don't know why but I'm just a bundle of nerves. I swear to God I've got stage fright. Could I have a drink?" I said, "What would you like?" He replied, "A brandy." I sent out for a

MOBY DICK (1956). Orson Welles as Father Mapple.

bottle of brandy. The glass was on the pulpit, and the bottle was on the pulpit [*laughter*], and Orson had a big drink. I said, "Well, shall we rehearse it, go through it once more?" "No, no, give me a little time, will you?" He had another drink. I said, "Whenever you're ready, Orson, we'll rehearse it." Finally he said, "Let's not rehearse it. Let's shoot it." Letter perfect—five minutes—absolutely perfect! I think we were supposed to take four days with this scene. Three days on Orson himself and the rest on the congregation. The whole thing was finished that day. Orson never made one mistake, never misread one word. We took first the whole scene, the congregation, Orson, the camera behind the congregation; moved in for a closer shot; moved in to a very close shot. Three takes! Three times letter perfect!

There was one story point in *Moby Dick* that wasn't covered in the novel which might interest you. We never succeeded in the original writing with Ray Bradbury in explaining the awe, the fear, and the sense of sin the crew felt in what Ahab was doing, why they thought it was a sin. Melville just makes the statement, but it needed dramatising. We worked on this and tried to show, in scenes, what convinced them that he was on an unholy mission, that the voyage itself was sinister and evil. Finally I remember one day I was driving to the set in the car and it came to me. It wasn't what he was doing, it was what he was not doing. The whaler men at that time thought that their mission was holy—bringing oil for the lamps of the world. Light that could be read by. By the oil lamp people read the Good Book. It was light to illuminate the minds and hearts of humanity. Ahab turns away from the herd of whales in pursuit of Moby Dick. In pursuit of one whale he is committing a sin. This was really the heart of that matter. Ahab saw Moby Dick as the embodiment of evil, and he sees God. This is, of course, in Melville: "When will the judge himself be tried before the bar?" He is assaulting the Almighty, it is his naked fist against the Deity.

MOBY DICK. 1954/56. *A Moulin* picture, released by Warner Bros. *Director and Producer:* John Huston. *Associate Producer:* Vaughan N. Dean. *Screenplay:* Ray Bradbury and John Huston. *Based on the novel by:* Herman Melville. *Photography:* Oswald Morris. *Second Unit Photography:* Freddie Francis. *Colour:* Technicolor. *Colour Style:* Oswald Morris and John Huston. *Editor:* Russell Lloyd. *Art Director:* Ralph Brinton. *Special Effects:* Gus Lohman. *Music:* Philip Stainton. *Sound Recording:* John Mitchell and Len Shilton. *Running time:* 115 minutes.
Players: Gregory Peck *(Captain Ahab)*, Richard Basehart *(Ishmael)*, Leo Genn *(Starbuck)*, Harry Andrews *(Stubb)*, Bernard Miles *(Manxman)*, Mervyn Johns *(Peleg)*, Noel Purcell *(Carpenter)*, Edric Connor *(Daggoo)*, Joseph Tomelty *(Peter Coffin)*, Philip Stainton *(Bildad)*, Royal Dano *(Elijah)*, Seamus Kelly *(Flask)*, Friedrich Ledebur *(Queequeg)*, Tamba Alleney *(Pip)*, Orson Welles *(Father Mapple)*, James Robertson Justice *(Captain Boomer)*.

Story
1840: Ishmael, a young sailor, arrives at the Spouter Inn, New Bedford, where he learns of the whaler "Pequod" and her·captain, Ahab, and makes friends with his chance bedfellow, Queequeg, a harpooner. Ishmael and Queequeg sign on the "Pequod," despite the ominous predictions of the ragged Elijah and the odd reputation of Ahab. When the ship has been some days at sea, Ahab—scarred in mind and body, with one live leg and one of whalebone—makes clear to the crew that the prime object of the voyage is to wreak vengeance on the monstrous white whale that took off his leg; and the crew,

MOBY DICK (1956). Gregory Peck as Captain Ahab.

despite the counsels of the wise mate Starbuck, are readily infected with Ahab's lust for revenge. At last—having set his purpose before everything else, including the capture of lesser whales and the appeals for assistance of the whaler "Rachel"—Ahab overtakes and meets Moby Dick. In his fury, Ahab leaps from the long-boat on the whale's back, and is pinned there by lines left by previous hunters. The whale, in agony and anger, attacks the ship; and all its crew, save Ishmael, are lost.

Comment
 Taking Melville's great novel about a man's obsessive quest for the white whale which has maimed him, Huston created an exciting version of this haunting, mysterious tale of revenge, agony and religious fervour. Compelling in its narrative, awe-inspiring in its settings, authentic in its period sense, this enormously difficult and expensive film is one of Huston's most magnificent achievements.

Tobago: **Heaven Knows, Mr. Allison** (1957)

After what we went through, it was a pleasure to go to an island and
make *Heaven Knows, Mr. Allison*. This was a fairly happy experience.
Bob Mitchum is a joy to work with. I think he's one of the really fine
actors of my time. His talents have never really been revealed. He
should have played King Lear and might still. There's so much morè
there than is allowed to meet the eye. He's never been given the
opportunity that such talent as his deserves. He's a great actor, Bob.
The film began with the novel, a very bad novel, sensational, depending for its drama on the idea of a marine and a nun and its shoddier
implications. John Lee Mahin had written a screenplay and taken
some of the curse off the novel. Then we went to work on it, and I
saw it as anything but seamy. Just a demonstration of decency, and
essential innocence and purity on both their parts. I thought it was
a *tour de force* in screenwriting. Contrary to some credits, Ring
Lardner to my knowledge did not work on the script.

Robert Mitchum and Deborah Kerr in HEAVEN KNOWS,
MR. ALLISON (1957).

I'd seen some of the drawings of Stephen Grimes, he worked with Disney, and I wanted drawings of the action sequences of *Moby Dick,* illustrations of what was required in order for the crew to build accordingly. This young man did those drawings, he was very talented and a beautiful draftsman. After *Moby Dick,* when I saw the extent of his talents, I had him design the production of *Mr. Allison* and he became an art director. Now he's one of the best art directors, and he's done most of my films. This was my first film for Twentieth Century-Fox and it was filmed completely in Tobago. It was one of those delightful locations, a pleasant contrast from a film where so many different shots with different characters were required to now working basically with two people, which is almost an alternate approach from one to the other, in technique. One only thinks of this in terms of the film one is doing. *Moby Dick* was gone, I cut myself off from it, here's another set of problems.

HEAVEN KNOWS, MR. ALLISON. 1957. *A* Twentieth Century-Fox *Picture.*
Director: John Huston. *Producers:* Buddy Adler and Eugene Frenke.
Screenplay: John Lee Mahin and John Huston. *Based on the novel by:* Charles Shaw. *Photography:* Oswald Morris. CinemaScope. *Colour:* Technicolor. *Editor:* Russell Lloyd. *Art Director:* Stephen Grimes.
Music: Georges Auric. *Sound:* Basil Fenton Smith.
Running time: 106 minutes.
Players: Deborah Kerr (*Sister Angela*), Robert Mitchum (*Mr. Allison*).

Story
Washed ashore on a small Pacific island, U.S. Marine Cpl. Allison finds it already inhabited by a young nun, Sister Angela. Their attempt to escape on a raft is frustrated by the arrival of a Japanese weather unit, whose storehouse Allison raids for food for himself and Sister Angela. When the weather unit leaves the island, Allison celebrates by getting drunk, and then tries to assault Sister Angela, who runs out into the jungle and spends the night in a tropical storm. Next morning Allison finds her feverish and incoherent. The island is occupied by a full Japanese task force, and the two are forced back into hiding. Attempting to steal blankets from the Japanese, Allison kills an officer. When the body is found, the Japanese set fire to the undergrowth in order to smoke out the fugitives, who are only saved by the arrival of U.S. troops. During the battle which follows, Allison manages to disarm the Japanese artillery. With the Americans in possession of the island, the injured Allison is taken aboard in a hospital ship, with Sister Angela praying by his side.

Comment

The interest here lies in the interplay of two opposed characters, a rough and tough marine and a devout young nun, who are forced to live together on a Pacific island. In part it seems to be another version of *The African Queen,* alone on an island instead of in a boat. The Japanese rather than the Germans are now the enemy. Witty and often moving, visually attractive, the film has two actors who hold the screen throughout.

A Farewell to Selznick: **A Farewell to Arms**

David Selznick was a very good friend of mine, a friend of long-standing, and we'd seen a great deal of each other socially over the years. I'd gone to his house and he'd come to mine, and we'd taken boats together. He was a wonderful companion and a very generous, kind-hearted man; but when it came to doing *A Farewell to Arms* with him, it was a slightly different story. I don't mean that his gen-erosity diminished, or anything of that kind, but David liked to run the show. I saw very quickly that, so far as he was concerned, the show was Jennifer. I felt that Hemingway's book was being destroyed; the idea, the story, in fact, was being distorted to serve what he believed to be her best interests. Everything came around to its being a show-piece for a star.

Well, no one had a higher regard for Jennifer than I did, I have great admiration for her talents and liked her enormously, so it wasn't that I was trying to diminish her function or part in the pro-ceedings. However, I thought David's approach would damage the picture, which would in turn damage her. My concern was for the picture itself. We had little disputes. Nothing came out in the open, but little differences of opinion kept cropping up. For instance, Rock Hudson. I wanted him to look more like a soldier than a lover. As you know, in the First World War, why, people had short haircuts, and David wanted his hair long and romantic-looking. Oh, there were things like that. He wanted to get as quickly to the story of the nurse as he could and cut short the opening of the story where we are with the Lieutenant for some time before meeting the girl. We were working with Ben Hecht, and Ben was trying to please both of us and not getting very far. It was frustrating, and I am sure it was equally frustrating to David, for he had his ideas. This was the first time, and the last time, I ever was head-to-head with a producer, and it was ironical that this producer was probably my best friend among all the producers! The one I found most amusing to be with, the best company; but this didn't deaden the impact, and finally I got a memorandum from David which I haven't read entirely to this day. I read a couple of pages of it. His production manager had called me and said, "John, I want to warn you—a memorandum that may not sit well with you is coming up to your room." It was early in the morning. I read two pages of the memorandum and called my secretary and said, "Pack!" There was an "out" in it, because David wrote, "if you feel, as you seem to feel, that this picture is not worthy of your best efforts," and so on, "why, you are at liberty to do as you please." I took that avenue of escape instantly. That's all that happened.

I had very little to do with Selznick afterwards. I was over here for the most part and David returned to the Hollywood scene. He was on location with us all the time and, even though he was there, he wrote these memos. He didn't believe in coming and sitting down and talking about the picture. He loved to write memos! He had a theory about it. I read a little bit of Sam Behrman's introduction to the book ["Memo from David O. Selznick"]. David thought the written word was taken more seriously than the spoken word and made a greater impression on the reader than if he was just told. I was sore at David. Not angry—sore! I continued to like him, but I was out of temper with him. On my next trip out to California I got a call from Jennifer. She wanted me to come to a party, as I always had. I said, "No, I'm still mad. Maybe next time I'll be over it. Ask me again later!" [laughter]. There was no next time.

I was disappointed not to do the picture for many reasons, the most important being that it was Hemingway. It wasn't going as I wanted it to and as I believed it should. I thought it was an important enough work to get the very best treatment. As it turned out, I was right. I might have been wrong, but it was a bad picture. It was done according to the measurements David set forth, and he was mistaken. His mistake was apparent at that time as far as I was concerned, and it wasn't going to come to anything if he didn't have his way. If he didn't have his way—well, there was no chance of him not having his way! I was butting my head up against a stone wall. The whole picture, after I left, was apparently a heart-breaking affair. He fell out with this person and that person. Ossie Morris left the picture. Stephen Grimes left the picture, not because of me, not at all, not out of any mistaken sense of loyalty. They felt Ossie wasn't doing as well by Jennifer as he might. Well, Ossie's only the best cameraman alive, and was then! But there was that general tense air. I think David liked to feel his impact. If you remember, he changed directors on *Gone With the Wind* several times. Everybody remained friends. Maybe David was right on that occasion, I don't know.

It has been said it probably hastened the end of Charles Vidor who finally directed the picture—one never knows, of course. It didn't do Jennifer any good, it didn't do David any good. Hemingway made fun of it, the whole thing was unfortunate. As it turned out, the earlier version remained the better one. I worked on the screenplay with Ben Hecht, but I didn't start shooting, I never made a shot. I'd already found the locations for the opening shots and they were all in the picture. Those opening shots had already been designed, and we came from the convoy down across the bridge, and things of that kind. I left a couple of days before shooting started. I forget where I came back to! I think it was then I went to Vienna to play Cardinal Glennon in Otto Preminger's *The Cardinal*.

Japan (Tokyo): The Barbarian and the Geisha (1958)

The Barbarian and the Geisha was originally called *The Townsend Harris Story,* and was proposed by the same man, Eugene Frenke, who produced *Heaven Knows, Mr. Allison,* and a very dear friend of mine who died just recently, Charles Grayson. I'd never been to Japan, and it all sounded rather attractive. The script wasn't all that good, I worked on it continually while we were making the film. Wayne was a very obedient actor. I had the feeling he wasn't entirely happy about doing this with me, but there were no quarrels or anything of that sort. We would never have become bosom friends under any set of circumstances.

It's one of the two pictures, when we were talking about *The Red Badge of Courage,* why I said I could understand what was done to it. I hated the title that Fox finally decided to use—*The Barbarian and the Geisha*. When the picture was delivered to the studio, I liked it. When I saw the film some time later, I was appalled. One error leads to another of course. What happened was this: in the meantime, Fox wanted to make another picture with me and I'd read the Romain Gary story of "The Roots of Heaven." They bought the book for me to film. Darryl Zanuck had the power to pre-empt material from Fox and he saw it as a medium for his star of the time, Juliette Greco, and Darryl proposed that I do it with him. With some misgivings, and reassurances from Darryl that I needn't have any, why, I agreed. I asked that a certain man be put on the writing of it, Patrick Leigh-Fermor, and that Stephen Grimes do the art direction—my people. Darryl went right along with this. But the screenplay of *Roots* wasn't very good, so I wrote my criticisms and Darryl, doing everything that I required, abiding by the letter of his word to me, kept every promise. It just didn't pan out. Darryl liked the script, and they tried to do the changes I suggested. Now

John Wayne and
Eiko Ando in THE
BARBARIAN AND
THE GEISHA
(1958).

I was occupied with the Japanese film, so I couldn't take a hand in it myself, but they tried to follow my suggestions, my ideas, and just came a cropper with them, that's all. The production was being planned and Darryl had certain people out in Africa. Presently they were waiting for me to finish the Japanese film and join them in Africa, where the company was making a very big investment indeed. The studio had some sixty people out there, and a village had been built for them. It was in a remote place, Fort Archambaud, and the whole enterprise was maintained at great expense.

When I'd finished *The Barbarian and the Geisha* and put it in their hands, I had to go immediately to Africa. So far as I knew, that was it. I didn't see the picture until I returned to Los Angeles from Africa, having finished shooting. I saw it in release and I was appalled. It wasn't the picture I'd sent them at all. They'd even re-shot certain scenes, and the whole idea of the picture was lost. God, the other night they were running it on television here and it was just awful what they had done. Wayne had apparently taken over after I left, and the man who was the head of the studio, Buddy Adler, was ill. Even at the late date I saw the picture, after it was in release, why, I would have had my name taken off the picture, except that Buddy Adler had died. What had been done was just wretched. You can only take my word for it. I'll tell you the pictures I made that were not good, and I was responsible for. This was a good film and it was made into a very bad film, a very poor film indeed. That's the story of *The Barbarian and the Geisha*. Wayne was the big star, and they wanted him for other pictures. Where he didn't look too well according to his own idea of himself in a shot, they re-shot the scene. All became an absurdity, it was just wretched.

When I went into the film and the making of it, I was interested in the effect this first American in Japan had on the Occidentals, on the Oriental culture, the exploration of these two completely different conceptions of life, not only religious and political, but different souls. Townsend Harris actually lived but the story was faithful in idea, not in fact, not in the events which are full of speculation anyway. He's become a legend, and the girl is almost a national figure in Japanese mythology. We shot all of it in Japan. I was always interested in Japanese art and while I was shooting I was collecting. It was fascinating. Making a picture in Japan is a very good way of going into the character of the people. The Japanese were very good, they gave me every assistance. There was no arrangement with any studio there whatever, yet they lent me men and helped to do things that would have been very difficult otherwise, without any benefit to themselves. This is a film, really, that depended a great deal on character and dialogue. There wasn't really very much action in a physical sense, but there was a lot to look at that was strange. The important part, dramatically, and which conveyed the theme, was the relationship between him and the girl. I loved the period, and the settings, and imagining what life in Japan was really like at that time.

THE BARBARIAN AND THE GEISHA. 1958. *A* Twentieth Century-Fox *Picture*.
Director: John Huston. *Producer:* Eugene Frenke. *Screenplay:* Charles Grayson. *Story:* Ellis St. John. *Photography:* Charles G. Clarke. CinemaScope. *Colour:* Eastmancolor. *Editor:* Stuart Gilmore. *Art Directors:* Lyle R. Wheeler and Jack Martin Smith. *Music:* Hugo Friedhofer. *Sound:* W. D. Flick and Warren B. Delaplain. *Running time:* 105 minutes.
Players: John Wayne *(Townsend Harris)*, Eiko Ando *(Okichi)*, Sam Jaffe *(Henry Heusken)*, So Yamamura *(Tamura)*, Norman Thomson *(Ship Captain)*, James Robbins *(Lt. Fisher)*, Morita *(Prime Minister)*, Kodaya Ichikawa *(Daimyo)*, Hiroshi Yamato *(Shogun)*, Tokujiro *(Iketaniuchi)*, Fuji Kasai *(Lord Hotta)*, Takeshi Kumagai *(Chamberlain)*.

Story
    Townsend Harris, the first diplomatic representative of the U.S.A. in Japan, arrives in 1856 in the tiny seaport of Shimoda. The local

governor makes life miserable for Harris by refusing to sell him food or offer the least hospitality. The governor also sends a spy to distract him from his official duties—a young geisha girl, Okichi. At first frightened of the foreigner, Okichi comes to respect and love him. When Harris burns down part of the town to stamp out a cholera epidemic, he is arrested by the governor, but later released and taken to the capital for presentation to the Shogun, at whose court rival factions struggle to decide whether the treaty between America and Japan should be recognised or not. An attempt to assassinate Harris is foiled by Okichi, and the would-be murderer commits hara-kiri. But Okichi realises that she must live by the Japanese code and leaves Harris, whom she sorrowfully watches being carried in triumph through the cheering crowds to the palace for the signing of the treaty.

Comment

Huston's wide and contrasting interest in life, art and history drew him to this strange and exotic tale of the clash between two totally different societies. Designed and photographed with all the skill of a Japanese period film, it presents John Wayne in his only attempt at true characterisation in the role of Townsend Harris.

Africa (French Equatorial Africa) : The Roots of Heaven (1958)

The Roots of Heaven didn't come up to anything like what it might have been. The quality of the novel that attracted me to the subject matter in the first place was never realised. Darryl Zanuck did everything that I asked, so it was my responsibility and, unlike Mr. Nixon, I accept the blame fully! The depths of the novel—a good, a very interesting book indeed—were not touched, became in our hands a kind of adventure story, a shoot-up. If you recall the beginning, there was a mystery about it and a provocative atmosphere. The protagonist is in a concentration camp, and he's among a number of others who have become thoroughly demoralised, who have all but lost their humanity. They invent a woman, they pretend that a woman is in their presence, and they behave accordingly as gentlemen. Where they had allowed themselves physically to go to hell, why, they washed, cut their hair, shaved, and they would rise when the woman came into the room. Very, very good as Gary wrote it. The Germans, their captors, discover the conspiracy, as it were, the existence of this phantom woman, and they execute this phantom. In desperation, then, this man turns it into a dream, and he dreams of these great beasts that wander across the land and move silently, in complete freedom and with enormous dignity. Coming out of this dream, on his rescue and deliverance, he goes to Africa to see his dream in the flesh. The picture should have been in that spirit and, as I say, it wasn't, it was a failure.

I felt all the time as we were making the film that we weren't in any way living up to what was required, and it was beyond my power to do anything about it. I was bowing for defeat in this, trying to make as good a picture as I could, but I couldn't. My powers weren't sufficient and my abilities weren't up to it, and this is in no way in extenuation when I said that *Moby Dick* was the most difficult picture to make physically. With *The Roots of Heaven* I don't suppose there's ever been a greater hardship on a company than what this unit was up against in making this film. The temperature never dropped below 100° at night, and in the daytime it was 125°. There were illnesses. People actually went off their rockers. It was a remote part of Africa, blasted, a strange environment, and to some of our people it was threatening, and there was so much serious illness. No-one died, but people came away physical wrecks and were months recovering from it, physical and mental wrecks a number of them. One man was sent back in a strait-jacket. Eccentricities flowered! It was dismaying going through all this and yet not getting what I really wanted. Darryl was there. He could, like other producers I have known, spared himself the experience. He drank the bitter dregs right through to the finish, spared himself nothing, was a marvel of splendid behaviour. He was only helping to the best of his abilities, to make things that little bit easier. He might have kept me from going mad myself. Fortunately I'm blessed with a good constitution and I'm lucky too. The actors saw what was happening to the crew and began to get pretty extraordinary in their behaviour and imagining themselves to be ill when they weren't. Oh, there were several bizarre occurrences! The lives of many people have never been the same since.

With all of this was Errol Flynn, and I knew then, we all knew, that Errol was on his last legs. His behaviour too, was exemplary. He couldn't have been better. We were talking about shooting and guns. Between locations I secretly set up a shoot for myself. The only person to know anything about it was Darryl himself. I didn't want anyone to come with me because they would just be excess baggage, and Errol smelled a rat. He said, "John, you're going on a safari, aren't you?" Well, I denied it at first, and then I couldn't conceal it from him any longer and said, "Yes." He said, "Well, I'm going to come along." I said, "No, you can't." He was ill. I said, "You wouldn't be up to this." He said, "Will you take me? I'm

Watched by Errol Flynn while directing THE ROOTS OF HEAVEN (1958).

asking you, it's a request." The way he put it, I couldn't say no.
Errol came, and he wasn't up to the rigours of this journey. It was
a hard safari, we'd walk as many as twenty-five miles in a day; but
Errol would go out in the mornings and then come back, and go
out in the evenings and then come back to camp. When the whole
thing was over he said, "Thank you. I'll never forget this. It's been
the best time I think I've maybe ever had." He did not have a
drink, or a pill, that whole period. I was always thankful that I had
Errol come along with me. Not very long after the film was finished
he died. Trevor Howard was one of the few survivors. Orson never
came out. Orson's scene in the hospital was done in Paris. Eddie
Albert, Paul Lukas, Herbert Lom—they were all there. In the circumstances it was hard not to get something that was of some
interest! It was never what it might have been.

I am asked sometimes, are there any pictures you'd like to re-
make. Well, I think the whole practice of re-making successful pictures is absurd. I would gladly re-make *The Roots of Heaven*,
however. The ending, where Howard just walks out of the gate,
was as it was in the novel too, but it had a much greater significance
in the novel. Everything was significant in the novel, whereas very
little was of significance in the picture. Many other directors have
had reason to complain because Darryl has re-edited their films. But
he left the film the way I edited it. I haven't a leg to stand on!

The animals gave us the least trouble. We went to where the
animals were, of course. This extraordinary concentration of elephants was photographed where we found them. Then there was a

place, Ganglia Nabodio, where we did a little shooting where the natives had domesticated, or semi-domesticated, the elephants. The African elephant is wild no matter what is done with him. He's not like the Indian elephant in any way, he's another creature entirely. If you know something about animal behaviour, it's not hard to work with animals. Animals do pretty well, if they have any sense, what you anticipate. If you think like an animal, why, you are seldom disappointed! They are very constant in their reactions. Why, if you understand a horse, you understand an elephant, more or less.

Ossie Morris was remarkable as usual, although here the photography was a quite straight rendering of the scenes; but still difficult, considering the circumstances and the heat. People fell down with what they called sun-stroke, heat exhaustion, virus infections, strange blood diseases, malaria, symptoms that couldn't be accounted for, which, much later the doctors of tropical diseases here recognised and treated. Ossie stayed reasonably healthy. He had his days off.

Trevor Howard, Errol Flynn and Juliette Greco in
THE ROOTS OF HEAVEN (1958).

Our problem was to get the film over to Africa and back to London, and under refrigeration. We always carried thermos jugs in the back of the car, one had ice cubes in it and the other was lemonade and we'd stop and have a drink. We used to give an ice cube to a native. They had never seen ice and they didn't know what this cold stone was! They'd dance with it in their hands. Then I took to giving them a Lily cup and they'd go home and show them what they had. Of course, by the time they got home any ice cube was a little water in the Lily cup!

THE ROOTS OF HEAVEN. 1958. *A* Twentieth Century-Fox *Release.* *Director:* John Huston. *Production Company:* Darryl F. Zanuck Productions. *Producer:* Darryl F. Zanuck. *Screenplay:* Romain Gary and Patrick Leigh-Fermor. *Based on the novel by:* Romain Gary. *Photography:* Oswald Morris. *Second Unit Photography:* Skeets Kelly, Henri Persin and Gilles Bonneau. CinemaScope. *Colour:* Eastman-color. *Editor:* Russell Lloyd. *Art Directors:* Stephen Grimes and Raymond Gabutti. *Music:* Malcolm Arnold. *Sound:* Basil Fenton Smith.
Running time: 125 minutes.
Players: Trevor Howard (*Morel*), Juliette Greco (*Minna*), Errol Flynn (*Forsythe*), Eddie Albert (*Abe Fields*), Orson Welles (*Cy Sedgwick*), Paul Lukas (*Saint-Denis*), Herbert Lom (*Orsini*), Gregoire Aslan (*Habib*), André Luguet (*The Governor*), Friedrich Ledebur (*Peer Qvist*), Edric Connor (*Waitari*), Olivier Hussenot (*The Baron*), Pierre Dudan (*Major Scholscher*), Francis de Wolff (*Father Fargue*).

Story
    Following the failure of his petition urging the French Government to introduce legislation against the slaughtering of elephants, Morel, a European dedicated to the cause, takes more positive action by wounding an American broadcaster, Sedgwick, who is about to set out on safari. Outlawed by the government, Morel takes to the hills where he is joined by a strange band of European idealists and Waitari, an African leader, who hopes to use Morel's campaign for his own political ends. Minna, a local club hostess, and Forsythe, a drunken ex-Army officer, also drawn to Morel and his cause, secretly bring ammunition and supplies. Morel's band successfully prints a clandestine leaflet and publicly chastises a lady elephant hunter, an action which causes a major uproar among the government set. Following the defection of Waitari, who feels that he has been betrayed, they are joined by Abe Fields, an American photographer sent to cover the story. Coming across a large herd of elephants, they attempt to thwart a group of hunters intent on killing, led by

Habib, a tusk dealer. During the ensuing battle, several of Morel's followers, including Forsythe, are killed and the rest taken prisoner by Waitari. After some negotiations, Morel secures their release and they set out for their hide-out. Minna having fallen sick, the party makes an arduous detour to the nearest hospital, where they are well received by the local administrator, a convert to Morel's cause. After saying goodbye to Minna, Morel and his followers, cheered by their moral victory, continue on into the bush.

Comment

This is an ambitious film which pleads its case for wild game preservation through statements involving humanist and political ideals. Although Huston admits that it failed, it is still an impressive, unusual and committed work, containing memorable character studies, magnificent animal photography, and a setting both strange and remote.

Mexico (Durango) : **The Unforgiven** (1960)

Hecht-Hill-Lancaster brought me the script of *The Unforgiven*. There was a little editing after I had finished which I didn't approve of when I saw the film. They dropped John Saxon, who had a more important role in the picture, and I thought it was a loss to the film. Except for that, as I cut it there was little tampering with it; but what they did was to the detriment of the picture. I suppose it could be called a western—people always think of a film set outdoors in pioneer days as being a western. What interested me about the story was the role the Indian played, and how the Indian was regarded by the pioneer. That gave the story whatever interest it had. Then there was the kind of Gothic figure of the nemesis, who appeared with his sword on horseback. These were interesting moments in the film, but I thought it got a little bombastic and over-dramatised itself on occasions!

Ben Maddow, who worked briefly on *The Asphalt Jungle,* wrote the screenplay from the novel by Alan LeMay. I'd never worked with Burt Lancaster, Lillian Gish and Audrey Hepburn before. Audrey Hepburn learned to ride in the picture. She had a fear of horses, but she was very good and a quick student. She was put under a teacher and rode a little Arab. One day it got away from her and she was thrown and cracked a vertebra. We had to call a halt until she recovered and was fit to go on. She was never on a horse again! We made the film entirely in Durango, Mexico. I must say I didn't feel myself thoroughly in command of the material, and I didn't approve entirely. It was not too well prepared and again I felt

Lillian Gish, Burt
Lancaster and
Audrey Hepburn in
THE UNFOR-
GIVEN (1960).

a sense of it not being what I'd liked to have had, mostly in the screenplay. Joseph Wiseman gave a marvellous performance as the Gothic figure. He's a fine actor. I liked his scenes in the film. I liked the pursuit of him, if you remember. There were things I admired about the film, but things I didn't. I'd known Lillian Gish. She was a great friend of my Aunt Margaret. Lancaster was a very professional actor.

In that picture and one or two others, I have come in like a surgeon just to do a job, you know. It's not a very good practice. I should work on the screenplay from the beginning. The pictures of mine which I like are the ones where I've done that, with the possible exception of *The Misfits*. I did very little work on that but I liked it. I only take screenplay credit when I have written the original script. When I haven't done that, I never feel the film is mine. At best it's an adopted child.

THE UNFORGIVEN. 1960. *A* United Artists *Release.*
Director: John Huston. *Production Company:* James Productions/
Hecht-Hill-Lancaster. *Producer:* James Hill. *Screenplay:* Ben Maddow.
Based on the novel by: Alan LeMay. *Photography:* Franz Planer.

Panavision. *Colour:* Technicolor. *Editor:* Russell Lloyd. *Art Director:* Stephen Grimes. *Music:* Dimitri Tiomkin.
Running time: 125 minutes.
Players: Audrey Hepburn *(Rachel)*, Burt Lancaster *(Ben Zachary)*, Audie Murphy *(Cash)*, Lillian Gish *(Mattilda)*, Doug McClure *(Andy)*, Charles Bickford *(Zeb Rawlins)*, Joseph Wiseman *(Abe Kelsey)*, John Saxon *(Johnny Portugal)*, Albert Salmi *(Charlie Rawlins)*, June Walker *(Hagar Rawlins)*, Kipp Hamilton *(Georgia Rawlins)*, Arnold Merritt *(Jude)*, Carlos Rivas *(Lost Bird)*.

Story
    Abe Kelsey, an old saddle-tramp unhinged by the grief and bitterness of the Civil War, spreads a story around the barren plains of the Texas Panhandle that Rachel, the dark-skinned girl adopted by the long-dead father of rancher Ben Zachary, is an Indian rescued as a baby from a massacre of Kiowas. Returning home after hiring hands for a cattle drive, Ben hears the rumour and asks his mother, Mattilda, if it is true. Though shaken when told that it is, for he lives in a community that fears and hates the Indians, Ben stubbornly defends Rachel against the Kiowas, whose spokesman is her brother; against his partner, Zeb Rawlins, whose family and hands want to sacrifice her to the raiding tribesmen; against his brother, Cash, whose love for his adopted sister is overwhelmed by hatred for her race; against Rachel herself, when she attempts to return to her people to save Ben's family. Eventually Rachel justifies Ben's confidence and love by shooting her brother when the Kiowas attack. Cash returns to find Mattilda dead and his young brother, Andy wounded. He and Ben drive off the remaining Kiowas, mourning their dead mother and the burning of their home, but resolved to face the future and public opinion together.

Comment
    A western of heroic proportions, telling a strong story of family tensions, racial bigotry, and sexual strife against post-Civil War settings, this is Huston's first film set in the U.S.A. since *The Red Badge of Courage*, with which it has many similarities, although not in looks. Again there is a strong visual style, this time characterised by statuesque photography, brooding night scenes, and a deep feeling for period and character.

U.S.A. (Reno): The Misfits (1960)

Marilyn was very grateful to me for giving her her first opportunity. One day I received a script in the mail with a very modest letter from a man I'd never met, but whose work I admired very much, Arthur Miller. It was the screenplay of *The Misfits*. He asked me if I would read it with a view to directing it, if I didn't find it thoroughly bad. I read it, was deeply impressed, and telephoned him. I had finished *The Unforgiven* and gone to Ireland, and I telephoned him at his home in New York. Arthur came over, we talked about the script and the few changes that he had in mind, and some that occurred to me, and he set about making them. That was the book we worked from. That was the script—our Bible! Very little was changed as we went along. The casting was done in a very short period of time. Marilyn, I think. was the first to mention Gable. She had adored him as a little girl, on the screen. We arranged for production by United Artists, and we went out to Reno and shot the picture.

Things went without a hitch, except where Marilyn was con-concerned. Very quickly one perceived that she was in difficult straits, she was taking drugs to go to sleep, drugs to wake up, and she was in a vicious circle. She was suffering from this physically, and the time it took to make the picture suffered because of this. She would be late on the set for the simple reason that she couldn't be awakened by a certain time, and we'd wait, sometimes for hours, for her. Eventually we had to close down and the writing on the wall was there to read. I knew that it had to come to a desperate conclusion, and where I thought it might take three or four years, or five or six years, why, it was a matter of months.

Arthur Miller was with her all through the shooting. He did everything he could. Finally he couldn't do any more. His efforts met with antagonism on her part, and she was no longer capable of helping herself. She went into hospital and we had to stop shooting for two weeks. It was ever so clear that the drugs were her undoing, and still it was possible for her to get the drugs. The company doctor wouldn't give them to her, but she was being provided with them by her own doctors out of Hollywood. This was criminal, an awful indictment of the medical profession, but they do it. Quite unforgivable in my opinion. There were times when we wondered if we'd ever get finished at all. Each time when we got a scene, why, it was a bit of a victory. Sometimes she'd be excellent, sometimes she would hardly know where she was, and we had to cut our cloth accordingly.

There was something deeply touching about Marilyn. We all loved her and knew that tragedy was impending. We had to re-shoot scenes occasionally and sometimes it would be impossible to make a scene, so we'd defer it, do something else, and wait until she had recovered sufficiently to do it. Occasionally she was just wonderful.

With Marilyn Monroe and Arthur Miller while shooting
THE MISFITS (1960).

It was said that Arthur should have seen to it that she never got
any drugs. There was an estrangement there, and they separated
during that period. I think Arthur made every attempt, and did
everything possible to assist her recovery, and finally they were living
in different hotels in Reno. This was her doing. I didn't enquire
too deeply as to what was going on between them but it was evident.
They would go home from the set in different cars. Gable was wonderful through all this. He couldn't have been better. Thoroughly professional, of course, and excellent. I liked him ever so much.

One thing I didn't mention, but this film was in black-and-white.
Colour would be a distraction. I don't think that the film-makers
should be denied a palette any more than a painter. After all, Picasso
chose to do "Guernica" in black-and-white, didn't he? There are films
which, I think, are better in black-and-white. More and more, however,
we have learned to adjust our palette to the requirements of the

story, to the idea, so that it's just not a straight colour rendering, but that we make the colour serve a special purpose, and more and more pictures can be done in colour without so distracting the eye that the sense doesn't come across.

The essence of *The Misfits* really concerns the environment, what civilisation does in the way of tarnishing the life around us and our souls. These people represented the holdouts, as it were, against the stamped-out, factory-made article. The ones who were in revolt against this movement, but who didn't know it themselves, were pursued and harried and put-down the way horses were and made into pet food instead of ponies for children. It was really very painful having to create some of the scenes.

This was my first film with Montgomery Clift. I think he was probably having emotional problems all the time, but they became progressively worse. Something nothing of us realised was that he

Marilyn Monroe, Clark Gable and Montgomery Clift in
THE MISFITS (1960).

was also in the process of going blind. He didn't know it either. He was very good in the picture, I thought, so good, and all the stories about troubles people had had with him in other pictures were refuted by his behaviour on *The Misfits*. The reassurance led me to doing *Freud* with Monty. In *Freud*, why, while we were doing it, everything caught up with him, and he was quite incapable of certain things.

With all the delays we were actually filming on a three-month proposition. It didn't drag out to six months, as some said it did. The one period of inactivity was when we closed down for two weeks, but I stayed on in Reno and visited the gambling tables! I like to gamble. I wouldn't call myself a great gambler by any means, but I like it. When the film was finished, I felt I had obtained the qualities I wanted, and which I liked in the script. It was released the way I wanted it. There are scenes in the picture I liked enormously. For instance, following the rodeo when they came home to the framework of that house, and Monty Clift's bandages are coming undone. Things go off tangently and these moments had a kind of shock and a vibration, a life of their own that I thought was extra-ordinary. This was the writing and the performance. When we talk about realism and reality we talk about two different things, but there it was—it was true. It was indeed a fact. It was not a difficult picture to make physically, and the only difficulty, as I have said, was with Marilyn herself. It was shocking, you know, that Clark Gable, like the gentleman he was, finished his last shot in the picture and went home and died. Almost unbelievable.

THE MISFITS. 1960. *A* United Artists *Release.*
Director: John Huston. *Production Company:* Seven Arts. *Producer:* Frank E. Taylor. *Assistant Director:* Carl Beringer. *Second Unit Director:* Tom Shaw. *Screenplay:* Arthur Miller. *Photography:* Russell Metty. *Editor:* George Tomasini. *Art Directors:* Stephen Grimes and William Newberry. *Music:* Alex North. *Sound Recording:* Philip Mitchell.
Running time: 125 minutes.
Players: Clark Gable (*Gay Langland*), Marilyn Monroe (*Roslyn Taber*), Montgomery Clift (*Perce Howland*), Eli Wallach (*Guido*), Thelma Ritter (*Isabelle Steers*), James Barton (*Old Man in Bar*), Estelle Winwood (*Church Lady*), Kevin McCarthy (*Raymond Taber*).

Story
Gay, a part-time cowboy, and Guido, a motor mechanic and former pilot, are both drifters in the shifting, casual society of Reno. When they take up with Roslyn Taber, a lonely, disconsolate showgirl who

has come to Reno for her divorce, it is because they recognise in her an instinctive sympathy, a "gift for life." Roslyn turns to Gay, and they live together for a few weeks in the little house outside the town which Guido left unfinished after his wife's death. Their existence is a kind of tranquil playing at domesticity. With Guido and Isabelle, Roslyn's landlady, they go to a local rodeo, *en route* picking up Perce, a rodeo-rider friend. He is thrown and injured, and Gay is as exasperated by Roslyn's revulsion from the cruelty of the show as she is hurt by his casual acceptance of it. All three men have unhappy relationships behind them—Gay has lost contact with his children, Perce's mother has remarried, Guido blames himself for his wife's death—and all three use Roslyn as a confidante. After a drunken evening, they set off next day on an expedition to rope and bring in a herd of wild mustangs. Once the mustangs were needed as children's pets, now they can only be sold for dog food; and it is the realisation of this that brings on Roslyn's final rebellion. She rounds on the men for their callousness, their indifference, their shabby pretence of a "free" life. Guido remains unregenerate; but Perce helps her to cut the horses free, and Gay, after fighting his personal battle in subduing the stallion, turns him loose. Together, Gay and Roslyn drive away. "Just head for that big star straight on," he tells her.

Comment

Marilyn Monroe's first, and last, important film, and Gable's last, made on a wave of publicity, and Arthur Miller's first, and last, screenplay, this is a thoughtful statement about the American conscience, the failures of personal relationships, the weakening of the belief that men can still live freely and keep the western myth alive; it is stark and terrible in its depiction of the dubious activity of rodeo riding, the slaughter of wild horses, and the complex and destructive relationships of human beings.

Austria (Vienna): **Freud: The Secret Passion** (1962)

Freud really started when I was at Mason General Hospital in Bethlehem, Long Island, doing *Let There Be Light*. I got a short course in psychiatry there, the best advice instantly available. I read, crammed as it were, all the time I was there making the film. I knew nothing about the subject, I'd read a little Freud like everyone else but only superficially, and I had a vague idea of what he was about, but working there his figure loomed large at every turn. His presence was always felt and it was the name that was uttered oftener than anyone else. This started me reading Freud, and reading about Freud, and then of conceiving his life and work as being a picture. Wolfgang Reinhardt had had the same thoughts. I'd known him at Warner Bros. originally. Gottfried Reinhardt was the producer of *The Red Badge of Courage*. They were brothers, the sons of Max Reinhardt.

We talked about who would write the script and it was my notion to get Jean-Paul Sartre. I had met Sartre before, and he agreed to do it. He wrote a script. First he described what he was going to do, and it sounded promising. He wrote a script about 400 pages long, with so many characters and so many incidents that it would have been impossible to contain them all in one picture. It was very interesting, but random and erratic. When I say it was interesting, at times it was fascinating. But Sartre, if you recall, was to write a preface to a book by Jean Genet, and the preface turned out to be 700 pages. There was a marvellous flow of words out of Sartre. He came to my home in Ireland to work with me there, and we went over the script and talked about cuts and changes. My God, what a worker, too—unbelievably fiendish in his pursuit of an idea. He wrote in French, and then we translated it. Then, when we had decided on these cuts, why, he went back to Paris and presently in about three to four weeks the next script appeared and it was over 600 pages long [*laughs*].

Well, it was just impossible to cope with this massive output. I set about trying to rewrite and reduce it down to a reasonable length of about 150 pages, still a long picture. I sent the script to Sartre and he disavowed it entirely. Charles Kaufman wrote an original treatment before Sartre and then he came on and worked a bit with Sartre's material. Charlie didn't have a great deal to do with it, actually. He was a screenwriter at Warner Bros. Sartre spoke no English. He speaks German fluently, and the French language. Sartre holds forth; as he writes he also speaks. I've enormous admiration for Sartre, enormous. As we all know, he has a profound intelligence and is a dedicated man, and does unerringly what he believes in, what he believes to be the right thing. On the other hand, he is not a particularly attractive individual to me [*laughs*]. He's not in any way a joyful companion! He works with a single-mindedness that's impressive and frightening, almost.

I remember the night after he left Paris to come over with me to Ireland he had a play opening. Being from that old New York world where people hung on the remarks of the critics, why, I expected Sartre to be on the telephone. Not at all! Three or four days later there came an envelope in the mail, brought in while we were in the midst of a conversation. I knew the envelope had the reviews of the play, and I was just waiting for him to open it and see what the reaction was. Not at all! This was in the mid-morning, and he didn't look at the envelope until lunch was called. Then he remained in the study, looked at the reviews, and then came into lunch. We'd had a conversation—well, it was scarcely a conversation. Sartre would hold forth, and then there would be the opportunity for a few comments. Sartre would then go upstairs to his room and write notes. He had a secretary there who would transcribe them for the screenplay, and the result of our so-called conversations would be twenty-five pages of notes. It was all valid material but, as I said, it was tangential, it would go off in too many directions, trying to tell too many things. Freud's relationship with his first teacher, and his second teacher, and his third, and fourth, and fifth, the theme being that he was seeking a father; but it just became inchoate through so many characters, fragmentary scenes, some of which were extraordinary, and some of them are in the film. He never referred to the reviews again. I said, "What about them?" and he said "Well received"—that's all. But he was a bit of a monster, Sartre—a monster of the mind.

A film-maker takes a risk when he decides to use someone like Sartre in the sense that film-makers are still looked upon as being despoilers of intellectual works. You decide to get, possibly, the man who is best suited to do the work. He then proves unsuitable only because he has really no idea of what the film medium actually requires. You have to then either use someone else, or cut down what that person has done for you, and then you run the risk of being criticised for having ruined what was originally given to you. I thought Sartre would be ideal for it. There's a little smell of sulphur about everything Sartre does, and he can be succinct in an extraordinary way, as in "Huis Clos" where every line is precise and like an arrow-point. But not so in *Freud*.

We cast it, went into production, and it was a very unhappy picture to make. I made it in Vienna, and Monty was very, very hard to work with. He was in physical distress. He couldn't remember lines, it was very difficult. I didn't want the tone of the script to sound modern, I wanted to have a certain quality of that time, even stilted in a sense. People spoke in rounded phrases. That and the scientific terminology was an interesting combination, but it quite defeated Monty who was always trying to be colloquial when Freud was anything but colloquial! He said exactly what he wanted and intended to say, and it was very difficult to do anything with him. He couldn't remember the lines. Finally we were writing the lines for him to read,

FREUD: THE SECRET PASSION (1962): with Susannah York, Larry Parks and Montgomery Clift.

off-screen, on boards, on little pieces of paper on doors, and tricking the scenes. Nevertheless, in the end, I thought he gave quite an extraordinary performance. Freud was a tortured man himself, a self-proclaiming neurotic. It was his own analysis of himself that led him to an understanding of neuroses. At least I got a tortured actor. With the worries about how he was reading lines, there was the possibility that this would affect the character portrayal itself, even visually. It was very difficult and ever so hard. The most ·difficult experience I have ever had working with an actor. I'd have to approach him one way one time, and another way another time, and I'd have to threaten him on occasions, cajole him, hold his hand, whatever was expedient.

Monty, among other things, as I said, was losing his eyesight and didn't know it. This came out in the scene in which his hat was knocked off, and he complained that something had happened to his eyes when his hat was knocked off. He was examined and it was discovered that he had dreadful cataracts, and that his vision was

FREUD: THE SECRET PASSION (1962). Montgomery Clift and
Susannah York.

such that he literally couldn't read. I would see him look at the
script very closely and wonder why. I thought he was just nearsighted.
It didn't ever occur to him to go and get them checked. In the meantime, Monty was also drinking, he was a torn creature. It was before
this that Clift had his car accident, and his condition was a belated
result. The picture was finished and I liked it. But not Universal.

To begin with, it was black-and-white, and it was almost two-
and-a-half hours long. It was very closely written, step by step, and
anything cut out of the picture was damaging because it was a suspense
story, an intellectual suspense story, and no step in its logic could
be removed without affecting the whole thing. Yet audiences, when
it was previewed, all said—"long, much too long." Now, here again,
I don't hold Universal responsible for this beyond a certain point.
Cuts were made and vital links are missing. On the other hand, to
ask an audience to sit and watch a syllogism for two-and-a-half hours
is asking one hell of a lot. Well, the picture was cut until it was just
under two hours. The audience still said it was too long. It wasn't any

longer at two-and-a-half hours than it was at two hours, so it might as well have been left as it was.

What is seen is a cut version, and nothing like as good as what was there. Sometimes the studios keep the parts they cut out. I wish to gosh Universal would reissue it now in its original version. By the way, that reminds me, I got a communication not long ago from Metro asking me if I had the original version of *The Red Badge of Courage,* as they would like to release it [*laughter*] in its original form. I haven't got it, and they haven't. Now, when this occurred, I took a silent vow that hereafter I will always keep the original version. When *Freud* was cut I did it myself, but left the bits with them. Do you know how hard it is to take out essential scenes, knowing the film is being destroyed? It's an unbelievable experience. I'm afraid I didn't foresee when making the film that this might arise. It seemed to me to be utterly fascinating, every inch of it! The film-maker who wants to be true to himself also hopes, of course, that he will have an audience for what it is he has made that he can remain true to. Showing the film to one audience in one place and taking their reactions into consideration is usually indicative of how audiences are going to be everywhere. There have been exceptions to this, but, more or less, an audience (not an audience of critics such as you will have at Cannes), an anonymous audience, reacts very much as one audience to another, very much the same. With your provision that between countries it can be quite different. I've noticed this. France will like a picture thoroughly which has no following in America. Sometimes this occurs in Italy.

I should mention that technically the dream scenes were challenging. Dreams played an enormous role in the Freudian conception, a revealing role, and he regarded them, of course, symbolically. To capture these in the visual sense we used old film that was explosive, so there was a shattering effect: the whites were whiter, and the black blacker. We photographed the scenes usually overexposed. We tried in some way to capture visually the shocking effect that dreams have.

I did say, when talking about *They Were Strangers,* that I wouldn't make a film about another country, using American actors. Since then I used American actors to play a Frenchman [*Moulin Rouge*] and here to play an Austrian, a Viennese. These were justified, I think, when there's a sufficient time interlude. Curtains between the audience and the past grant permission to do this, but, if it's a contemporary story, I am always embarrassed by having them speak. Ideally, if the story had been completely and utterly authentic it would have all been in German! The cast of players on the whole was splendid. It was very hard to find a Joseph Breuer who was, how can I say it, a conservative man, highly conservative, but with a certain fundamental weakness. Larry Parks was good at this. I had seen Parks, during his brief time as a Columbia star, turn in some very good performances. He was a solid actor—what I needed, I thought. It was a solid performance.

With the deaths and difficulties, one after another, I found myself getting rather depressed. I'm often asked, when talking about Marilyn Monroe and Montgomery Clift, why did their lives go like this? Why, when they seemed to have everything, was there such unhappiness? With Monty his life took a curve downwards with an automobile accident, so I think that played a role in the decline of Monty Clift. With Marilyn, as with many others not so strikingly demonstrated, here was a child, scarcely educated, her upbringing a pretty scattered proposition, ill-prepared for the role she was to play, that of sex symbol. It takes background and character to stand the assault on that kind of career. Marilyn certainly had nothing good in the way of background. Little disasters had begun when she was still a child. Her mother was in an institution. She had a very early child marriage that soon went on the rocks, with rumour of some sexual incident with some older, male relation. It was this kind of world she had behind her. She had no mental preparation of what was to come, just a great innocence, a childishness, the kind of faith that was very often betrayed, too, because people began to exploit her, use her. The studio used her to its purposes, individuals tried to get her to serve their purposes, a variety of purposes—some carnal, some fiscal—and Marilyn was a victim of that system. One wonders why it doesn't end tragically for more of them. Maybe it does. Perhaps their tragedies are not so apparent. It's almost like an allegory in which innocence has attracted evil. The quality of innocence was so innocent that it failed to recognise evil, possibly, and the evil then destroyed her.

FREUD: THE SECRET PASSION. 1962. *A* Universal-International *Picture*.
Director: John Huston. *Producer:* Wolfgang Reinhardt. *Associate Producer:* George Golitzin. *Associate Director:* Gladys Hill.
Assistant Directors: Ray Gosnell Jr. and Laci von Ronay.
Screenplay: Charles Kaufman and Wolfgang Reinhardt. *Story:* Charles Kaufman. *Photography:* Douglas Slocombe. *Editor:* Ralph Kemplen.
Art Director: Stephen Grimes. *Music:* Jerry Goldsmith. *Electronic Music:* Henk Badings. *Sound:* Basil Fenton Smith and Renato Cadueri.
Medical Consultant: David Stafford-Clark. *Technical Adviser:* Earl A. Loomis Jr.
Running time: 140 minutes

Players: Montgomery Clift (*Sigmund Freud*), Susannah York (*Cecily Koertner*), Larry Parks (*Dr. Joseph Breuer*), Susan Kohner (*Martha Freud*), Eileen Herlie (*Frau Ira Koertner*), Fernand Ledoux (*Prof. Charcot*), David McCallum (*Carl von Schlosser*), Rosalie Crutchley (*Frau Freud*), David Kossoff (*Jacob Freud*), Joseph Fürst (*Jacob Koertner*), Alexander Mango (*Babinsky*), Leonard Sachs (*Brouhardier*), Eric Portman (*Dr. Theodore Meynert*).
Prologue and Epilogue read by: John Huston.

Story

Vienna, 1885. Dr. Sigmund Freud, a young neurologist, is in conflict with his colleagues about the nature of hysteria. He goes to Paris to study under Professor Charcot, who has demonstrated by hypnosis that some hysterical symptoms are mentally induced. Encouraged by Martha Bernays, whom he later marries, and Dr. Joseph Breuer, Freud returns to Vienna and continues to use hypnosis in treating hysterical patients—in particular a young girl, Cecily Koertner, who broke down completely after her father's death, and Carl von Schlosser, a youth who has made a homicidal attack on his father. During his treatment of Carl, Freud realises that the boy's hatred of his father springs from incestuous love of his mother. Horrified, he drops the case but later, when the boy has died in an asylum, he begins to understand that he abandoned Carl because he was afraid of uncovering a similar neurosis in himself. While trying to find the way into his own unconscious, Freud perseveres with Cecily. He has now given up hypnosis and is patiently developing a technique of analysis. Convinced that all neuroses have their origin in sexual traumas, he finally uncovers Cecily's repressed desire for her father and releases her from her physical symptoms. He also traces in his own childhood memory of the incident in which his guilt towards his father was rooted. He is now able to formulate his theory of sexuality in infancy, and expounds it in a lecture. This time not even his old friend Breuer is convinced, but Freud is more determined than ever to go on with his researches.

Comment

Underrated when it was first shown, this is another of Huston's masterpieces, not a biography of Freud but a remarkable genesis of his basic theories and methods. In conveying the atmosphere and mentality of late-19th century Europe and the reluctance of the medical profession to accept Freud, Huston and his excellent players have shown a passionate, concerned and fascinating interest in the life, beliefs and discoveries of this tormented genius. Four imaginative dream sequences brilliantly convey the workings of the inner mind, disturbed, startled and tortured!

Ireland: **The List of Adrian Messenger** (1963)

The List of Adrian Messenger is a trick film, *a tour de force*. Tony
Veiller and I again wrote the script and it was perfectly simple. I
thought it was rather an amusing picture! Well done with no problems.
I was surprised it wasn't better received than it was. I thought it a
good mystery-thriller. George C. Scott was good in it, everybody was
good in it. It had an idea, it had a point, and the picture served it
rather well. It followed the novel, by Philip MacDonald, more or less.
Fox-hunting played a greater role in the picture. I don't think it
played any role to speak of in the novel, but then the way the villain
met his end wasn't as in the novel. The *idea* was in the novel: this
protean change of faces, that was the main thing. Edward Lewis, the
producer, came to us with the idea. It was his notion to have well-known
actors, not let the audience know who they were, and then reveal

THE LIST OF ADRIAN MESSENGER (1963).
Kirk Douglas and George C. Scott.

them at the end. I was one of the members of the hunt. Tony, my boy, was about ten years old, I think, at the time and I needed a child who could ride well, and Tony rode very well indeed. That's why I had him in the picture. I remembered Herbert Marshall and Clive Brook from way back, and Clive Brook was, I thought, beautifully cast. He's that sort of person. I cast them for their personalities. The same with Bert Marshall. There are special requirements here, because with a mystery film one must decide how much the audience is to know, or not to know. The problem is with presentation: the suspense of this picture was, who was who? Not knowing if the villain was among those present, because of his ability to change faces.

The picture was shot in Ireland for the best part. A little shooting here, but mostly in Ireland. Just a scene or two in the States. Just one gathering, I think, of the hunt. This was for Universal, and black-and-white, too. It *could* have been in colour. I didn't have any difficulty with the studio over it. That's the sort of picture they leave alone, because they believe there are no difficulties with it as far as audiences are concerned. It's usually different if you want to do something a little out-of-the-ordinary.

THE LIST OF ADRIAN MESSENGER. 1963. *A* Universal-International *Release*

Director: John Huston. *Production Company:* Joel. *Producer:* Edward Lewis. *Second Unit Director:* Ted Scaife. *Assistant Directors:* Tom Shaw and Terry Morse Jr. *Screenplay:* Anthony Veiller. *From the novel by:* Philip MacDonald. *Photography:* Joseph MacDonald. *Editors:* Terry Morse and Hugh Fowler. *Art Directors:* Stephen Grimes and George Webb. *Set Decorator:* Oliver Emert. *Make-up:* Bud Westmore. *Music:* Jerry Goldsmith. *Music Director:* Joseph Gershenson. *Sound:* Waldon O. Watson and Frank Wilkinson. *Running time:* 97 minutes
Players: George C. Scott (*Anthony Gethryn*), Kirk Douglas (*George Brougham*), Jacques Roux (*Raoul Le Borg*), Dana Wynter (*Lady Jocelyn Bruttenholm*), Walter Tony Huston (*Derek*), Clive Brook (*The Marquis of Gleneyre*), Herbert Marshall (*Sir Wilfred Lucas*), Bernard Archard (*Inspector Pike*), John Merivale (*Adrian Messenger*), Gladys Cooper (*Mrs. Karoudjian*), Marcel Dalio (*Max*), Anita Sharpe Bolster (*Shopkeeper*), Noel Purcell (*Farmer*), John Huston (*Huntsman*), Robert Mitchum, Burt Lancaster, Frank Sinatra, Tony Curtis (*Guest Stars*).

Story
Shortly after a man has been murdered in a West End office lift, a clergyman spies on the country seat of the aged Marquis of Gleneyre. Inside, writer Adrian Messenger, one of the Marquis's fox-hunting

guests, asks retired intelligence officer Anthony Gethryn if he will check on the whereabouts of eleven men on a list he has compiled, all former acquaintances, while he is away in America. At the airport, Messenger engages in conversation with the vicar, then boards his plane. While the vicar goes into a washroom and exchanges his disguise for that of a pedantic, balding old gentleman, the plane which he failed to catch blows up. Gethryn, having discovered that practically all the names on the list have died over a number of years in suspicious circumstances, is now certain that a cold-blooded mass-murderer is at large. He contacts Raoul Le Borg, the sole survivor of the plane explosion, who helps him make sense of Messenger's garbled last words before he died. Their conclusions take them to Messenger's flat and then to Messenger's typist, but they are too late, for she has just been gassed by the old gentleman. Similarly, Gethryn is unable to prevent the murder by a scruffy East Ender of the last surviving name on Messenger's list. A statement by Mrs. Karoudjian, dipsomaniac widow

George C. Scott in THE LIST OF ADRIAN MESSENGER (1963).

of an earlier victim, gives Gethryn the connecting link between the eleven names, and sends him back to the Marquis's house. Here, during a fox-hunt, he meets the killer, by now so confident of his ultimate goal that he not only eschews any kind of disguise but flirts openly with the Marquis's beautiful, widowed daughter-in-law, Lady Jocelyn Bruttenholm. Nevertheless, it is in yet another disguise that the killer is finally unmasked and meets his death in the horrible manner he had planned for his next victim—the pertinacious, keen-eyed Gethryn.

Comment

With a typical change of pace, Huston turned to another quirky detective tale, this one with lots of jokes and well-known actors playing guest roles in make-up. The depiction of the aristocratic country life, the upper-crust characters, their polite rituals and violent fox-hunting, are beautifully, knowingly and lovingly set. The use of players from a past era adds to the charm and nostalgia of this casual yet absorbing thriller.

Mexico (Puerto Vallarta) : **The Night of the Iguana** (1964)

Ray Stark had spoken several times to me about making a film of Tennessee Williams's "The Night of the Iguana." I had seen the play and liked it, with reservations. I was a great admirer of Tennessee Williams. Tony and I wrote the script and we changed the finish. It seemed to me that Tennessee had wrenched it around to suit his own philosophy of the spiderlike qualities of womankind when Maxine Faulk (the role Ava Gardner played) consumed her lover, as it were. He thought about it, we had a difference of opinion. No quarrel or anything of that kind, but he maintained his opinion. Finally, I accused Tennessee of twisting his characters to his own purpose and he didn't deny this. I said it in defence because I liked the girl and I didn't see any reason for an unhappy ending. In fact, it was a distortion. I don't know whether Tennessee ever brought himself to agree with me, but he couldn't disagree and he certainly didn't accuse me of doing damage to his play. Here's a wonderful example of his genius: Tony and I wrote a scene, a fairly good scene, and on reading over the script, Tennessee said, "I'd like to have a crack at that scene. Let me see what I can do with it." Well, it was just the difference between night and day. He had Burton with a glass and a bottle on his dresser, standing before his dresser, and when the young girl came into his room, why, in his agitation he knocked the glass off the bottle, and it broke on the floor. There was broken glass on the floor, and he was barefoot, and he walked on the broken glass without

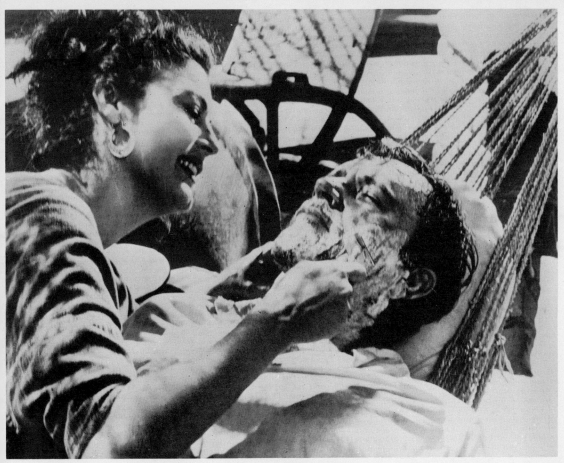

Ava Gardner and Richard Burton in THE NIGHT OF THE IGUANA (1964).

realising it. That was his state of mind. The girl sees him doing this, and finally she takes off her shoes and joins him, walking on the broken glass. It just lifted the scene on to another sphere. The theme of *The Night of the Iguana* is of loose, random souls trying to account for themselves and finally being able to do so through love. The old man, when he read the poem, expressed the feeling of the whole work, the night of the old man's death. It was that and the execution and the demonstration of it which attracted me to the play. Very moving.

I thought Deborah was wonderful in the picture. I liked Burton enormously, he was lovely to work with, full of gaiety and immediate appreciation of the quality of something good. He didn't take himself all that seriously, but took his work very seriously, he was a joy. Ava's one of my favourites. I've had Ava in as many pictures as there were opportunities to have her. Elizabeth Taylor was present, she was on the scene, and in spite of all the publicity these powerful person-alities' received, why, it was never a more peaceful occasion. Every-

Richard Burton and
Deborah Kerr in
THE NIGHT OF
THE IGUANA
(1964).

body got along famously. I went down to Mexico and the reason I got Gabriel Figueroa was because I remembered the quality of his photography, and I thought it suited the subject very well. I thought it was exactly right for *The Night of the Iguana*. There's a dreamy quality to it, and yet it has definition. He can sharpen, soften, create haloes, there's a mystery to his work. There were no hitches whatever. Tony and I went down and visited Tennessee in Key West, and stayed down there for a while. Then Tennessee came and stayed with us in Mexico. He took no credit and I would gladly have given it to him because his contribution to the screenplay was enormous. By the time it was finished it filled the bill completely as far as I was concerned. It was distributed by M-G-M. That was the only time I came back to M-G-M, but the scene had changed there entirely. It had the same name, that's all. Everything was done in Mexico, everything on that location, right near Puerto Vallarta. This was before the boom occurred, and I think making the film there had something to do with the boom, it's now become one of the great resort places of the western world.

THE NIGHT OF THE IGUANA. 1964. *An* M-G-M *Release.* *Director:* John Huston. *Production Company:* Seven Arts. *Executive*

Producer: Abe Steinberg. *Producer:* Ray Stark. *Associate Producer:* Alexander Whitelaw. *Assistant Director:* Tom Shaw. *Associate to Mr. Huston:* Gladys Hill. *Screenplay:* Anthony Veiller and John Huston. *Based on the play by:* Tennessee Williams. *Photography:* Gabriel Figueroa. *Editor:* Ralph Kemplen. *Art Director:* Stephen Grimes. *Music:* Benjamin Frankel. *Sound:* Basil Fenton Smith and Leslie Hodgson.
Running time: 118 minutes.
Players: Richard Burton *(Rev. Laurence Shannon)*, Ava Gardner *(Maxine Faulk)*, Deborah Kerr *(Hannah Jelkes)*, Sue Lyon *(Charlotte Goodall)*, James "Skip" Ward *(Hank Prosner)*, Grayson Hall *(Judith Fellows)*, Cyril Delevanti *("Nonno")*, Mary Boylan *(Miss Peebles)*.

Story

The Rev. Laurence Shannon, an Episcopal clergyman locked out of his church after a scandal involving a pretty young parishioner, is now courier to a party of American women teachers on a coach tour in Mexico. They include Charlotte Goodall, a teenage girl, who although travelling with one of the teachers as chaperone, makes insistent passes at Shannon. Afraid of losing his job and at the end of his spiritual tether, Shannon is drinking heavily and trying to resist Charlotte's advances. He strands the party in a remote hotel run by an old fisherman friend of his, only to find the friend dead and his widow, Maxine, in charge. Maxine, a happy-go-lucky extrovert, agrees to take the party in and also finds room for two more guests who appear from nowhere. These are an itinerant artist, Miss Jelkes, and her ninety-seven-year-old grandfather, reputed to be the oldest poet in the world. This curious *ménage* is soon in uproar, with Miss Fellowes, the chaperone, chasing her charge and threatening Shannon, while he flees, fearing for his job and his sanity, to the protection of Maxine and Miss Jelkes. Eventually Miss Fellowes hears of Shannon's scandalous past and manages to get her party away in the coach. Shannon goes berserk and tries to drown himself. During the night that follows Miss Jelkes calms him, her grandfather completes his last poem and dies, and Shannon frees a captive iguana which the servants had been fattening for food. In the morning Miss Jelkes goes on her way alone and Shannon decides to make his home at the hotel with Maxine.

Comment

A wildly hilarious farce with tragic overtones, it shows Huston perfectly at ease with Williams's erratic and extravagant characters, their wild behaviour and exaggerated dialogue. A truly peculiar crowd, they are nevertheless brilliantly portrayed by a clever cast, as with all Huston's films, and bring a strange, compelling life to the run-down hotel in Mexico where their outrageous and ridiculous eccentricities take on a passionate sense of humanity.

Italy (Rome) and Egypt: **The Bible . . . in the Beginning** (1966)

I was down in Mexico and this was just before we started shooting *The Night of the Iguana.* Luigi Luraschi came with Dino De Laurentiis and Paul Kohner to see me, with a proposal that I do one sequence of a film they were going to make called *The Bible.* They had a script by Christopher Fry, so I was very interested. I forget what sequence I wanted to do, and said, "Yes, by all means." Then they said, "Would you yourself choose the other directors and co-ordinate it?" Well, that was right up my alley, something I very much wanted to do and I would have enjoyed that enormously. Then the next I heard was, "Would you make the picture?" [*laughter*]. Well, this gave me reason to pause, because I could see it being a very long race indeed, with a lot of big timber jumps and open ditches. However, it was a challenge and Christopher Fry's script was very fine, written beautifully, which isn't at all surprising. I worked on it with him and that in itself was an education. Discussions with scholars, not the C. B. DeMille kind of research! But it was all very interesting indeed and the various interpretations of the Scriptures were challenging.

Of course, *The Bible* consisted of about half the book of Genesis, and marched under false colours. I did indeed try and persuade them to change the title, but they had advertised it too much by the time I came on to the picture to make the change. The name had been bandied about and advertisements had been taken and published three years before the picture was ever released! "Dino De Laurentiis produces *The Bible.*" It sounded big, that was what Dino wanted, and, of course, it brought a lot of jokes too! [*laughs*]. It was, my God, something! A book could be done on *The Bible,* believe me.

First, I wanted a special introductory sequence about the spirit of Creation. I sent for Ernst Haas, a very fine photographer who has had exhibitions at the Museum of Modern Art and other galleries, and we talked about the idea of the Creation sequence. I didn't want it to be a trick proposition, something done in the special effects department of a studio, but an interpretation. The idea was that each morning is the creation of the world. The Creation, you know, is something that is infinite and forever and instantaneous, now and forever. When a land mass appears out of the deeps, why, that too is creation, and still occurs today. That was the approach to the Creation sequence, and I thought Haas did some very beautiful things with it, going around the world to various places, South America, the Galapagos, Iceland, North America, taking moving pictures of nature with his little crew. Then came the Creation of Man. Where was there such a garden? What interpretation should it have? We thought there was a garden in Portugal; there were wild gardens in Ireland; some I was familiar with and some I went and saw. Finally— this was good so far as the cost of the picture was concerned—there was a place outside Rome owned by a very noble Italian family, the Oedascalci. It was a kind of sward, grasses with wild flowers and beautiful trees, big, wonderful looking trees, with a special quality, a kind of majesty to them, nothing formal, of course, but a restrained wilderness. So I said, "Yes, I think this would be the place." There were open fields and I saw that, by putting just a few animals in it, we would create the impression of the Garden of Eden. We were there in the wild flower season and so I said, "Let's get seeds now and scatter them so that when we go to shoot in three months' time there will be new wild flowers growing." I cautioned the workers to be very careful about the grass because I wanted everything to be fresh and new, untouched, untrammelled, virginal. Then we talked about waters, deep waters. There was no lake or running water on the place. I left that for the time being and went and worked with Kit on the script. Then I had to go around to other places and loca- tions, deciding where other sequences were to be shot, because once underway we couldn't stop, we had to keep going.

Finally, the hour was approaching, and I went back to see the Oedascalci garden and good Christ! It must have looked something like Passchendaele after the battle! Mud up to the hips. They'd made an artificial lake [roars of laughter] and in making the artificial lake, of course, everything for a hundred yards around was knocked to hell! They brought in earth-movers and diggers to make the lake, they put up a metal fence around the whole place so that the wild animals wouldn't escape. Then they had planted trees, and put artificial flowers on the trees, and the place was full of flamingoes and ospreys [roars of laughter]. Oh Jesus! Oh God! It was my idea of Hell, not Eden! [laughter]. Also, those beautiful trees were changed, they'd gone quite mad [laughter]. I called Prince Oedascalci and when he saw it, oh, he went off his rocker! It's a wonder he didn't sue everybody! He had every right to [laughter]. They peeled the bark off the trees. I tell you, it was devastation [roars of laughter]. What remained, when I looked through the camera at the one angle at which I could take any pictures at all, was a picture-postcard night-

mare! It was just utterly hopeless, and so we moved the whole operation into the middle of Rome, where there's a Zoological Garden
the authorities had allowed to go to seed. A wild place with thickets,
trees, bushes, everything we needed. Had I seen this before, I'd have
contemplated using it even before the Oedascalci estate, and I can tell
you they sought out corners to destroy in that place, it was unbelievable what happened. Where I had cautioned them to put down
walks, elevated walks so as not to disturb the grasses, it was mud!

I had the great good fortune of finding another magnificent cameraman, Lupino Rotunno, and miracles can be accomplished that
way. This is a typical example of the difficulty of a director keeping
control of an enormous production like this. The art director was
inspired, and with Italian energy he assaulted the citadel, you know!
[*laughter*]. He was, come hell or damnation, going to make it the
most beautiful place that had ever been on film! He was "disappointed"
and no doubt couldn't understand why I didn't like it. He felt, rather,
I think, that I'd let him down! [*laughter*]. Oh, I still have affection for
him, of course, and in some ways he was a very good art director. In
some ways, full of ingenuity. For instance, the Tower of Babel—that
was extraordinary in its conception. It was a combination of locations,
models, and glass shots. The base of it was in Italy and the top, the
peak of the tower, was in Egypt poised on a precipitous incline, so
that we looked down from this place. It was a few storeys high built
on the top of this perpendicular mountainside, rising above the desert,
hundreds of feet. The sides were absolutely straight down, so that the
audience couldn't see anything. We were at the top of a great tower,
and we could shoot down on to the desert where the figures were
diminutive. It was really quite a triumph of ingenuity, the designing
of the Tower. The same man who was guilty of one thing was also
responsible for the other, which was very, very good. The Cain and
Abel sequence was done in the south of Italy, where the grain was
grown.

There were parts of the picture I liked very much. I think it
suffered from over-publicising; first its name, and then a little bit
old-fashioned in its approach to the public as a spectacle. It wasn't
shot as a spectacle. It was very seriously conceived and everything that
was done had thought behind it. Some things were more successful
than others, but I felt that some sequences were quite extraordinary.
For instance, the sequence where the three angels visited Abraham,
and Ava Gardner, you remember, played his wife, was, I thought, one
of the most interesting sequences I have ever seen in a film. I can
detach myself from it! It was full of mystery. The book, in Genesis,
is full of mystery. The argument with God; the bargaining with God;

THE BIBLE . . . IN THE BEGINNING (1966).
John Huston as Noah, ark at left.

the horse-trading with God, as it were, over Lot and the destruction
of the city; the announcement of his having a son; the laughter of
Sarah—all these things are strange and have a mysterious beauty as
well as a pagan, savage spirit. When it came to choosing the actor
to play Noah I tried various people, among them Charlie Chaplin.
Charlie, I think, wanted to do it. I telephoned him and sent him a
script, and Charlie played with the idea very briefly, and then finally
said no. I was sorry, he'd have been wonderful. Then I tried three or
four other people. Orson would have been fine, but he was engaged
in something else though. I tried Alec Guinness, and I thought
maybe of making it a comedy sequence, to bring out the humorous
aspects of it. It's the child's book of the Bible. Children respond to
that story, and it is *the* story in the Bible that kids know best. I thought
to make that part of the film for children, for the child that's in all of us.

Finally, I was reduced, really, to doing it myself. We were at the
studio, we had to go, we had to shoot, and I couldn't really get anyone
I wanted, so I played the role myself. It's difficult to direct and act,
but the approach was that I'd put somebody else in and direct the

John Huston as Noah
in THE BIBLE . . .
IN THE BEGIN-
NING (1966).

scene and get the camera, the shot, and then step in and enact the
part. Then I would look for approval to my assistant director and the
cameraman, and see whether I'd been all right or not, and what they
said. There, by the way, I thought the Ark itself was a beautiful
thing, an object of beauty. The building of the Ark was done on the
back lot and it was, my God, a big thing. They went all out on that!
The interior of the Ark was on a studio stage and the atmosphere of
that stage was quite extraordinary. The animals were in the Ark, and
visitors were enchanted. Two or three times this remark was made:
"It's very revealing, it seems to me. You see, I've never been in an
Ark before"! [*laughs*]. They felt as though they were returning to a
place that was familiar, and the animals got along famously. The only
timid creatures were the elephants, and now and then when a bird
would fly too close to the elephants, why, they'd get restless and

trumpet. Otherwise they all got used to each other. The savage beasts were kept behind glass, of course, which you couldn't see.

The shot of Noah leading the animals into the Ark was a bit of a trial! Nobody really, except me, thought it could be done. They didn't see how you could get animals to go two-by-two, and the only way to do it was through a trick. There was even talk about drawing it, animating it; but I was sure it could be done. Finally I got a circus owner who knew animals very well, who agreed with me. Everyone else disagreed, but this one man who knew animals, he said, "Oh, I think it can be done." What he did was to build a road with a ditch on either side of it. The road led into a false front of the Ark. The entrance led right out on the other side of the Ark to a road, so that it was all a circle. One animal or two animals were brought out that could be led, and they were led on this road, around the road into the Ark. Presently it would be four animals, and they got to know the pattern of this. Some animals pick up habits very quickly, and fall into habits very quickly. I had bridles made for other animals, and the men who led them with a little nylon rope walked in the ditch, leading the animals. More and more were added to the train over a period of many weeks, and finally while there were two, four, six animals finally they'd take off the halters and the animals moved along the road and through the Ark until at last the great day came and we had them all there. This training had gone on for some weeks and we got it the first shot! The animals followed the walk exactly, did precisely what they were supposed to do, and we couldn't believe we had it! A great shout went up, and we did it again, and the animals did it again [laughs]. They were as well rehearsed as Orson Welles! I felt a great deal of satisfaction at having that, but when the film came out, in the reviews, whatever, nobody commented on it, because they assumed that if animals went in two-by-two, they *should* go in two-by-two. It was what was expected of them!

I took as a pattern for the Flood the Da Vinci drawings of water, and the dynamics of the wave, and that was the inspiration for the treatment of the Flood. Some shots were miniatures, some things were done on the set, waterfalls were photographed. Then real dams were opened up, and the ground flooded with this onrush of water. The sequence was a combination of many things.

I've got another very interesting story to tell you about *The Bible*! When we went to do the Creation of Man, various ideas were put forward and finally I went to the sculptor, the living sculptor whom I most admire, Giacomo Manzu, who was living outside Rome. I knew Manzu and he was busy on the doors of St. Peter's at this time, and there hadn't been a work of his for sale for years. He'd done nothing except work on the doors for the past two years. I scarcely hoped he would do what I was going to ask him, and I was quite prepared for him to say it was impossible. I wanted him to do the Creation of Man out of the earth and in three stages, the idea being then to put dust around it, the dust, the clay of that earth, and let the wind shape it and reveal, as the winds blew, the Creation of Man. We required four pieces of sculpture and, to my surprise and delight, Manzu said, "Of course." It was one of the most extraordinary things I have ever witnessed, literally an act of creation. He came to the place, mined the clay right there, modelled the figures in their development, and it was wonderful to see this work in process. Of course, they were priceless, and they were to be destroyed. I'd left it to the business people to talk to him about payment, and Dino was quite prepared to pay anything for this. Dino's business representative approached Manzu and said, "Maestro, what are you asking for this work?" Manzu said, "Nothing, it's for my friend Huston." They tried to argue with him and he said, "No, please, it would ruin the whole thing if you talk like that." In order to get the effect that I wanted, we had wind machines to blow the dust, so that the figures would be obscured briefly and then, as the dust would clear, the development of the figure could be seen, creating the impression that it took form right before our eyes. The cameras had to turn with great speed to get this effect, and the motors burned out. The figures were on the verge of collapsing when we got it. To have failed was just unthinkable! Manzu didn't stay to see it photographed. Having done it, he walked away, went back to his studio. Yet it took him several days to do it, and he gave it as much attention as though they were to be permanent. The abstract shapes of Adam before he was formed were equally interesting, and the shape of the earth was a fascinating piece of abstract sculpture. Each one was consummately good. I went and saw Manzu and said, "Thank God we got it," and told him how near we were to not getting it, and he said, "Well, if you hadn't, I would have come out and done it again. Why are you so concerned?"

Throughout the filming, Christopher Fry was everywhere. He came to Ireland; I stayed with him here in England at a hotel and had frequent meetings with him; he came to Italy; we took trips together, we were down in the South of France together. He is a poet, as you know, and one of the kindest, dearest men alive. Without any pretensions. What he did was an act of devotion. Every moment with him was ever so valuable as an experience. He works very quietly, lives in the country, writes poems, does translations. Money is not his object, he lives for his work.

I completed the editing and so forth, and the finished film is as

I wanted it, with some reservations. There were little moments of disappointment in it; but, on the whole, it filled the bill of requirements as far as I was concerned. There were no arguments with De Laurentiis. We were in complete harmony. I love Dino, he's dynamic, a man who's fascinating to watch in action. He's got fine taste and excellent judgement, and he knows what's good and what's not good when he exercises his judgement and exercises his taste. Sometimes I think he blinds himself and proceeds on what he thinks is commercial and only that, but when he's called on to render an opinion, it's a good one. He took a great risk, too, because the whole time he was producing that film and pouring money into it, he had no distribution arrangements. It was not until it was completely finished that Fox agreed to distribute it. He's nothing but a gambler. He's a high roller, Dino, and I take my hat off to him in many ways.

He gambled on *The Bible* and won. It not only managed to earn its costs back, but it showed a very fine profit. Now, for instance, *The Misfits* was such an expensive film that, although it made its costs back, it didn't make a profit. It was so expensive because of the great above-the-line costs for all these ever so expensive people who were being paid their full amounts. Very often the money that is paid into the making of the film is never apparent on the screen. *The Misfits*, as far as the making of the picture was concerned, was comparatively cheap. I mean, the below-the-line cost, the actual making of the film, was quite cheap; but the cost of the cast, and so on, made it a very expensive film.

The Bible was as fascinating to me as "The Golden Bough." I'm not an orthodoxly religious person, and I don't profess any beliefs. If I were to, I'd feel guilty of an impertinence—the mystery of life is too great, too wide, to do more than wonder at, as far as I'm concerned. On occasion, I envy those people who have it all down pat [*laughs*]. That was my approach to the material from mythology to legend, the emergence of the myth. I remember when production began, and while we were filming, there was controversy over such silly things as what was the actual fruit Eve ate, what was the size of the Ark, did Adam have a navel [*laughs*]—well, everybody knows today there was no Adam and Eve, and we are supposed to have had our beginning in the ocean. I coped with all of that by ignoring it largely, and also by treating everything with a certain credence. My friend, Buckminster Fuller, is of the opinion that man appeared on the planet earth in his present form, and that other species are degenerations of that [*laughs*], and that he came first as a visitor from another planet. Whatever Buckminster Fuller says must be given due thought [*laughs*]. No, my approach to it was, as I said, the emergence out of myth and legend, with facts from the Bible. The measurements for the Ark are laid down in the Bible. They are old-fashioned measurements which no one is quite' sure about, but there are those scholars who claim to know what the measurements were, and the Ark was according to that size. Or course, we could make it twice the size with the lens of a camera, or half the size! The apple was a golden fruit that seemed to have a magic about it. One of the most difficult things was the Serpent, and the form of the Serpent. Serpents were modelled; costumes were made to fit over a man; serpents' heads like masks were made. The tree was designed and re-designed twenty times. Eventually a very fine artist, Corrado Colliea, an Italian painter, worked on the tree, and we decided on a very simple rendering of it, and the fruit, and the Serpent, which was just a shape. You saw its shape in the leaves in the tree and it spoke in a whisper, a sibilant sound, something like the hissing of a serpent. All of those things went through all the pangs of birth. Many of them were in other forms before the final ones that are seen on the screen were decided on. The entire cast was splendid. I don't remember how long exactly it took to make. It was a long time, I know that! [laughs]. It was like doing several pictures—each picture presented a whole new set of problems. I was ever so surprised to be finished! [laughter]. The very fact that we were finished was something.

THE BIBLE . . . IN THE BEGINNING. 1966. *A* Twentieth Century-Fox *Release.*
Director: John Huston. *Production Company:* Dino De Laurentiis.
Producer: Dino De Laurentiis. *Associate Producer:* Luigi Luraschi.
Production Supervisor: Bruno Todini. *Second Unit Director (for "The Creation"):* Ernst Haas. *Assistant Directors:* Vana Caruso and Ottavio Oppo. *Screenplay:* Christopher Fry. *Script Assistants:*
Jonathan Griffin, Ivo Perilli, Vittorio Bonicelli. *Photography:*
Giuseppe Rotunno. *Colour:* Technicolor. *Print by:* DeLuxe.
Editor: Ralph Kemplen. *Art Director:* Mario Chiari. *Set Decoration:*
Enzo Eusepi and Bruno Avesani. *Special Effects:* Augie Lohman.
Music: Toshiro Mayuzumi. *Music Director:* Franco Ferrara. *Costumes:*
Maria De Matteis. *Choreography:* Katherine Dunham. *Sound:* Fred Hynes. *Sound Recording:* Basil Fenton Smith and Murray Spivack.
Zoological Consultant: Angelo Lombardi.
Running time: 175 minutes (70mm).
Players: Michael Parks (*Adam*), Ulla Bergryd (*Eve*), Richard Harris (*Cain*), John Huston (*Noah*), Stephen Boyd (*Nimrod*),
George C. Scott (*Abraham*), Ava Gardner (*Sarah*), Peter O'Toole

Huston directing Richard Harris for THE BIBLE . . . IN THE BEGINNING (1966).

(*The Three Angels*) , Zoe Sallis (*Hagar*) , Gabriele Ferzetti (*Lot*) ,
Eleonora Rossi Drago (*Lot's Wife*) , Franco Nero (*Abel*) ,
Alberto Lucantoni (*Isaac*) , Robert Rietty (*Abraham's Steward*) ,
Adriana Ambesi and Grazia Maria Spina (*Lot's Daughters*) , and
Claudie Lange, Luciano Conversi, Pupella Maggio, Peter Heinze,
Angelo Boschariol, Anna Maria Orso, Eric Leutzinger, Gabriella
Pallotta, Rosanna De Rocco. *Narrator:* John Huston.

Story

Episodes from the Old Testament: The Creation; Eden and the
Expulsion; Cain and Abel; Noah and the Ark; Nimrod and the Tower
of Babel; Abraham and Sarah; Abraham begets Ishmael upon Hagar;
Sodom and Gomorrah; Lot's Wife; The Birth of Isaac; The Lord asks
Abraham to sacrifice Isaac.

Comment

All during its long production schedule, and pre-opening publicity,
it became an enormous joke ("read the book, see the film") , but
throughout the making of this enormous, expensive undertaking,
John Huston worked quietly and patiently and created a respectable,
spectacular, and intelligent film which makes no concessions to the
kind of religious nonsense and sentimentality once associated with
Hollywood films. Huston himself excels as Noah and is completely
at home with the animals, whom he directs with as much persuasion
as the humans.

England (Pinewood) : **Casino Royale** (1967)

I did the first sequence of *Casino Royale;* there were several directors,
and I didn't have to take over the whole thing! The producer, Charlie
Feldman, an old friend of mine, asked me if I'd do a sequence about
a grouse shoot. Every friend he's ever had in his whole history of the
business was in that picture, or had something to do with it—and so
I couldn't be left out! [*laughs*]. It ended up with me *not* doing a sequence about a grouse shoot, but the whole first sequence of the
picture. I thought the idea of the first sequence was amusing. I never
saw any of the rest of the picture until the opening [*laughs*], and I
was rather surprised at the directions it took; but I thought the first
sequence with Deborah Kerr and David Niven was amusing. It was
a take-off, of course. David Niven was supposed to be the real original
Bond, then another one came after him. It became very rapid, I must
say! I didn't take too long on this, and my part was done entirely in
the studio, with a little bit of exterior in Ireland. It was amusing,
colourful as written, I thought.

Directing Deborah
Kerr and David
Niven in CASINO
ROYALE (1967).

CASINO ROYALE. 1967. *A* Columbia *Release.*
Directors: John Huston, Ken Hughes, Val Guest, Robert Parrish, Joe
McGrath. *Production Company:* Famous Artists. *Producers:* Charles
K. Feldman and Jerry Bresler. *Associate Producer:* John Dark.
Production Managers: Douglas Peirce, John Merriman and Barrie
Melrose. *Additional Sequences:* Val Guest. *Second Unit Directors:*
Richard Talmadge and Anthony Squire. *Assistant Directors:* Roy
Baird, John Stoneman and Carl Mannin. *Screenplay:* Wolf Mankowitz,
John Law and Michael Sayers. *Suggested by the novel by:* Ian Fleming.
Photography: Jack Hildyard. Panavision. *Colour:* Technicolor.
Additional Photography: John Wilcox and Nicolas Roeg. *Editor:*
Bill Lenny. *Production Designer:* Michael Stringer. *Art Directors:*
John Howell, Ivor Beddoes and Lionel Couch. *Set Decoration:*
Terence Morgan. *Special Effects:* Cliff Richardson and Roy Whybrow.
Music/Music Director: Burt Bacharach. *Title theme played by:* Herb
Alpert and The Tijuana Brass. *Song: "The Look of Love" by:* Burt
Bacharach and Hal David. *Sung by:* Dusty Springfield. *Choreography:*
Tutte Lemkow. *Titles/Montage Effects:* Richard Williams. *Sound:*
John W. Mitchell, Sash Fisher, Bob Jones and Dick Langford.
Running Time: 131 minutes.
Players: David Niven (*Sir James Bond*), Peter Sellers (*Evelyn
Tremble*), Ursula Andress (*Vesper Lynd*), Orson Welles (*Le Chiffre*),

Joanna Pettet *(Mata Bond)*, Daliah Lavi *(The Detainer)*, Deborah Kerr *(Agent Mimi)*, Woody Allen *(Jimmy Bond)*, William Holden *(Ransome)*, Charles Boyer *(Le Grand)*, John Huston *("M")*, Kurt Kasznar *(Smernov)*, Terence Cooper *(Cooper)*, Barbara Bouchet *(Moneypenny)*, Angela Scoular *(Buttercup)*, Tracey Crisp *(Heather)*, Elaine Taylor *(Peg)*, Gabriella Licudi *(Eliza)*, Jacky Bisset *(Miss Goodthighs)*, Alexandra Bastedo *(Meg)*, Anna Quayle *(Frau Hoffner)*, Derek Nimmo *(Hadley)*, George Raft *(Himself)*, Jean-Paul Belmondo *(French Legionnaire)*, Peter O'Toole *(Piper)*, Stirling Moss *(Driver)*, Ronnie Corbett *(Polo)*, Colin Gordon *(Casino Director)*, Bernard Cribbins *(Taxi Driver)*, Tracy Reed *(Fang Leader)*, John Bluthal *(Casino Doorman/M.I.5 man)*, Geoffrey Bayldon *("Q")*, John Wells *("Q's" Assistant)*, Duncan Macrae *(Inspector Mathis)*, Graham Stark *(Cashier)*, Chic Murray *(Chic)*, Jonathan Routh *(John)*, Richard Wattis *(British Army Officer)*, Vladek Sheybal *(Le Chiffre's Representative)*, Percy Herbert *(1st. Piper)*, Penny Riley *(Control Girl)*, Jeanne Roland *(Captain of Guards)*.

Story

The power of SMERSH is growing to such proportions that the heads of the British, French, American and Russian secret services get together to see what can be done about it. Their solution is to force agent James Bond, now Sir James Bond, out of retirement to deal with the situation. This they do by blowing up his country house; in the bombardment "M" is killed. Bond's first duty is to console "M's" widow in Scotland, "M" proving to be McTarry of the Glen. McTarry's own family is replaced by a band of SMERSH agents, with the intention of sullying the fair name of Bond, hitherto incorruptible. But Bond enchants "Lady Fiona" (Agent Mimi) and escapes the murderous intentions of her "daughters." Back in London, Bond decides to designate all agents "James Bond" or "007" to confuse the enemy. He reaches an agreement with Vesper Lynd, the richest spy in the world, and sets her to seduce Evelyn Tremble, inventor of a fool-proof system for winning at baccarat. Others co-opted at this time include Cooper, a muscle-man, and Bond's daughter, Mata Bond, his child by Mata Hari. Mata Bond goes to Berlin, foils an attempt by SMERSH to extract money from the major powers, and returns. Bond's plans for Tremble are put into effect when he and Vesper go to the Casino Royale so that he can beat Le Chiffre at baccarat and thus prevent SMERSH's attempts to replenish their finances at the tables. Tremble wins, but Vesper is kidnapped as they leave. Following her, he is captured and tortured and finally shot by Vesper. All seems to be over, but there is still the fiendish Doctor Noah. Mata

As an actor in CASINO ROYALE (1967)
with Charles Boyer, David Niven, William Holden and Kurt Kasznar.

Bond is kidnapped in a flying saucer, and Sir James sets out in pursuit. The trail leads to the Casino, which proves to be a front for Noah's secret headquarters. Noah himself turns out to be Jimmy Bond, Bond's scapegrace nephew. Bond and his secret weapon against Noah, the glamorous "Detainer," manage to rescue Mata and Cooper, and get as far as the Casino. They are followed by Noah, whom the Detainer has fed an explosive capsule, and in the end everyone is blown up, along with the Casino.

Comment

A chaotic and expensive send-up of James Bond turns out to be a wild and wacky extravaganza without trace of planned coherence, style or approach. Huston's opening sequence emerges as the best of the work by five directors, in which Sir James Bond's Scottish adventures are recounted with an assured lunacy at which Huston is not unsurprisingly adept in view of his past excursions into various styles of comedy. His two players, Deborah Kerr and David Niven, are delightful.

Italy (Rome): **Reflections in a Golden Eye** (1967)

We are moving now into what has since become known as the "permissive" age, where at least a film-maker could approach subjects with a little more freedom than before. Here we could indicate homosexuality. I admired Carson McCullers' work enormously and it had been suggested that I film "Reflections in a Golden Eye." I'd read everything she'd written. I hadn't thought of making this film particularly, I don't read with that idea in mind. Then again, Ray Stark said, "Would you like to do this?" and I immediately said "Yes." My long-time associate, Gladys Hill, and I worked on the script, showed it to Carson McCullers, who made a few suggestions, but otherwise found it almost completely to her satisfaction. Carson—she was an invalid—then came to Ireland. The trip marked her first time out of bed in several years. She was inspired to come to Ireland. I had talked to her about the country and she longed to see it. She came and she was, of course, in bed there instead of in her place in New York.

The picture, I thought, was beautifully played. I liked it very much, quite wholly. I like things about some pictures and don't like things about others. I find very little to fault in *Reflections*. Now, more and more, people include it among my best pictures. It's mentioned oftener and oftener, I see what's happening to it. The story itself, the characters, the theme fascinated me, and that detachment with which Carson McCullers writes, the understanding with which she views these people impressed me. There is no hatred, there is no moral condemnation, no moral evaluation even. She records with dignity rather than reports. The behaviour of these humans is recorded. There's something *lasting* about her prose, considered and deep. I felt it was an important book, and we followed it very closely.

Among the characters, Major Penderton, played by Marlon Brando, was the most commanding, doubting his own manhood, his own yearnings, his contempt for himself, his aspirations, his attempt to prove himself in his own eyes, and the pathos of the failures, such as his ride on the horse where he had some image of himself as a conqueror and failed himself. The most sympathetic figure in the picture is that of the woman next door and her own neuroses, and her association with the Filipino, the unawareness of Brando's friend the Major, who is sleeping with Brando's wife, who wasn't a neurotic. She was quite the opposite. Nor was her lover, he wasn't neurotic, nothing strange about him. I think the whole is not a dramatic convenience, but a pretty fair reflection of the neurotics among us.

Some of it was done in New York, out on Long Island where there was an army installation that was about to be torn down, because we couldn't use a real army installation. All the interiors and some exteriors were in Italy, because Elizabeth Taylor didn't want to work in the United States. It's to her advantage, where income tax is concerned, not to work in the States. It was done at the De Laurentiis studios, and the outside of the two houses were put up on an estate. Everything in the ride was done in Italy, too. I would have preferred to have done it all on actual locations, even the interiors, but in this instance it was perfectly all right to do the interiors in a studio. It facilitated it, although we built the two houses on this location next to the studio, and we often worked inside the house. Very little of the time were we actually inside the studio.

At first it was difficult to get Brando to appear in the film. Brando came over to see me in Ireland. He had read the book, he had various

REFLECTIONS IN A GOLDEN EYE (1967). Robert Forster (left) and Elizabeth Taylor.

ideas, and he talked for quite a long time about them. While he was talking, why, the script was being typed. When he was all through, I said, "Well, Marlon, in a couple of hours I'll give you the script and this will answer many of your questions." I did, he read it, and took a very long walk in a thunderstorm at night [*laughs*] and came back and said, "I want to do it, yes." He didn't attempt to change anything, and Heavens no, he didn't try to direct. I'm of the opinion that Brando is one of the finest actors alive. He reaches down to some recess, at the end of some cavern in his spirit and comes up with a revelation of something that's new and unexpected and shocking. When somebody asked Cocteau, "When you make a picture, what do you look for? What should a picture do?", he replied, "Astonish." Brando does this. He always for ever astonishes. It's not a *cliché* that he produces, but some oblique observation that is valid. He provides a reality, something that's almost tangible. He is extremely intelligent and perceptive, completely and wonderfully satisfying. I ask something of him, I give him some little idea, and it comes back ten-fold. Then he thanks you profusely for having given it to him, something that was insignificant until he worked on it and transformed it.

This was another film where we experimented in colour. Ossie Morris was really the cameraman. Very rarely has this ever happened to me, but there was a change of cameraman on the picture and Ossie came on. In the meanwhile, we'd been experimenting in the lab to get this colour effect, and weeks and weeks went into this. The Italian lab was very good. They worked on this process and finally came up with it after many, many failures and disappointments, to them and to me. It was just through their own invention and determination we were able to achieve success. I take my hat off to them. We finally got it. Then it was disavowed by a man whose mother must have seen a beer ad when she was pregnant! [*laughs*]. He was the head of the Sales Department of Warner Bros. at that time. I forget his name, but he fought us bitterly. As a result, very few prints were released with our original colour. I think about a third. I had the promise of Elliot Hyman that it would be released in the original version. He kept to the promise but he lost control and this other opinion prevailed.

What we were actually striving for was a golden effect. It was a psychological story and I didn't want to have the distraction of too many colours. I wanted to have a few rather than be multi-coloured. This was achieved in the printing. Ossie Morris shot fairly straight, kept colours down, and then played with this process and each scene was separately developed. In the book and in the film the significance of "reflections in a golden eye" was found in the boy who watches the

REFLECTIONS IN A GOLDEN EYE (1967). Zorro David and Julie Harris
(back to camera).

behaviour of the characters, and it's rather the eye of Pan, the eye
of nature that beholds all this, and he's the boy who is finally murdered.
Then the little Filipino makes a drawing, makes a painting, of an
imaginary bird. The bird has a golden eye, a kind of Phoenix bird.

REFLECTIONS IN A GOLDEN EYE. 1967. *A* Warner Bros.-Seven
Arts *Picture.*
Director: John Huston. *Producer:* Ray Stark. *Associate Producer:*
C. O. Erickson. *Production Managers:* Milton Feldman and Mario
Del Papa. *Assistant Director:* Vana Caruso. *Screenplay:* Chapman
Mortimer and Gladys Hill. *Based on the novel by:* Carson McCullers.
Photography: Aldo Tonti [and Oswald Morris]. Panavision. *Colour:*
Technicolor. *Editor:* Russell Lloyd. *Production Designer:* Stephen
Grimes. *Art Director:* Bruno Avesani. *Set Decoration:* William
Kiernan and Joe Chevalier. *Special Effects:* Augie Lohman. *Music:*
Toshiro Mayuzumi. *Music Director:* Marcus Dods. *Costumes:* Dorothy

Jeakins. *Sound:* Basil Fenton Smith and John Cox. *Horse Master:*
Friedrich von Ledebur.
Running time: 109 minutes.
Players: Marlon Brando (*Major Weldon Penderton*), Elizabeth
Taylor (*Leonora Penderton*), Brian Keith (*Lt. Col. Morris Langdon*),
Julie Harris (*Alison Langdon*), Zorro David (*Anacleto*), Irvin Dugan
(*Captain Weincheck*), Robert Forster (*Private Williams*), Fay Sparks
(*Susie*), Gordon Mitchell (*Stables Sergeant*), Douglas Stark (*Dr.
Burgess*), Al Muloch (*Old Soldier*), Ted Bennides (*Sergeant*),
John Callaghan (*Soldier*).

Story

A peacetime army camp in Georgia. Major Weldon Penderton
and his wife Leonora have a house at the edge of the camp. Leonora
is having an affair with their neighbour, Lt. Col. Morris Langdon,
whose own wife Alison finds consolation for the loss of a baby in the
companionship of her effete Filipino houseboy, Anacleto. As dawn
breaks one morning, Alison, standing at her window after a sleepless
night, notices a soldier leaving the Penderton house. The soldier is
Private Williams, who works in the camp stables, rides naked through
the woods near the camp by day, and at night steals into the Penderton
house to sit at the foot of Leonora's bed as she sleeps. One day
Penderton, who unlike his wife and Langdon is a poor rider, takes
out Leonora's stallion to prove himself. But he rides the horse too
hard, is thrown into a bramble, and in retaliation beats the horse
with his crop. He returns home to join a party which Leonora is
giving; but in the middle of the party Leonora goes out to the stables,
sees her stallion's wounds, and returns to whip her husband across
the face. Believing that the man she has observed entering the Penderton house is her husband, Alison finally confronts Penderton; and
when she sees Williams in Leonora's room, she tells her husband that
his mistress is deceiving him and announces that she is leaving with
Anacleto. On medical advice Langdon takes her to a sanatorium with
Anacleto; but before he gets back to the camp, Alison has died of
a heart attack, and her death casts a shadow over his relationship with
Leonora. Penderton, meanwhile, has become increasingly fascinated
by the elusive Williams. One night he sees him enter Leonora's room,
takes his pistol, and shoots him as he sits by the bed.

Comment

A claustrophobic, peacetime U.S. army camp setting ("a dull
place") accommodates a hot-house of neurotic, erotic characters, most
of whom would be absurd were it not for Huston's great skill and
understanding in making them and their behaviour completely con-

vincing. The director transfers the novel faithfully to the screen, and makes every part of it work by treating the eccentricities with understatement, compassion and sensitivity.

Ireland: Sinful Davey (1968)

Here again was a picture I thought of as just a lark and a romp, a sort of prank, which I could make entirely in Ireland. It was a very good picture until it came under the artistic domination of the producer, Walter Mirisch. Some of these men, you know, long to get their fingers in the pie. They don't realise they are quite inadequate! [*laughter*]. He had promised not to interfere. He had proposed certain things and I had been against them and finally he gave me his word that the film would be as I wanted it. He betrayed his word. It was a very good picture when it was turned over. He had too much time on his hands, he fiddled with it, and he really ruined it. He changed the sequence of events. He put a frame around it. He took a scene out of the middle of the picture and put it at the beginning. It became just a mess, a complete mess. He put a narration over it—dreadful, dreadful! What was a rather blithe, amusing, unserious but sheer rendering became clotted and cluttered and distasteful. The original screenplay was the idea of James Webb, quite a good idea, and he wrote quite a good screenplay. We made some improvements and it was a *good* film, not a great film, but very good with an almost Chaplinesque quality about it at times. It was just cut so badly and changed around after I'd finished, the music and everything else. The whole was a finished picture. The people, the chase, the humour, the late 18th century settings. It was easy and light, quick and refreshing, and delightful. And *this* happens. There were two occasions when pictures I'd made were really ruined. One was the picture with John Wayne [*The Barbarian and the Geisha*] and the other was this one.

I understand that the film was not particularly successful commercially, yet it might well have been if it had been left the way it was finished. Pictures like *The Red Badge of Courage* and *Freud* were cut for different reasons, but it doesn't bring about the results desired by those who do the cutting. Just shortening a picture doesn't serve to make time go by, and if the logic is reduced, why, that's another way of making it slow, too. Even in the theatre and certainly in the concert hall there is not that one point, one area, of concentration. Where attention and concentration is so complete, the time seems to move slower, so the film-maker has to manipulate time on screen. It must necessarily move faster. The factor changes. There

John Hurt in SIN-
FUL DAVEY (1968).

cannot be any surpluses. Everything must be significant and pointed. This just occurs to me that in the old silent films, where fewer frames were shot per second, the action was speeded up on the screen and this was quite acceptable. There was a different time then. It's always struck me, though we are getting into the area of generalities now, that in watching the screen, it's as though one were projecting one's own thoughts; as though the reel were unwinding from behind our eyes, and we are seeing what we wanted to see. A kind of wish-fulfilment in its best sense. That's what occurs with a successful picture. There's a unity on the part of an audience. When its attention is compelled, and held completely, it reacts as one person, united by the film. For the film-maker himself, it is the result of an unreeling of the thought process.

SINFUL DAVEY. 1968. *A* United Artists *Release.*
Director: John Huston. *Production Company:* Mirisch/Webb.
Executive Producer: Walter Mirisch. *Producer:* William N. Graf.
Associate Producer: William Kirby. *Production Manager:* E. J. Holding. *Assistant Directors:* Tom Pevsner and Jim Brennan.
Screenplay: James R. Webb. *Based on the book "The Life of David*

Haggart" by: David Haggart. *Photography:* Ted Scaife and Freddie Young. Panavision. *Colour:* Eastmancolor. *Print by:* Technicolor. *Editor:* Russell Lloyd. *Production Designer:* Stephen Grimes. *Art Director:* Carmen Dillon. *Set Decoration:* Josie MacAvin. *Special Effects:* Richard Parker. *Music/Music Director:* Ken Thorne. *Title Song:* Ken Thorne and Don Black. *Sung by:* Esther Ofarim. *Costumes:* Margaret Furse. *Sound:* Basil Fenton Smith. *Master of Horse:* Frank Hayden.
Running time: 95 minutes.
Players: John Hurt *(David Haggart)*, Pamela Franklin *(Annie)*, Nigel Davenport *(Chief Constable Richardson)*, Ronald Fraser *(MacNab)*, Robert Morley *(Duke of Argyll)*, Maxine Audley *(Duchess of Argyll)*, Fionnuala Flanagan *(Duke of Argyll's Daughter)*, Fidelma Murphy *(Jean Carlisle)*, Noel Purcell *(Jock)*, Francis de Wolff *(Jock's Friend)*, Donal McCann *(Sir James Campbell)*, Leon Collins *(Dr. Gresham)*, Eddie Byrne *(Yorkshire Bill)*, Niall MacGinnis *(Boots Simpson)*, Mickser Reid *(Billy the Goat)*, Derek Young *(Bobby Rae)*, John Franklin *(George Bagrie)*, Eileen Murphy *(Mary Kidd)*, Paul Farrell *(Bailiff of Stirling)*.

SINFUL DAVEY (1968). Fidelma Murphy, John Hurt and Ronald Fraser.

Story

Scotland, 1821. Young Davey Haggart deserts from the army, determined to equal or excel the exploits of his father Willie, who was hanged at the age of twenty-one. He joins forces with MacNab, a small town pickpocket, but their efforts at crime meet with small success and they soon find themselves in Stirling Jail, from which Davey is bailed out by his childhood friend Annie, who has never given up hope of reforming him. Davey next attempts to hold up a coach, but he loses most of the loot and is himself nearly robbed by a villainous innkeeper. Posing as a gentleman, Davey helps another young man beat off some thugs. This new acquaintance, Sir James Campbell, introduces him to the Duke of Argyll, in whose household —under the name of Donald Forsythe—Davey becomes an honoured guest. But Davey's past is catching up with him. Chief Constable Richardson is in pursuit, as are Annie, MacNab and a Stirling trollop called Jean Carlisle. Davey arranges with Jean and MacNab to rob the Duke's guests during a ball, but Annie discovers their plans and foils them. And after a wild chase Richardson captures Davey, laid low by a fiercely driven golf ball. In prison, Davey writes his memoirs, accompanied on the bagpipes by the Duke, who has remained his friend. Tried and condemned to death, Davey admits on the scaffold that he repents his wicked ways. But with MacNab's help, Annie contrives to cheat the hangman, and she and Davey set off together for the distant hills.

Comment

Because it looks like Ireland and we know it was filmed in Ireland, it is hard to believe this story is set in Scotland! Not that it really matters. This is a series of improbable adventures which befall a likeable, amorous rogue, all told tongue-in-cheek, laced with jokes, robust and enthusiastic, tasteful and enjoyable. And this despite what the producer did to it!

Austria: A Walk with Love and Death (1969)

Not consciously, but unconsciously certainly, when I go from one film to the next, I want to have something different from what I did before. Because I have been served by my previous film, the next picture is very rarely like the one that preceded it. I read "A Walk with Love and Death." I liked the story very much. The script was brought to my attention, in fact, by a young man, Carter De Haven, who had come over to Ireland to see me about doing something else. I had been looking for a picture to do with my daughter. I read

Anjelica Huston and Assaf Dayan in A WALK WITH LOVE AND
DEATH (1969).

this script and it seemed to be ideal for her, and that's why I made it.

The theme is that of two young people during the One Hundred
Years War who were trying to find a place for themselves away from
the murder, the anarchy, the unsettling time. I think Koningsberger,
the real author of the book, certainly intended readers to find a
similarity with what is happening today, with young people doing
the same thing. The setting seems to be Europe but actually it's any
place and every place. The time seems to be in the middle of the
fourteenth century but it's just as much now, today, this moment.
Young people of today think that their problems are unique and
extraordinary. I sympathise with them. But the facts are that there
has always been a generation gap. There were student disorders in
the Middle Ages just as violent as those of today. Young people
throughout the centuries have always thought that their parents
made the wars and then sent off their own sons to die in them. Was

war really any less terrible in medieval times than it is today? Despite the bomb, I truly doubt it. In its day the crossbow was a devastating weapon that staggered the imagination. Moreover, young people in the throes of first love have always felt and will always feel that they are sharing an experience that can never be understood by any other than themselves. These are the considerations behind Hans Koningsberger's little book, "A Walk with Love and Death," that have made it a minor classic. Small wonder then that a cult of young people has grown up around this book all over the world. It seems to express a philosophy peculiar to their plight today. But actually the philosophy expressed is timeless and universal. My great wish was to make a film that will be faithful to that idea. I am the parent of two young people of exactly the ages of the leading characters of this story. So you can understand my personal concern in this undertaking.

I had intended to film the story in France, but there was a strike of some kind that made shooting there quite unfeasible, so we did it in the Austrian countryside and used the castles around Vienna. I was rather pleased with the picture. It had no success whatever in the States. It did in Europe, and particularly in France where critically its reception was extraordinary. We were talking about the difference between reactions in different countries and here was an example of it. It was played in three theatres there simultaneously and I think almost recovered its original cost in France. We were able to make it on a fairly modest budget, and I thought my daughter did rather well. I chose young Dayan without knowing about him. I saw his photograph, I didn't know who he was and I said, "I'd like to see this young man," among others, and he came and spoke to me. We talked and I was very interested in him, and said to the casting director, "Yes, this is our man." He said, "Do you know who he is?" and then it came out that he was Moshe Dayan's son. I think that both he and Anjelica portrayed the effort of youth today to find its place in a torn, turbulent world. One almost has a sense of time that it is doomed. Our recent history hasn't been to the great advantage of this new generation, it's almost as though we plotted its downfall. We are now trying to make some recompense, readjustment. I quite agree that the world we've left them isn't a very good one, and this is what the picture's about.

A WALK WITH LOVE AND DEATH. 1969. *A* Twentieth Century-Fox *Release.*
Director: John Huston. *Producer:* Carter De Haven. *Screenplay:* Dale Wasserman. *Adaptation:* Hans Koningsberger. *Based on the novel by:* Hans Koningsberger. *Music composed and conducted by:* Georges

With daughter Anjelica Huston during production of A WALK WITH
LOVE AND DEATH (1969).

Delerue. *Photography:* Ted Scaife. *Colour by:* DeLuxe. *Production
Designer:* Stephen Grimes. *Editor:* Russell Lloyd. *Art Director:*
Wolfgang Witzemann. *Costumes:* Leonard Fini. *Associate Producer:*
Dale Wasserman. *Production Manager:* Laci Von Ronay. *English
Lyrics and Associate to John Huston:* Gladys Hill. *Sound:* Basil Fenton
Smith. *Assistant Directors:* Richard Overstreet and Wolfgang Glattes.
Set Decorator: Josie MacAvin. *Wardrobe Supervisor:* Analisa Rasalli-
Rocca. *Costumes executed by:* Rotislav Doboujinsky.
Running time: 90 minutes.
Players: Anjelica Huston (*Claudia*), Assaf Dayan (*Heron of Foix*),
Anthony Corlan (*Robert*), John Hallam (*Sir Meles*), Robert Lang
(*Pilgrim Leader*), Guy Deghy (*Priest*), Michael Gough (*Mad Monk*),
George Murcell (*Captain*), Eileen Murphy (*Gypsy Girl*), Anthony
Nicholls (*Father Superior*), Joseph O'Connor (*St. Jean*), John Huston
(*Robert the Elder*), Frank Franklyn (*Whoremaster*), Francis Heim
(*Knight Lieutenant*), Melvyn Hayes (*1st. Entertainer*), Barry Keegan
(*Peasant Leader*), Nicholas Smith (*Pilgrim*), Antoinette Reuss

(*Charcoal Woman*), Gilles Segal, Med Hondo and Luis Masson
(*Entertainers*), Eugen Ledebur (*Goldsmith*), Otto Dworak (*Innkeeper*), Max Sulz (*Peasant*), John Veenenbos (*Monk*), Paul Hoer
(*Peasant Boy*), Myra Malik (*Peasant Girl*), Michael Baronne
(*Soldier*), Yvan Strogoff (*Soldier*).

Story

The Northern European countryside of 1358 is ravaged by a war
that has been going on for decades. Heron of Foix, a nineteen-year-old
student who has been expelled from college, is heading for another
university in another country. Seeking food and shelter, he is directed
to the Chateau Dammartin, owned by the Count of Vallois, who
represents the King of France and is apparently safe from disturbance.
Heron meets the Count's sixteen-year-old daughter, Claudia, and falls
in love with her on sight, asking her to be his lady. As a token she
gives him a blue scarf which he wears as he continues his journey,
joining a band of pilgrims on a river journey. Later he learns that the
peasants have risen and sacked Dammartin. He rushes back to find
it burned to the ground and Claudia taking refuge in a nearby church.
Possessing only the clothes on their backs, Heron and Claudia set off
for her father's cousin's place in Ermenonville where Robert the Elder
reveals that he has deserted his rank in the nobility to lead one of
the peasant armies. Claudia is angered that Heron does not kill the
traitorous Robert. She and Heron are captured by peasants but freed
by a band of knights led by Sir Meles. Heron reluctantly fights alongside Sir Meles in attacking a castle taken over by peasants. Escaping a
later peasant ambush, Heron and Claudia return to Ermenonville
which is attacked by knights. They become refugees in an abbey
where, left alone but deliriously happy in each other's company, they
hear death approaching and sing their last love ode.

Comment

Another totally unexpected Huston film. Its style is that of a saga,
set in the time of the One Hundred Years War. Many directors of the
older generation have been pandering to the "youth audience" by
making superficial films which are supposed to appeal to them in
troubled times and assure a box-office return. Huston has made a film
of warmth, modesty and existential appeal, sustained by a compassion
for innocence and optimism attempting to endure amid chaos.

Finland (Helsinki) : **The Kremlin Letter** (1969)

I thought almost certainly *The Kremlin Letter* would be a box-office
success. Not only was it diverting and sensational but it seemed to

me to have all the ingredients that would go to make a successful picture. It struck me it was about time to do that. A film-maker can't be entirely free from the thought that, well, perhaps I ought to look for a subject or make a film that seems to have an appeal which is popular at the moment, even though by the time the film is finished it may no longer be popular. This is a pressure that is there. A director can't resist it.

In this instance, it was a mistaken idea. The picture seemed to me to have the ingredients of popularity, and the mystery-spy drama has now become almost as much a classical form as the western. It had its little portion of violence, and sexuality, and an inventiveness in the story, in the plot, that I thought would be very attractive to audiences. I was quite mistaken! [*laughs*]. I read the novel and I thought it very entertaining, an amusing idea, you know, of the old-fashioned spy brought back into service, who didn't hold with the computer approach to international intelligence, and whose motives were purely revenge. I worked on the screenplay. I think Gladys Hill and I did the whole screenplay as I recall.

What everybody is looking for with a film partly set in Russia is, of course, how we are going to fake the background, because

Bibi Andersson and Patrick O'Neal in THE KREMLIN LETTER (1969).

Russia is a difficult place to duplicate. We couldn't go to Russia to film it, so we went to Finland, Helsinki, where their architectural features are similar to Russia. The same French architect who designed many of the buildings in Finland also designed buildings for Petrograd. I enjoyed making the film, and I thought it was a good picture. Maybe it was too complicated, maybe that was the answer—it's the best one I can come up with anyway! The performances were good, it was a well-designed picture, well-mounted, and the camerawork was interesting and on occasions rather dazzling, I thought.

THE KREMLIN LETTER. 1969. *A* Twentieth Century-Fox *Picture.*
Director: John Huston. *Producers:* Carter De Haven and Sam
Wiesenthal. *Production Manager:* David Anderson. *Assistant Directors:*
Gus Agosti and Carlo Cotti. *Screenplay:* John Huston and Gladys Hill.
Based on the novel by: Noel Behn. *Photography:* Ted Scaife.
Panavision. *Colour:* DeLuxe. *Editor:* Russell Lloyd. *Production
Designer:* Ted Haworth. *Art Director:* Elven Webb. *Set Decoration:*
Dario Simone. *Music/Music Director:* Robert Drasnin. *Costumes:*
John Furniss. *Sound Editor:* Les Hodgson. *Sound Recording:* Basil
Fenton Smith and Renato Cadueri.
Running time: 121 minutes.
Players: Richard Boone *(Ward)*, Bibi Andersson *(Erika Boeck)*,
Max von Sydow *(Colonel Vladimir Kosnov)*, Patrick O'Neal
(Lt. Commander Charles Rone), Orson Welles *(Aleksei Bresnavitch)*,
Ronald Radd *(Potkin)*, Nigel Green *(Janis, alias "The Whore")*,
Dean Jagger *("The Highwayman")*, Lila Kedrova *(Madame Sophie)*,
Barbara Parkins *(B.A.)*, George Sanders *("The Warlock")*, Raf
Vallone *("The Puppet Maker")*, Michael MacLiammoir *("Sweet
Alice")*, Sandor Eles *(Grodin)*, Niall MacGinnis *(Erector Set)*,
Anthony Chinn *(Kitai)*, Guy Deghy *(Professor)*, John Huston
(Admiral), Fulvia Ketoff *(Sonia)*, Vonetta McGee *(Negress)*, Marc
Lawrence *(Priest)*, Cyril Shaps *(Police Doctor)*, Christopher Sanford
(Rudolph), Hana-Maria Pravda *(Mrs. Kazar)*, George Pravda *(Kazar)*,
Ludmilla Dudarova *(Mrs. Potkin)*, Dimitri Tamarov *(Ilya)*, Pehr-
Olof Siren *(Receptionist)*, Daniel Smid *(Waiter)*, Victor Beaumont
(Dentist), Steve Zacharias *(Dittomachine)*, Laura Forin *(Elena)*,
Saara Rannin *(Mikhail's Mother)*, Rune Sandlunds *(Mikhail)*,
Sacha Carafa *(Mrs. Grodin)*.

Story
    An official in American Intelligence mistakenly signs an agreement enjoining his country to help Russia destroy China's nuclear weapons. Polakov, a Russian counter-intelligence agent sent to buy back the document from the Kremlin, is captured and kills himself under torture; his interrogator is Colonel Kosnov. In the United States,

Lt. Commander Charles Rone is suddenly discharged from the navy and drafted into the intelligence team assembled to retrieve the treaty; trained by the celebrated agent Sturdevant, missing since 1954, the team is now led by "The Highwayman." Ward, Rone's immediate superior, sends him to enlist other agents, including Janis, "The Warlock," and B.A., the daughter of an expert safecracker. She and Rone soon become lovers. Meanwhile, the Russians are equally baffled by the letter's disappearance; Bresnavitch, a high-ranking Soviet official, tells their American-based agent, Potkin, to give him priority over Kosnov when making reports. The American espionage team kidnap Potkin and persuade him to lend them his Moscow apartment as an operational base. In Moscow they trace Erika Boeck, once Polakov's wife and now married to Kosnov. Masquerading as a male prostitute to ensnare her, Rone gains access to the Kosnov secrets, which invariably lead to Bresnavitch whose inveterate smuggling record now comes to light. When Bresnavitch discovers the team's Moscow base and seizes Janis and B.A., Rone blackmails him into giving himself and Ward safe conduct out of Russia, telling him also that the "Kremlin Letter" is now in Peking. Settling last debts, Ward murders Erika and Kosnov, and then reveals himself as the long-lost Sturdevant, now Bresnavitch's agent. He will hold B.A. hostage until Rone has completed his last mission—to fly to New York and murder Potkin's wife and daughter.

Comment

Star turns here are no substitute for dramatic coherence. A well-shot, well-acted and cynical spy story is somewhat lessened in effect by a complicated narrative in which a band of professionals are seen following their orders to help Russia destroy China's nuclear weapons. It becomes too involved, but Huston's familiar theme of the society misfit, here a spy, being sold out by forces outside his control, is expressed with a new violence, fast-paced editing, lively camerawork—a film quite unlike the many other spy pictures of the time.

A Run That Never Started: The Last Run

The Last Run was an unfortunate experience. I didn't like the script that was given to me. I agreed to make it—that was a mistake to begin with. I should never have got into it. The actor, George C. Scott, liked the script but I found it wanting and what I was doing was having to rewrite the script as we went along, so I suppose they were exchanging something for what they knew not of! "They" were M-G-M, sitting several thousands of miles away in Hollywood. I was working with a producer of sorts! It was really a collision between Scott and me. I thought I could change it and make it something acceptable. The possibilities of the story appealed to me. What was done in black-and-white didn't appeal to me very much, but I saw an opportunity to do something with it, changes which would have made it acceptable and interesting. Scott wanted to do something rather nostalgic which would bring to mind the old Bogart films, I think. This is exactly what he said. I didn't agree with this. It just proved that I should never have got into it in the first place! The picture, by the way, when it came out had nothing to recommend it and I don't remember who took over [Richard Fleischer]. I had shot a few exterior scenes of automobiles, and scenes like that, in and around Malaga, Spain, down the coast. Then I went very gratefully to the U.S.A. and *Fat City*, which was an atmosphere that was quite different.

U.S.A. (Stockton, California) : Fat City (1972)

Ray Stark sent me the novel to read. A very good book by Leonard Gardner, who had also written the script. He didn't know all that much about screenplay writing, but his impulses were all good and right, and again I worked on the script. I liked the performances

Stacy Keach and Jeff Bridges in FAT CITY (1972).

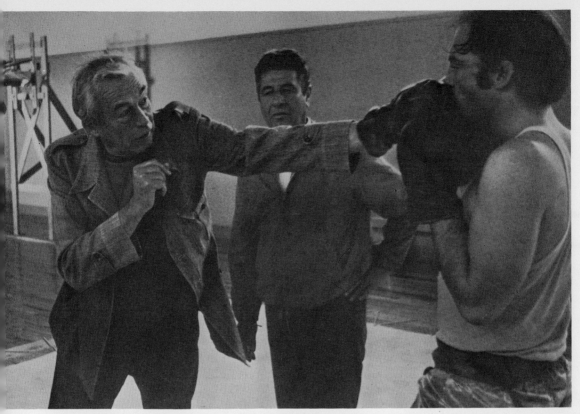

Directing Stacy Keach in FAT CITY (1972).

enormously. I liked the subject. It harkened back to the days of my youth when I was boxing in California, and so it was a scene with which I was quite familiar, and it hadn't changed very much. In fact, there were old friends of mine I'd known when I was boxing, old boxers, long, long retired. I liked Stacy Keach, a man of splendid talents, again that mysterious quality that very few of them have, who can come up with a revelation, as I've said before, reach down somewhere and produce a miracle. I like the girls. I liked everything in it. It is a picture about hope and failure, great misery alongside great wealth. Like *The Misfits,* it is one of those allegorical stories concerning the condition of man which I like so much. I went to Stockton, California, and used all actual locations and interiors, the interiors of the bars, the hotel rooms. There is nothing simulated.

This is what the critics called "A return to form for John Huston." Whatever that means! I don't examine too deeply those things. I proceed blithely ahead! Onwards and perhaps downwards . . . ! [*laughs*]. I suppose they were talking about the American look of it, with which I was identified many years ago. It was in the American grain surely, an aspect of life that hasn't been explored all that deeply.

Then, of course, if I'd been doing that all along, all my films would be alike and the critics would then say there was no progressing, or advancing, or whatever it is!

Basically, my approach to all my films is the same, from the point of view of doing them as well as I am able. With many of them, everybody finds them satisfying. Yet another one isn't. Is it due to story, treatment, actors, the fact that some chemistry doesn't work, some magic doesn't come off? I think that very often, particularly in my instance, it's due to the times. One is just as mistaken in being before the times as being old-fashioned or after the times. It's when one is right at the right moment that a great positive response comes from the public. It's happened to me so often that pictures that were not well-received have later become classics, as it were.

FAT CITY. 1972. *A* Columbia *Release.*
Director: John Huston. *Production Company:* Rastar. *Producer:* Ray Stark. *Associate Producer:* David Dworski. *Production Manager/ Assistant Director:* Russ Saunders. *Screenplay:* Leonard Gardner. *Based on the novel by:* Leonard Gardner. *Photography:* Conrad Hall. *Colour:* Eastmancolor. *Editor:* Margaret Booth. *Production Designer:* Richard Sylbert. *Set Decoration:* Morris Hoffman. *Special Effects:* Paul Stewart. *Music Supervisor:* Marvin Hamlisch. *Song:* "Help Me Make it Through the Night" by Kris Kristofferson. *Sung by:* Kris Kristofferson. *Titles:* Wayne Fitzgerald. *Sound:* Tom Overton and Arthur Piantadosi.
Running time: 96 minutes.
Players: Stacy Keach (*Billy Tully*), Jeff Bridges (*Ernie Munger*), Susan Tyrrel (*Oma*), Candy Clark (*Faye*), Nicholas Colasanto (*Ruben*), Art Aragon (*Babe*), Curtis Cokes (*Earl*), Sixto Rodriguez (*Lucero*), Billy Walker (*Wes*), Wayne Mahan (*Bufford*), Ruben Navarro (*Fuentes*).

Story
Stockton, California. Billy Tully, a former boxer now out of training and recovering from a drinking bout induced by his wife's desertion, visits the local gym in a half-hearted bid to return to competitive fitness. Here he meets young Ernie Munger and, impressed by his boxing potential, sends him along to his former manager Ruben, who signs him on. Ernie loses his first small-time professional fight, and Tully, who has temporarily abandoned his hopes of a return to the ring, finds consolation in an affair with Oma, a scatty, heavy-drinking girl also suffering bereavement pangs through the imprisonment of her negro lover Earl. The two set up together in an apartment, but a series of semi-drunk quarrels soon persuades Tully that

he is better off on his own. Ernie meanwhile, after losing his second fight, further dismays Ruben by running off to get married. The bride is Faye, a schoolgirl whom Ernie has dated several times in his car and who has now declared herself pregnant. Ernie and Tully meet up again and take a brief job together on a fruit farm but, with Ernie's encouragement, Tully soon decides to return to training. His first big fight, against an ageing and patently unfit Mexican opponent, ends in victory. But the result does nothing to restore Tully's self-respect and he abandons boxing entirely. Some time later, Tully—now virtually a hobo—waylays Ernie, who has recently returned to training, and persuades him to have a drink. The two sit together in the local diner, talking uncomfortably into the night.

Comment

Characters searching for a way of life in which they cannot be used or exploited is the main concern of Huston in this thoughtful, deceptively casual, deliberately slow chronicle of hope and failure among the boxing fraternity. Yet it is not a film about boxing; rather, life's futile cycle of work, drink, makeshift relations, and continual defeat form the substance of this deeply observed and sympathetically knowing film. It brought Huston great praise from all the critics, but the public found it too sad for its liking.

U.S.A. (Tucson, Arizona) : **The Life and Times of Judge Roy Bean** (1972)

This might have something to do with the success of *The Life and Times of Judge Roy Bean*: here I very consciously made a concession to a technique which has become popular today, and which I had never used before, which I call a "fragmented" technique, in which all sorts of things can be happening without necessarily justifying them logically; things appear, things happen, from being funny to being sad, from going to drama to comedy, being outrageous one minute, and perhaps being sober the next. This is the chief characteristic of this film, and I saw this "technique" or quality applied more to *The Judge* than perhaps others did. It seemed to reflect the old American spirit, the outrageous character, that was capable of doing so many unlikely things, in a way that, say, Twain was. There was a breadth and a generosity, and a carelessness about it that I fostered in the picture. It seemed to me it was an allegory, and the vengeance of the past was interesting to me. My God, I'd love to see Wyatt Earp and Doc Holliday, in their long black coats, walk down one of our streets today! [*laughs*]. This was something, from hearing my grandmother's stories, I was familiar with, this world, this atmosphere. My grandfather was part of that world, John Gore, the gambler who won the Water and Power of Nevada, Missouri. Grandfather would have been quite capable of coming back and destroying a place the way the Judge did. I loved the audacity of the film. I liked it better than most, it's been very successful, and it's been very well reviewed by the reviewers I like most, and by others who sometimes don't like what I do at all. But there are those I take seriously, and they chose to like *The Judge* which delighted me.

I enjoyed bringing Ava Gardner in as Lily Langtry. She looked marvellously beautiful. Langtry would have looked a lot older, but that was all part of the fantasy. There were ideas that took form as we made the picture. The writer of the original script, John Milius, was there all the time, we'd work at night. He was a joy to work with, and entered into new ideas with great enthusiasm. It turned out to be one of those pictures that we wrote as we went along. We were not all that well prepared. The general shape of it was there, but the entire finish is completely different from the one that he wrote originally, and it was a matter of a couple of weeks before the finish of the picture that we wrote that section. The whole episode was a joyous occasion, and I loved the people, and I loved what they were doing, and I loved the parts they were playing. I loved Bad Bob [*laughs*], and the little horse thief who was hanged without ceremony, and stammered, and had a kick. The whole, I thought, was good and amusing, and with a certain old-time sweep to it, with everything filmed about an hour-and-a-half out of Tucson, Arizona. I lived on the location, quite alone, by the way. I was the only one who did, except a watchman. The others went back to the town, but I stayed there all the time in a trailer. I've been on so many locations, and I've often wondered why everyone takes fatiguing, back-breaking journeys backwards and forwards, day after day, sometimes an hour's journey over rough roads, and I've often thought why not stay there, with the comfortable trailers you can live in today? Isn't it true today, not only of motion pictures, but of life itself? When I see the traffic on the roads, when I think all we've got is time and men are spending an hour driving alone in a great car, wasting the earth's treasures and their own limited time to get to their jobs, and then an hour, hour-and-a-half, coming home—there's something wrong with a civilisation that puts up with this.

Judge Roy Bean is not fantasy, no. While there's a large element of truth, there is no element of fact in the story. There was a judge, of course. but the judge was just a small-time con man who made a living out of short-changing customers who got off the train to slake

Paul Newman in THE LIFE AND TIMES OF JUDGE ROY BEAN (1972).

their thirsts at his bar. We chose to make him the figure that he is in the film. This was purely creative, we had little or no material to go on in this way. No, I think we put the judge into the legendary class. When I talk about the distinction between fact and truth, there is no fact but I think quite a great truth about our feeling for that past, reflecting our feeling for that past. In fact, the truth of that past is that the gestures were large and the spirit was big and people were good and bad, and we didn't indulge them with the understanding that we do today. It was before we knew about neurotics and the effect of environment. If a man was bad, why, he got shot down in the barroom, and that proved he was bad if he was the one who got shot! [laughs] Very rarely was a decent man killed! It was always the bad man who was killed [laughs]. It is from this that has really sprung what is now referred to as "conventional morality," especially in films and literature where the bad man dies and the good man wins. I've come a long way from my first film, all through these years, and among my responses to Fat City was the fact that it made me think of when I was young. Now also, Judge Roy Bean was part of my father's world and my grandfather's world.

THE LIFE AND TIMES OF JUDGE ROY BEAN. 1972. A National General Release.

Director: John Huston. Production Company: First Artists Productions. Producer: John Foreman. Associate Producer: Frank Caffey. Assistant Director: Mickey McCardle. Screenplay: John Milius. Photography: Richard Moore. Panavision. Colour: Technicolor. Special Photographic Effects: Butler-Glouner. Editor: Hugh S. Fowler. Art Director: Tambi Larsen. Set Decoration: Robert Benton. Music: Maurice Jarre. Song: "Marmalade, Molasses and Honey" by: Maurice Jarre, Marilyn and Alan Bergman. Sung by: Andy Williams. Sound Editor: Keith Stafford. Sound Recording: Larry Jost. Sound Re-recording: Richard Portman.
Running time: 124 minutes.
Players: Paul Newman (Judge Roy Bean), Jacqueline Bisset (Rose Bean), Ava Gardner (Lily Langtry), Tab Hunter (Sam Dodd), John Huston (Grizzly Adams), Stacy Keach (Bad Bob), Roddy McDowall (Frank Gass), Anthony Perkins (Reverend LaSalle), Victoria Principal (Marie Elena), Anthony Zerbe (Hustler), Ned Beatty (Tector Crites), Jim Burk (Bart Jackson), Matt Clark (Nick the Grub), Steve Kanaly (Whorehouse Luck Jim), Bill McKinney (Fermel Parlee), Francesca Jarvis (Mrs. Jackson), Karen Carr (Mrs. Grubb), Dolores Clark (Mrs. Whorehouse Jim), Lee Meza (Mrs. Parlee), Neil Summers (Snake River Rufus Krile), Jack Colvin (Pimp), Howard Morton (Photographer), Billy Pearson (Miner/Station Master), Stan Barrett (Killer,), Don Starr (Opera House

Manager), Alfred G. Bosnos (*Opera House Clerk*), John Hudkins (*Man at Stage Door*), David Sharpe (*Doctor*), Barbara J. Longo (*Fat Lady*), Frank Soto (*Mexican Leader*), Roy Jenson, Gary Combs, Fred Brookfield, Ben Dobbins, Dick Farnsworth, LeRoy Johnson, Fred Krone, Terry Leonard and Dean Smith (*Outlaws*), Margo Epper, Jeanne Epper and Stephanie Epper (*Whores*), Bruno (*Watch Bear*).

Story

Texas, 1890. Roy Bean, wanted for rape and robbery, seeks refuge in the outlaw town of Vinegaroon where instead of being welcomed he is beaten up and left to die. Aided and supplied with a revolver by a sympathetic Mexican girl, Marie Elena, Bean returns to Vinegaroon and takes his revenge. Having buried his victim with the help of LaSalle, a travelling clergyman, he proclaims himself "Judge" Roy Bean and vows to bring law and order to the town. Marie Elena moves into a shack next door to the judge's saloon-cum-courthouse, which Bean dedicates to Lily Langtry, his feminine ideal. Bean also swears in five itinerant outlaws as his marshals, and before long they have tried and hanged their first wrongdoer, Sam Dodd. Vinegaroon prospers under Bean's rough justice and is renamed Langtry, but as the town acquires respectability, so the Judge begins to feel out of place. His pet bear is killed saving him from an assassin hired by Frank Gass, a prissy lawyer with a grudge against him. He makes an ill-fated trip to San Antonio to see Lily Langtry in person. And Marie Elena dies giving birth to his daughter. Disillusioned, he rides out of town. Twenty years pass. Oil has been discovered and Langtry has become a boom town, tyrannised by Gass and his hoodlums. Rose Bean, the Judge's daughter, faces eviction, but decides to defend her father's property. Shortly before the showdown, a grizzled Roy Bean returns on horseback and rounds up his ex-marshals. A fierce gun battle ensues in which Gass's men are routed, although Bean himself perishes under a blazing oil derrick. Years later, when the oil has dried up and Langtry has reverted to a desolate backwater, a train stops here. Lily Langtry descends and is shown round the Judge Roy Bean Museum, where she pays homage to her late admirer.

Comment

Back to the 1800's again, this time in Texas, and—as usual with Huston—from a sombre story to an amusing tale: in this instance, a celebration of the indomitable and undiluted spirit of the pioneers of the West, and, at the same time, a burlesque of the cinema's greatest myth, the western. Here, the characters who are considered heroes become the victims of the society they created out of the wilderness.

Ireland, London, Malta: The Mackintosh Man (1973)

I'm always working, or occupied. In fact, I don't think making pictures is work, any more than a painter thinks he's at work. It's what I *do*. Someone made the observation: "Blessed is the man who finds his work"—because it stops being work then, it's what we do. Having finished *The Judge,* I had nothing to go into immediately, nor did Paul Newman or John Foreman, the producer, or the whole group who had worked on *The Judge,* and I think it was a reluctance to separate. Here was the opportunity to go on and do another film and have a good time! [*laughs*]. We certainly won't be guilty of the same mistake we made in *The Kremlin Letter* of being overcomplicated. This is very simple and easy to follow indeed.

The screenplay was proposed to Newman, they brought it to Paul, and then he turned to me with it and to John Foreman. It comes from a novel, and I did quite a bit of work on the script myself. I haven't the faintest idea if there is any relationship to what's happening in the film to what really happens to spies and counter-spies and people who chase them. In fact, it's a glorious fantasy from the mind, almost entirely that! The few occasions on which I have had any connection with spies have been pretty sordid ones and quite unpleasant. People I've known have nothing to do with these films. They were people who were planted to preach Hitler's philosophy, and that sort of thing. No, this film is a slender object indeed. We've hung some invention on it, and I hope it's stimulating to the eye and the ear. It plumbs no new depths, but I think it's probably going to be quite entertaining, and the cast is delightful. I get a good deal of pleasure and satisfaction from actors, especially those actors I know already and who are going to respond in certain ways and give me the performances I want. That's the way I cast, according to personality so that when it comes to actually directing them, why, there's very little involved. They do pretty well what I know they will do. When I undertake a script originally, why, I know, I'm thinking only of the script, and then the casting comes after; but in an instance like this, of course, I don't write *for* the actor. I do the writing and then the actor, the artist, adapts himself to it. It would be very hard for me to write "a vehicle" for someone. I think of the storyline rather than the actor. Then if someone brings me a more-or-less finished screenplay, and the producer says, "I think so-and-so would be great for this," it's a case of reading it and visualising the actors projected in these parts. If the producer suggests somebody that I like too, then it's a matter of accord, or I might insist on actors

Paul Newman and Dominique Sanda in THE MACKINTOSH MAN (1973).

for the parts because I visualise them. Different films call for variations of this.

The Mackintosh Man is a world that we imagine, rather than a
world that is. Now that doesn't make it any the less real. If it subscribes
to the requirements of our imagination, fulfils that, why, it's as real
as if we were just reporting events. I don't think that fact makes for
reality, any more than *vice versa*. It's what we think. I think, therefore
I am, is the bottom of it, isn't it? What we believe is so, no matter
how mistaken our belief may be; if we believe it, so far as we are
concerned, it's the truth. I enjoy challenges, and it was a joy making
it with the people involved. In a film like this there are so many
things to make authentic or make probable. Whatever may be happening may be completely unlikely in real life, but it's got to look likely
on the screen. In this case we are constantly moving, playing with
boats, cars, aeroplanes, all of these things. For this kind of picture

I enjoy manipulating them, and juggling them around, and fitting them in. This approach would be unacceptable in another kind of picture, in a *Fat City*, say.

THE MACKINTOSH MAN. 1973. *A* Warner Bros. *Release.*
Director: John Huston. *Production Company:* Newman-Foreman/ John Huston Productions. *Producer:* John Foreman. *Associate Producer:* William Hill. *Second Unit Director:* James Arnett. *Assistant Director:* Colin Brewer. *Screenplay:* Walter Hill. *Based on the novel "The Freedom Trap" by:* Desmond Bagley. *Photography:* Oswald Morris. *Colour:* Technicolor. *Editor:* Russell Lloyd. *Production Designer:* Terry Marsh. *Art Director:* Alan Tomkins. *Set Decoration:* Peter James. *Special Effects:* Cliff Richardson and Ron Ballinger. *Music/Music Director:* Maurice Jarre. *Sound Editors:* Les Hodgson and Don Sharp. *Sound Recording:* Basil Fenton Smith. *Sound Re-recording:* Gerry Humphreys.
Running time: 99 minutes.
Players: Paul Newman (*Joseph Rearden*), Dominique Sanda (*Mrs. Smith*), James Mason (*Sir George Wheeler*), Harry Andrews (*Angus Mackintosh*), Ian Bannen (*Slade*), Michael Hordern (*Brown*), Nigel Patrick (*Soames-Trevelyan*), Peter Vaughan (*Brunskill*), Roland Culver (*Judge*), Percy Herbert (*Taafe*), Robert Lang (*Jack Summers*), Jenny Runacre (*Gerda*), John Bindon (*Buster*), Hugh Manning (*Prosecutor*), Leo Genn (*Rollins*), Wolfe Morris (*Malta Police Commissioner*), Noel Purcell (*O'Donovan*), Donald Webster (*Jervis*), Keith Bell (*Palmer*), Niall MacGinnis (*Warder*), Eddie Byrne (*Fisherman*), Shane Briant (*Cox*), Michael Poole (*Mr. Boyd*), Eric Mason (*Postman*), Ronald Clarke (*Attendant*), Anthony Viccars (*Salesman*), Dinny Powell (*Young*), Douglas Robinson (*Danahoe*), Jack Cooper and Marc Boyle (*Motorcyclists*), Marcelle Castillo (*Madeleine*), Nosher Powell (*Armed Guard*), Terry Plummer (*Dark Man*), Joe Cahill (*1st Guard*), Gerry Alexander (*2nd Guard*), John McDarby (*Old Man at Bus Stop*), Donal McCann (*1st Fireman*), Joe Lynch (*1st Garda*), Seamus Healy (*Countryman in Pub*), Tom Irwin (*2nd Fireman*), Pascal Perry (*2nd Garda*), Steve Brennan, Vernon Hayden and Brendon O'Duill (*Pub Customers*).

Story
Provided with a false identity as a thief by the mysterious Angus Mackintosh and his "secretary" Mrs. Smith, Joseph Rearden carries out a daring diamond robbery. Picked up by the police after an anonymous tip-off and sentenced to twenty years imprisonment, Rearden is eventually contacted in gaol by a fellow convict, Soames-Trevelyan, who offers to include him—at a price—in a break organised

by a gang called Scarperers. During a pre-arranged riot, Rearden and another prisoner, the Communist spy Slade, are lifted over the wall, transported to a house in Ireland, and sedated for several days. Rearden's imprisonment had in fact been organised by Mackintosh— a government security man—and his daughter Mrs. Smith in the hope that Rearden would be able to break the Scarperers organisation and expose its leader, the eminent M.P., Sir George Wheeler. In an effort to force Wheeler to reveal himslf, Mackintosh hints that a government agent was involved in the escape. Rearden's rescuers turn sour on receiving the information, but he fights his way clear after firing the house and contacts Mrs. Smith, who flies to join him in Ireland, bringing the news that her father is dying after a deliberate hit-and-run incident. Deducing that Slade must now be on board Wheeler's yacht, Rearden and Mrs. Smith pursue the craft to Malta. Joining a reception party given by Wheeler, Mrs. Smith sees Slade in a cabin and manages to warn Rearden, but is then drugged and captured by Wheeler. Rearden persuades the local police to search the yacht, but is forced to escape when Wheeler manages to bluff his way free of suspicion. Returning to the ship, Rearden forces one of the crew to take him to Slade and Mrs. Smith, and in a nearby church he is confronted by Wheeler holding Mrs. Smith at gunpoint. Wheeler suggests that they all simply go their own ways, to which Rearden agrees. But as Slade and Wheeler prepare to leave, Mrs. Smith guns them down, then walks away from the shocked and bewildered Rearden.

Comment

Returning to the ethics of international espionage, and to European locations after two films in the U.S.A., Huston examines the ambiguous actions and motives of political villains and shady spies. Brilliantly played out and shot, exciting and always intriguing, it is a divertissement proving that truth in human behaviour makes all fantasies seem believable.

Morocco: **The Man Who Would Be King** (1975)

I've wanted to bring Kipling's story to the screen for more than twenty years. I think it's one of the greatest adventure stories ever written. James Barrie once called it "the most audacious thing in fiction" and Somerset Maugham considered it one of Kipling's out-standing stories.

When we were in Ireland filming *The Mackintosh Man,* John Foreman was browsing in my library when he came across this big

portfolio of drawings by Stephen Grimes for *The Man Who Would
Be King*. Years ago I had been to India and Afghanistan, and Stephen
went to the Atlas Mountains, but it was impractical to make the film
there. So he went to Morocco and made drawings. He's a fine painter,
and they were beautiful, very impressive, undoubtedly the best I've
ever seen. John saw these and said, "What's all this about?" and then
read the Kipling story. I had several scripts already written but none
of them really came off. He read them and we talked about the film
and I said, "It should be done." When *The Mackintosh Man* was
finished, he went to work on it, and he was almost entirely responsible
for bringing it off.

It is set in India, Afghanistan and Kafiristan during the 1880's,
yet it has something to say about the corruption of man. This is
nothing new, of course, but look what's happening in political and
business circles today. It also has some spiritual meaning which
becomes clear towards the end of the story. The original tale by
Kipling runs to about 12,000 words and forty pages. From its first
frequently-quoted line, "Brother to a Prince and fellow to a beggar if
he be found worthy" to its last line "And there the matter rests" it
contains everything a good story should have: excitement, colour,
spectacle and humour, adventure, high drama, tragedy, good conversation. There is truth, honesty and irony. Gladys Hill and I have
expanded Kipling's original for our film adaptation, but we have
kept close to the story and remained faithful to his speech, characters
and imagery. I was attracted too, to the friendship and relationship
between the two men, likeable rogues who are loyal to each other
and to their ideals and beliefs. Although Kipling has been out of
favour in the so-called literary circles, he still has a very large reading
public. I came to love his stories and verse, his humour and spirit of
adventure, and, above all perhaps, his love of humanity and his
fellow man. I think he ranks as one of the major writers and influences
of the century. So, too, did T. S. Eliot. Most people associate Kipling
with two things: the British Empire in general and India in particular.
He was born in India and it was this country which fed his imagination. He was forever intrigued and deeply fascinated by her enormity
and variety, her mystery and loveliness as well as by her poverty and
superstition. Christopher Plummer, who plays Kipling, has also been
a life-long admirer of the author and went to enormous time and
trouble to look, sound and behave like him. We borrowed a BBC
recording of Kipling making a speech in the early Thirties. Kipling
wrote "The Man Who Would Be King" when he was working as a
young journalist in India. Many of his earliest short stories appeared
originally in "Allahabad Pioneer," which he edited between 1887

Christopher Plummer as Rudyard Kipling in THE MAN WHO WOULD BE KING (1975).

and 1889, when he was about twenty-two and twenty-four years of age. This was one of them. Soon after their appearance in "The Pioneer," these early stories were published in small collections in what must have been some of the first paperback books. The firm of A. H. Wheeler & Co. held the contract for Indian railway bookstalls, and in 1887 they had the idea of issuing cheap reprints, selling at one rupee each, for reading on the train. Six volumes of Kipling's short stories were issued as the first six numbers of Wheeler's Indian Railway Library. "The Man Who Would Be King" was included in "The Phantom Rickshaw and Other Tales." Fittingly, we have Kipling, as the first-person story-teller, meet Carnehan in an Indian train compartment. This was an actual experience in Kipling's life. Again, the scenes where Kipling meets Dravot and Carnehan in his newspaper office have the smell of printing ink about them, since Kipling was a journalist and editor himself.

We found our locations in Morocco and I think they have the feel and smell of India as it was then. Bringing Kipling's story to life has been a challenge naturally, but no matter how authentic we are, why, it all rests on the characters. If the audience isn't going to be attracted to and involved with the characters, then we have failed Kipling. These two men, close friends and fellow-soldiers in

John Huston directs Sean Connery and Michael Caine in THE MAN WHO
WOULD BE KING (1975).

Victoria's army in India for many years, are practically brothers, having long and generously shared their money, their drinks, and no doubt their women. One's success has been the other's and one's failure similarly the other's, too. They have a deep affection for each other, and a lusty sense of humour. They tell Kipling: "The less said about our professions, the better, for we have been most things in our time. We have been all over India. We know her cities and her jungles, her palaces and her jails. Therefore we are going away to another place where a man isn't crowded and can come into his own. We're not little men and there's nothing we're afraid of." This refers not only to their physical appearance and bearing, which is imposing and fiercesome enough, in all conscience, but to their mental make-up and attitude. They think and act large. Not many leaders are this way today. Now that it's become a motion picture, one of my cinematic ambitions has come to fruition and I'm very happy indeed.

I used Kipling as a character in the book because he wrote in the first person. He became the "I" in the film. I know that Kipling's stories and his way of writing are far removed in time, fashion and style from Williams, Hemingway, Hammett, Burnett, but I've loved his tales since I was fifteen years old, and to this day I can recite reams of Kipling doggerel and verse [laughs]. I remember one time I was on Hemingway's boat with him, and he said there were just two authors who wrote as well, if not better, about combat than himself. One was Tolstoy, the other Rudyard Kipling. Kipling did go out of fashion, but he was sent into that exile by the intelligentsia at the time of the Boer War when they thought he was mistakenly colonial. The way events have turned out, I'm not sure they were right with their opinion. But every now and then there is a new appreciation of his work that puts him where he belongs—in the front rank of writers in English. Mark Twain and Kipling met, you know, and afterwards Twain said that he, Twain, had explored all the realms of human knowledge, but his stories left off where Kipling's began [laughs].

. The casting of Connery and Caine is indicative of the great changes, thank heavens, which have taken place in the star system and movie-making in general. They bring a reality to it that the old stars, much as I loved Gable and Bogart, could not do. But in their time, they would have been acceptable—even I think to British audiences. Today they would seem synthetic, so in a way I'm glad I didn't make the picture with them. Caine and Connery ring true, and I think they are simply marvellous. Sean is simply wonderful, especially when he thinks he's Alexander. These two men are like the opposite sides of a coin. They are a unit, I wouldn't know how to divide them. One starts a line of dialogue, the other finishes it. They always speak as two, and they are identical until the moment when they divide and separate.

Then there is Plummer. I can't speak too highly of him. He was simply perfect as Kipling. So precisely convincing and so very human. I've always admired Plummer, a fine actor, a skilful actor, and he gives a superb performance, so much so that audiences don't recognise him. He does the picture a great service. He tells the audience what to think about these two men and they are coached into seeing them through his eyes.

I had some difficulties with the backers. They had a mistaken idea of the kind of picture it was going to be. They saw it more in the current tradition of violence, blood and thunder, and sex, and there was a misapprehension on the part of both Allied and Columbia, who saw it as a British "French Foreign Legion desert adventure" with slow motion violence and that sort of thing [laughs]. They as much as told me this. Then some of the dialogue, which is faithful to its time, to the colloquialisms of the period, they wanted changed. Among them, they wanted "sporan" changed to "money bag." There were others. Eventually, they came around and agreed with what was written.

There were great difficulties for Alex Trauner. His was a monumental job. Stephen Grimes still very much wanted to do the picture, but he was working on another film. Every shot was made on location. The only set we built on location was the temple, and that was a triumph, a beautiful set, done with great taste and a knowledge and understanding of the deeper and symbolic meanings of the picture and the story. There was a culture in that part of Afghanistan that extended down to Bijar, after the advent of Alexander. There was a Greek-Indian art form and there are remnants, little glimpses of Greek culture, still there. The Buddhas are rendered in a Greek way, and all this was fascinating to me, and undertaken by Alex Trauner with a thorough understanding and deep knowledge. The temple was done in proportion with all the details of the period.

Edith Head did one of her very best jobs with the costumes. It was an enormous undertaking to do all this from Morocco, and whatever the final cost of the picture, every bit of it is on the screen, and more. I was very glad to be with Ossie Morris again. His photography was superb. And we were fortunate in getting the Moroccan actor, Doghmi Larbi, to play Ootah. It's a marvellous, bravura, rococo, baroque performance [roars with laughter]. The Indian actor, Saeed Jaffrey, who plays Billy Fish, was also excellent. He plays with a great sense of comedy. We were fortunate with the entire cast. The ancient, who plays the High Priest, was an old man, well over 100, whom we found. We talked, through translators, and we warmed to each other, the old man and I. He pulled my beard and I pulled his, and he and two other very old men played the priests. The armies, the crowds, were all natives from the Atlas Mountains. They had no idea what was going on. They spoke only in Berber, so all the translations were done from English into French to Arabic to Berber and on the way something was lost [*roars with laughter*], but they were wonderful. We were there three months, it was very hot and very cold, and there was one curse. Drought! There had been no rain for months. There were dust storms, and dust was raised by our crowds and by the animals. Many of our people had to wear masks throughout the shooting. Everyone coughed.

Knowing Kipling as well as I do, I drew on him not only in spirit but in fact. A lot of the dialogue is Kipling's ("such as we" for example) which I took from his writing and slipped in wherever I could. We go into the mythology of the Masons, and use the Masons to begin the relationship between Carnehan and Kipling. While much of this is not Kipling directly, it's certainly in the spirit of Kipling, and, not to flatter ourselves, I think Kipling would have approved of the script.

The story has a trajectory. There is a wideness and handsomeness to it, and of the men; it echoes some dream that I think is in all our hearts, even as we grow older. That continual longing for the great adventure. They confirm something that is in our yearning souls, and there is a bravery there, that kind of courage that we aspire to, and an affirmation that if you are brave enough the Gods will be with you; if you dare enough, you will be aided and abetted; and if you are brought up short (and this is in the story) , why, it's because once you attain the place you seek there is the danger of becoming high and mighty, of falling victim to the disease of power that most of those who live in a rarefied atmosphere are assailed with, once you begin to believe that you yourself are indeed the supreme being, issuing the orders and making all the decisions. It has that sweep to it, and an underlying deep truth, which I hope and pray audiences will discover.

It's not a perfect picture, however. I wish it were, but it's grand, not in spectacle, but in spirit. It's difficult to create exactly on the screen what one imagines, particularly under the conditions we had to work. What one hopes for is to demonstrate the spirit of the work. Oh, I was frequently despairing at times, but I learned long ago to box my way out [*laughs*]. It has become a *cliché* to say that a story works on several levels, but it happens to be so in this instance. It's a ghost story, an adventure story, it contains history in the mythological sense, it's largely funny and only in its tragic moments is it not funny—when Dravot goes off course. And it has a physiological level as well and they all come together, they aren't random, they work together, and the picture stands as a whole. I am glad indeed to have done it; I hope it will be successful but one never knows, of course.

THE MAN WHO WOULD BE KING. 1975. *An* Allied Artists *Release.*
Director: John Huston. *Production Company:* An Allied Artists/ Columbia Pictures Production, A Persky-Bright/Devon Picture. *Presented by:* Emanuel L. Wolf. *Producer:* John Foreman. *Associate Producer/Stunt Director:* James Arnett. *Production Supervisor:* Ted Lloyd. *Screenplay:* John Huston and Gladys Hill. *Based on the short story by:* Rudyard Kipling. *Photography:* Oswald Morris. *Colour:* Eastmancolor. *Production Designer:* Alexander Trauner. *Editor:* Russell Lloyd. *Wardrobe Designer:* Edith Head. *Art Director:* Tony Inglis. *Camera Operator:* Eris Van Haren-Noman. *Assistant Director:* Bert Batt. *Assistant to the Producer:* Annabelle King. *Sound Mixer:* Basil Fenton-Smith. *Horsemaster:* Bob Simmons. *Special Effects:* Dick Parker. *Music:* Maurice Jarre.
Running time: 132 minutes.
Players: Sean Connery (*Daniel Dravot*), Michael Caine (*Peachy Carnehan*), Christopher Plummer (*Rudyard Kipling*), Saeed Jaffrey (*Billy Fish*), Karroum Ben Bouih (*Kafu-Selim*), Jack May (*District Commissioner*), Doghmi Larbi (*Ootah*), Shakira Caine (*Roxanne*), Mohammed Shamsi (*Babu*), Paul Antrim (*Mulvaney*), Albert Moses (*Ghulam*), Kimat Singh (*Sikh Soldier*), Gurmuks Singh (*Sikh Soldier*), Yvonne Ocampo (*Dancer*), Nadia Atbib (*Dancer*).

Story
Rudyard Kipling, a young journalist working in Lahore, India, is immediately interested when he meets by chance two shrewd former British army sergeants, Daniel Dravot and Peachy Carnehan, especially when he learns they are brother Masons. They tell him of their plan to set off for wild and primitive Kafiristan, through Afghanistan, to seek their fortunes by setting themselves up as Kings of a primitive country. After many adventures, Dravot and Carnehan arrive in the Kafiristan village of Er-Heb, meet a former Gurkha soldier, Billy Fish, who becomes their loyal friend, and Er-Heb's headman, Ootah, whom they help to defeat the rival town of Bashkai in battle. Because of Dravot's courage, battle prowess and apparent invincibility, the men of both armies hail him as King and God and he and Carnehan lead an ever-growing army into more victories.

Sean Connery and Michael Caine in THE MAN WHO WOULD BE KING (1975).

Dravot is eventually summoned to the Holy City of Sikandergul where, after initial doubts, he is confirmed as King and God of all Kafiristan and given priceless treasure: an entire chamber filled with gold, silver, pearls and jewels. He holds absolute power. But power can corrupt even the best man and, despite Carnehan's warnings, Dravot comes to believe that he is, indeed, a God directly descended from Alexander the Great. When he decides to take a beautiful local girl, Roxanne, as his wife and Queen, the people are doubtful, and during the wedding ceremony their doubts are confirmed when the terrified girl proves Dravot is not an immortal God but an ordinary man. Feeling betrayed, the people chase Dravot and Carnehan from the city. In a final battle, the soldiers of fortune fight to maintain their exalted status and to save their lives.

Comment
    The most striking aspect of this remarkable and memorable film is that it is an epic, John Huston's first, yet unlike most epics it never seems like one because the vast canvas on which it is laid, the im-

pressive landscapes and crowds of people, never once dwarf the story and its characters. So well has Huston cast his actors and used them that not for one moment does an audience lose them in the epic nature of this triumphant undertaking. It has all of Lean and Eisenstein at their best, yet through it runs the sure and expert hand, the subtle and reflective intelligence of Huston. It is filled with humour, sadness, imagery and poetry. The dialogue is splendid to hear, the players a pleasure to watch, the atmosphere strong and seductive. This adventure-parable, which takes Huston back in some respects to *Sierra Madre,* in this case shows the corrupting effects not so much of wealth, used to gain power, but of adulation going so far that the recipient begins to feel that he is divine, and uses the worship of the people to wield power over them. The two seekers here provide a lively and human account of themselves and find some triumphs before the payment that destiny demands is exacted. Huston has created a feeling for the period when the Raj ruled, and made it possible for two somewhat ignorant yet far from stupid men, brought up to believe in their superiority over others, to become fired with the ambition to create their own Empire. It is a magnificent achievement in visual concept, design, settings, sound and music, based on a beautifully written screenplay and acted to perfection. Some things are left too long in their realisation but this film is all the better for having been made twenty years late.

U.S.A. (Independence Hall, Philadelphia) : **Independence** (1975)

I was approached by the producer, Lloyd Ritter, who wrote the script with his wife, Joyce, on behalf of the National Park Service and he told me of the spirit and intention of the enterprise, and asked if I would direct the picture. It was to be done in eight days and the final running time just under half an hour. I approved of the idea, I thought it an excellent way to mark the Bicentennial, and I saw it as a way to make my obeisance to the progenitors of Uncle Sam [*laughs*]. I was asked how it felt to be making a "small film" after making "big pictures," but really, I don't know the difference between a major or a minor film. The fact that the narrative takes half-an-hour to tell doesn't change my thinking or the effort. If the film conveys a strong and meaningful message, then I'm quite satisfied that it's a major film. "The Gettysburg Address" is not as long as "War and Peace." The only difference, I suppose, is that one is not working for quite such a long time in actual shooting days as one would be on a longer film. I feel very much at home with this subject, with the historical background and the characters. I was born and raised as a child in the federalist tradition. My great grandfather was a general in the Civil War; my grandfather, on my mother's side, was a drummer boy; and my entire background was in this grain. My grandmother was an authority on the Constitution and the Bill of Rights, and I used to visit an aunt's house in Cincinnati and I don't remember how many times I was taken up to the study to be shown my great grandfather's sword and other mementos from his regiment, the 25th Ohio. I was raised in this atmosphere and whether this is reflected in the picture I have no idea. The founding fathers were all hallowed figures so far as I was concerned and I still look at them through the eyes of a child. Today, the United States needs to return, and has indeed returned, I think, with the outcome of Watergate, to the document they drew up and has lasted two hundred years, and

INDEPENDENCE (1975). Left to right,
William Atherton, Huston, Gladys Hill.

which has come into active service again. There haven't been many films made about 1776 and the events leading up to it because, I think, of the lack of information. The written history made it all so thoroughly disinteresting, with Paul Revere and other such banalities. More has been written and filmed about the opening of the west, which inflamed people's imagination. I think, too, that as it was the British against each other, as the Civil War was about the Americans against each other, we don't want to recall too much of the war itself, only the aftermath which, in the case of 1776, brought about independence. That's what this film is about. Before his death, Benjamin Franklin is said to have made a wish to "observe the state of America in a century or two," so we bring him back, with the other founding fathers, to give them a look at us today in this place, and for us to see a "re-play," as it were, of what they did here. We cover twenty years in a kind of montage effect. Franklin, played by Eli Wallach, says, "I must re-live those first days, now two centuries past. We must begin in 1774. I'm sixty-eight. How excellent it is to be young again." Eli is most infectious with his lively air and flourish. I haven't seen him since *The Misfits,* but he is still a splendid actor, as are the others who bring the fathers to life with their knowing portrayals. The costumes are beautiful and accurate, the dialogue has a great ring to it. There is a danger that in so short a time the characters could be seen as caricatures, but we know that the audience knows these figures from history, and we are seeing them in vignettes over twenty years, in moments that took place or might have taken place here in these historic buildings. The characters should also be known to the director when he starts filming, whether fictional or real, so consequently, there shouldn't be a contradiction in terms as to what to expect from them, and how they are to be portrayed. Some of this of course, is legend, but it's interesting to play with legends and see what else they have to say. Most audiences know what is legend and what is more or less true.

The future? Well, I have yet another unfulfilled ambition. This is to film a Hemingway story. As you know, I did not direct my script for *The Killers,* I could not go on with *A Farewell to Arms* under the conditions I described earlier. I was asked to direct *The Old Man and the Sea,* but I couldn't see the old Cuban fisherman played by an actor, and the studio couldn't risk doing it without one. Now Gladys and I are finishing the screenplay for *Across the River and Into the Trees.* I hope this will be my next film.

Pat Hingle as John Adams in INDEPENDENCE (1975).

INDEPENDENCE (1975). Eli Wallach as Benjamin Franklin, Patrick O'Neal as George Washington.

INDEPENDENCE. 1975. *Director:* John Huston. *Production Company:* Twentieth Century-Fox for the National Parks Service. *Producers:* Joyce and Lloyd Ritter. *Screenplay:* Joyce and Lloyd Ritter and Thomas McGrath. *Historical Consultant:* L. H. Butterfield. *Photography:* Owen Roizman. Panavision. *Colour:* Eastmancolor. *Second Unit Direction and Photography:* Lloyd Ritter. *Art Director:* Stephen Grimes. *Costumes:* Ann Roth. *Running time:* 28 minutes. *Players* (in alphabetical order) : William Atherton *(Benjamin Rush)*, John Favourite *(John Lansing Jr.)*, Pat Hingle *(John Adams)*, Ken Howard *(Thomas Jefferson)*, Anne Jackson *(Abigail Adams)*, Donald C. Moore *(Benjamin Harrison)*, Scott Mulherne *(Alexander Hamilton)*, Patrick O'Neal *(George Washington)*, John Randolph *(Samuel Adams)*, Joe Ritter *(Congressional Page)*, Paul Sparer *(John Hancock)*, Tom Spratley *(George Mason)*, Donald Symington *(Richard Henry Lee)*, James Tolkan *(Tom Paine)*, Eli Wallach *(Benjamin Franklin)*. *Narrator:* E. G. Marshall. *(Independence* is shown thirty-two times a day, seven days a week, in two specially built cinemas in Independence Hall National Park, Philadelphia. It will be shown here until the end of this century. Lloyd Ritter writes: "It will by then have been seen by more than seventy million people, and may well be the last of John Huston's works to be seen in theatres on a continuing basis.")

Story

Amid the usual daily life of Philadelphia, with groups of tourists visiting Independence Hall and listening to the guides reciting historical dates and events, the Founding Fathers, led by Benjamin Franklin, return to relive in brief episodes the years before and after the Declaration of Independence.

Comment

This is a film of great good humour, of robust spirits, of dignity and respect, beautifully staged and filmed, never stiff or stilted, never in awe of itself or the figures it portrays. Huston, with lovely camerawork and colour by Roizman, has captured the feeling of past and present in a series of easy-flowing vignettes, all the images being framed in a mist of recollection. The acting is vigorous and sure, the dialogue, much of it from actual statements, is direct and pointed, pure and exhilarating. Huston never panders to false patriotism, there is no flag-waving, rather, a fast-moving and thoughtfully dramatised historical tract which admirably suits the purpose for which it was made.

Huston as Actor

SOME CRITICS have written that I would prefer to be an actor than a director. This is nonsense. I don't take the acting seriously for a moment, and when I do appear in one of my own films I'm always my third or fourth choice. I'm reduced to being in it!

My first screen appearance was in a two-reeler called *Two Americans,* made at the Astoria Studios in Long Island, New York. I went along with my father—he was in it—and I played a young lieutenant. It was a good way to earn $200. I forget the date. During the War, I went back to the Astoria Studios. The Signal Corps. was based there and I worked on my war films.

After *Sierra Madre,* I didn't appear on screen again until *The Cardinal* (1964). My sole reason for appearing in this was in response to my old friend, Otto Preminger, asking me to play the part. I was happy to accept. For *Candy* (1968) I went down to the studio in Rome for one afternoon's work to play the doctor, the same thing for *De Sade* (1969) filmed in Berlin. I happened to be there. I went into *Myra Breckinridge* (1970) as Buck Loner because I thought it would be amusing. I read the book, but not the script. It would be done, they assured me, in a very limited period of time, which it was, and I went into it as a very well-paid lark [*laughs*]. I didn't see the finished film, I only heard about it, and that was enough to keep me away. Maybe unjustly, because occasionally someone now tells me, someone whose case I listen to, that they liked the whole picture very much, and that it had a surrealist kind of bizarre quality that was unusual. The largest role I have played was that of Sleigh, an old drifter living in Mexico, in *The Bridge in the Jungle* (1970). I did this because the story is by the mysterious B. Traven and it was directed by Pancho Kohner, the son of my old friend, Paul Kohner. Also, it was filmed entirely in Mexico, which suited me just fine. Of course, people made comparisons between me as the old man and my father's role in *Sierra Madre.* There is not much resemblance. I appeared as a film director in Orson's film, *The Far Side of the Wind,* which he hasn't finished as yet. I forget how *The Deserter* (1971) came about. It was a western shot in Spain. I played a general in a cavalry regiment. *Man in the Wilderness* (1971) was also shot in Spain. This time I was a captain. There, by the way, is a very good

Huston as actor: CHINATOWN (1974).

Huston as actor: above with Albert Salmi and Bekim Fehmiu in THE DESERTER (1970), below in THE WIND AND THE LION (1975).

director: Richard Sarafian. Only rarely do I see real talent demonstrated for me, and this is certainly an example. The next year, I
think, I went over to Fox for J. Lee Thompson and put on a ginger
wig to become the Lawgiver in *Battle for the Planet of the Apes*—an
orangutan Moses, you might say, giving forth with some semi-Biblical
phrases. *Chinatown* came along while I was waiting to start *The Man
Who Would Be King,* and this was followed by *Breakout* (1975)—
both somewhat villainous roles. Then John Milius asked me to play
John Hay in *The Wind and the Lion* (1975)—a much more pleasant
character. I enjoy playing these parts, I get a boot out of it and being
in front of the camera without any responsibility whatever is a
welcome change.*

* Since John Huston talked about his acting roles, he has played Moriarty in a
TV feature, *Sherlock Holmes in New York,* and read the narration for *Hollywood
on Trial.* Besides the films he mentions, Huston has also appeared in *The Mad-
woman of Chaillot* (1969) and *Breakout* (1975).

Some Reflections

I HAVE MADE these comments many times. After a while, why, I wonder if I believe them any more. This book will be useful if only as a permanent record of what I think about film-making. In future, I can refer interviewers to it and I won't have to say it all over again [*laughter and coughing*]. The things a camera does ideally are very much like the things our minds do, and indeed, our bodies. There's a physiological comparison. We were speaking of the cut instead of the pan. We do cut in life constantly. When I look from one place to another, if the two were any distance apart, why, usually I blink. I close my eyes ever so briefly in making that transition so that, in fact, it becomes a cut if I look from one side of the room to the other side of the room. My eyes don't remain open and sweep evenly over the distance separating the two corners of the room, but I close my eyes and the effect is that of a cut. By the same token, if someone is speaking and they are saying something very revealing, my inclination is to go, if not physically closer to them, to give them more of my attention, so that unconsciously, I lean closer to them with my mind if not my body. There's another thing, for instance—the conversations we are having now. We wouldn't be having this conversation, talking as we are, if you were at one end of the room and I was at the other. This is the proper distance for it. If I were to come back here [*moving away*], it would change the tone of our remarks. So the distance, the size of the figure on the screen, must be in accordance with what we are saying and doing. We even dissolve with our minds, one thought overlapping another. In preparing to do a scene I very often sit in, put myself in, the position of the actor and reckon what the sizes of the people should be, and act accordingly with the camera. I even think of the camera almost as another actor on the set. The relationship between the characters, the people who are moving and saying lines, is ever so important, and the camera can be every bit as eloquent as the finest actor. It's very important that the director uses the camera at exactly the right distance—the significant distance, let us say—from the actor when he says his line. Very rarely has my best camerawork been remarked on by either an audience or a critic. I'm trying to remember a single instance. And that's very flattering so far as I'm concerned, because the moment the camera becomes obtrusive and the audience is aware of the camera, I think (like dramatic scoring that becomes obvious) it ceases to perform its most important function. There are numerous theories about the

use of the camera, and I marvel at what we continue to discover
with it. I like to see one scene develop into another scene, one set-up
change and develop into another set-up, without anyone's knowing
it. A movement of the camera makes this possible. In fact, it's rather
a ballet between the people, the scene and the camera. I move the
camera only when it is required. Tracking, dollying, any movement,
depends largely on the material, on the subject matter, and on the
story. It's a way of telling a story, and a scene tells me how to shoot it.
Each film is conceived as the story of it needs telling. Instead of saying
to an actor "You come here" and "You go over there," I always begin
a scene by saying "Let's see it" and see how they sort themselves out.
A good part of the time, why, they do something of themselves that
calls for little or no correction. Sometimes they have to be arranged.
I would say, with most of my films, about half the time the actors,
without my telling them, fall into the set-ups of themselves, a quarter
of the time they did something that was better than I imagined, and
the rest of the time I had to manoeuvre them. This applies to great
actors, or personalities, or familiar characters, or new players in
small roles. The scene tells me of itself, if it's a good scene. But if
it's a bad scene it doesn't tell me a damn thing. A bad scene is the
most difficult to shoot. The better the scene, the way it has been
written and conceived and set-up for directing, the easier it is to
shoot and the quicker it instructs me.

This is in many respects a motion picture age, rather than an age
of the novel, of the magazine, or of the theatre, certainly of the theatre.
The origins of the cinema, although close to us in terms of time,
are as deep as any other artistic means of expression. It's not by
accident that the men and women who appear on the screen take on
the aspects of minor deities. Those great shadows projected on the
screen are surely not flesh and blood, why, they are more than that.
It must always be remembered that this has a bearing on the star
system. Audiences come to worship in the motion picture theatre.
It's in a sense a religious exercise. The medium itself is peculiarly
biological and physiological, I should say, and film itself is kind of
magical. It's almost as though we see what we want to see. And as
long as the picture is good, that's what's happening. It's only when
something wrong occurs that the audience is snapped out of this
trance in which we usually view a film—I mean a good film. The
camera does things the audience is not aware of; and when it does
become aware, why, these are failures. I can look at bad films and
still feel that enchantment, that almost hypnotic effect that the
screen exerts. It's almost impossible for me to sit through a bad performance at an opera. I've got to get out, and that's pretty well true

of the theatre. I have a great sense of confinement if the play isn't very good. For the reasons I have tried to explain, I don't feel this way in the cinema. It's almost as though it were a thought process. Let's consider the camera panning from one person to another, or from one object to another. What does a pan shot consist of? It establishes relationship, the spatial relationship, between two objects. There may be suspense involved in that motion of the camera. Now when the camera cuts, when the image changes instantly on the screen, that's also a physiological manifestation, a phenomenon if you like. To give an example, look at that group of technicians over there from this side of the studio, and then from that side of the studio from this identical pillar. First there, and then glance over there. Do it a time or two, and you will blink your eyes, that's the cut I mentioned. We know what the spatial relationship is, we close our eyes to rest them, or not to bore them, in between. So that, when we are interested, when we are fascinated by something, we move in on it, we move closer to it. That's what we call a dolly shot. Never try to make a man funny, never try to get an effective comedy shot, with the camera looking up, because that's against something very deep in our natures. We didn't laugh at our fathers or mothers or at a policeman. To get a comic effect we should look down a little bit, be superior to the thing we are laughing at, but not in a cruel way. I could go on at greater length in all this, but my point is simply to show the profound role the camera plays in the presentation of motion. But to go one step further, it's always seemed to me that the perfect motion picture is the one which we seem to be projecting with our own eyes. It's not a machine doing this for us. We ourselves are looking at an oblong of light which is the expression of our own thoughts, and our own dreams, and we fill it with our own images, with our own dream images. It's as though the reel of film was behind our eyes. The fact that the people on the screen aren't flesh and blood but shadows and colours, two-dimensional, allows us to read into them wonderful qualities—as I said before, they are gods up there, a pantheon, that screen is Parnassus, we are privileged to witness the behaviour of these deities. More concentration is required of audiences, although it's unconscious, in the viewing of a film than in reading a novel. An audience sits in a tunnel, ideally, looking at what it projects on a screen. With a bad film, pretty soon the muscles begin to weary and the physical requirements are such that it can become agony.

One of the questions most asked of me is how do I write a film and how do I direct a film. There's really no difference between them, it's an extension, one from the other. Ideally I think the writer should go on and direct the picture. I think of the director as an extension of the writer. There should be no innate antagonism between them. Rather, the director takes over beyond the written word and attempts to put in the things that are between the lines of dialogue. I think that a director who writes or is at least deeply involved with the script before it goes on the screen is at a peculiar advantage. He knows a little bit more about what the written word is attempting to convey— the spirit of the word. This is the reason why as a writer I eventually turned director. Now if, as the director, I am working from another writer's screenplay, why, in my experiences I've attempted to identify myself with the script. This hasn't happened very often, and I always say that it won't happen again. I want to have something to do with the writing of any screenplay which finds its way to the screen under my direction. I never saw a great dividing line between writing and directing. It's been pointed out to me that, although I have written plays and stories, all my films have been adapted from novels. They argue that an original screenplay is the purely creative act. Perhaps it is. My very good friend Bergman was going to direct *Peer Gynt* and had every intention of proceeding with it. My God, it's a great undertaking! Then he spoke to the sponsors and said, "Please forgive me, I have too much of my own work to do." I have the deepest respect for a man who has as personal a message to convey as Bergman. However, I'm contemplating making a film from an original screenplay written by myself, and I'll direct and produce it as well. So far as the theatre is concerned, I may write another play or direct one, it all depends. What can I do on the stage that I cannot do in the cinema? I work a great deal from novels perhaps because there is much less difference between the cinema and the novel than the cinema and the theatre. They are, after all, real people on the stage, and people are shadows on the screen. I don't see that, when it comes to thought and ideas, the cinema is any more divorced from the stage than the theatre is divorced from the novel. There is undoubtedly material better suited to the theatre than to the novel, or *vice versa*. Like the folk song, there is a place for tradition and convention. I hate to see—and this is the child in me, the same child I believe is in all of us—the distortion of the western. I hate to see a new-fangled western. I like to see the old western, that epic convention unfolded once again in reassuringly antique terms. In this sense, our people are cowboys and become heroes, and their lady-lovers, goddesses. I think that this is a role that's distinct to films.

Many people and critics ascribe to me a distinct style. Believe me, I am not conscious of any such thing. Whenever I undertake to direct a film, I do so out of the deep feeling it inspires in me. It is precisely this feeling that dictates the way in which I direct a picture. It is a matter of spontaneous sensitivity. There is so much talk of style and technique, of my "unifying technique," of "a Huston scene," and I've always been fascinated to hear what it was. I myself haven't the vaguest idea. Critics are so fond of talking about "a personal film," or "a personal style." I don't really know what they mean. I don't think they've really thought about it. I think that when they imagine the realism of the film is something the director has actually experienced, as, in my case, with certain elements in *Fat City,* then that becomes a personal film. I suppose that's what they mean, but I'm not at all sure. There is really just as much of me in all the films I have made, yet *The Bible* has been described as an "impersonal film." When I do something "personal," why, it's a "return to form" [*laughs*]. More seriously, it seems to me that each picture calls for a specific approach, or treatment. Obviously a horror tale and a pastoral should not be photographed through the same lenses. With *The Maltese Falcon* I attempted to transpose Dashiell Hammett's highly individual prose style into camera terms, with sharp photography, geographically exact camera movements, and striking, if not shocking, set-ups. I have tried to do this with every film since. There is a wide variety in the kinds of films I make so instead of trying to discover the qualities in one film that are similar to those of another, I try to make each one as differently as I possibly can, and to discover the things about the particular film that are innately its own. I always try to discover the point of any scene, and this, if you like, creates style or technique in the manner in which it's portrayed. Feelings, tensions, conflicts, relationships must be created between characters, they must do and say natural things, they cannot simply sit or stand in a scene, they must be things which the audience thinks are right because they have seen people behave this way. These actions and that sort of behaviour belong to the characters, to the scene and the idea, rather than to myself.

Whether a director holds a shot or breaks it with the frequent use of reverse angles, cutting after every few words, depends entirely on the scene itself. I've played scenes in several pictures that lasted five minutes or more. It depends in every instance on what's in the scene. How good is the actor, how effective his dialogue, what kind of mood and atmosphere have we established; all these elements have some bearing on the length of the scene and when cuts should be made. One must be careful not to bore audiences, but by the same token, fear of being tedious can inhibit a director and force him to deprive the audience—unnecessarily, I feel—of the time to enjoy and search out the details and colours of any given scene.

Some of the "directorial touches" that have accrued to my credit have not been my own at all, but the contributions of an actor, a writer. Let me say that I do try to lay myself open to fortunate accidents! I don't consciously try to make each film different. I adapt myself to the material. *Casino Royale* is like telling an anecdote or a story at dinner time, that's the spirit of it. *The Bible* is a rather different proposition. The entire enterprise, the making of a film, begins with an idea, mine or someone else's, and the expression of it on paper in the form of a screenplay. I may write it myself or get others to write it. It may be a book or a play which appeals to my imagination, and the first task is to prepare a screenplay. Then we say, "Who would be best to appear in this film, to work on it?" Finally, we have a finished script, a cast and a unit. We decide how to do it, where to do it. The actual making of a film is perhaps the easiest part of it, or should be. Making it is demonstrating what one has done—the proving of it. In all this, I don't see how a director can help but put himself in the film—even if it's just bloody awful and conventional!

Ideally, of course, to write, produce and direct a film oneself is theoretically to have full control over one's picture. The billing looks grand, but this itself is immaterial. I think the function should be as integrated as much as possible, but it is more important to write than to produce. I personally prefer to write the pictures I direct. Sometimes I can be all three, sometimes I'm the director only, and due to the exigencies and the expediencies of film-making, why, these shifts are possible. I don't think they are profitable, and I don't mean economically, but rather aesthetically.

When it comes to the producer, it depends on what kind of producer we are talking about. In the making of a picture in the old days of the major studios, there was an overall producer and under him would be a number of other producers. This executive producer would be given, probably by the front office or studio head, a story, a novel, a play and, in some rare instances, an original script (rare because they were considered something of a gamble, lacking a successful background) and he in turn would give it to the producer he thought would be most suitable for the kind of story it was. He would then put a writer on the script, work on the budget, decide what contract players and stars would be used, hire the director and so on. He was more of a co-ordinator, and the major studios employed up to twenty of them. When the picture was shot, the director had nothing to do with the editing or what happened afterwards. It was entirely in the hands of the studio, and the man who ran the studio had the final authority.

On the other hand there were independent producers who would hire a very good writer, hand the script over to a very good director, who doesn't need to write on a script, and in that way, a producer's name, a director's name and a writer's name appear on the screen, each in splendid isolation. Some writers could work well under the studio system and still have their work respected and others simply could not accommodate themselves to the system. Or they might with one film, and not another. Scripts were broken down into scenes and shots and camera angles, but most of these and other directions were ignored by the directors. I say this as a writer at that time. Now and then the director would take cognisance of specific instructions, but as a rule he simply read, and the writer himself didn't take the instructions all that seriously. I think I made the point before that, when the writer was finished, why he wasn't even invited to the set, except in extraordinary instances, and very often, when the director was finished, why, his presence wasn't required in the cutting room.

Today, of course, it depends on who the producer is and who the director is. Most directors have no authority whatever, although the system under which films are made today gives the director more freedom and if the film he has made pleases the producer, or the distributor, and stands a good chance of making money, then it will likely stay the way he edited it. We have, as the Screen Directors' Guild has written it out, the authority of a first cut. From that moment on, the picture no longer belongs to the director. There are today about a dozen of us whose authority goes beyond that. The common denominator, of course, is how much are the director's services worth in terms of money? If they are worth as much money, in terms of cash, as the producer put into it, why then he has his equal in say. I've had my battles, defended my films doggedly, and fought to keep them the way I finished them, and except for two instances, *The Barbarian* and *Sinful Davey,* I've come out on top. Of course, there is just nothing a director can do if he has made an expensive film that is not doing well at the box-office, and the studio decides after the opening to make cuts in the picture. The director may be asked by the studio to make the cuts, but more likely than not, his advice will not be sought. The old studio system was a synthetic way of making films but, surprisingly enough, a great number of excellent films emerged from it. That method rarely takes place any more, particularly in top-bracket pictures. I suppose there are some producers who still turn out films on the assembly line in that fashion, but they are getting fewer in number all the time. The function of the producer today is rather vague. It can be so many things. It can either be that he's concerned with the physical requirements of the picture, or the economic side of production, or the aesthetic considerations. Unless the producer is exceptional, the aesthetic requirements should rest rather with the writer and the director. I frequently hear it said that a director should have a producer to gain the benefit of a "second pair of eyes." My reply to that is, "If they are clear-sighted enough and are in front of a sufficiently good intelligence."

Producers are supposed to know what the public wants. They are supposed to know what entertainment for the public should be like. I have always been confused by questions as to what was entertainment and what was educational. I suppose that what is entertainment for one person is educational for another, and it depends on who and what the individual is, and what his background may be. But there is no easy line of demarcation that I can see. Entertainment is anything that is fascinating and I suppose one could almost put education under the category. Education if it is fascinating is also entertainment.

What about art in all this? Is all art entertainment? Can entertainment be art? Shakespeare's greatest play is not art, entertainment or education, if it is so badly staged and acted that audiences are bored by it. Once again, it depends on the individual work, and how it is created. Is the film an art form? It can be. It depends on who's doing it. Painting is considered to be an art, but very few paintings are works of art. But I'm lost when it comes to answering these questions, although everything is so apparent to me. The only question is: what is one to say? Is it better said in motion pictures or in some other medium? Motion pictures lend themselves to a certain kind of statement. There is a certain amount of snobbery among higher forms of society in accepting films as an art in the same easy, confident way symphony music or the theatre, and ballet and opera, are considered to be art. This is largely because films appeal to such a great audience, and because pictures must make money—unless the film-maker is subsidised by the state. A film must make roughly twice what it cost in order to break even. And making a picture is a very expensive proposition. If it were paints on a palette, why, elisyran crimson would be $140,000 and cobalt blue would be $160,000—a tube! There is, then, let's say, a requirement that the picture has a good chance by appealing to a large enough audience of making money. If it doesn't, the film-maker's chances of continuing to make what he believes in become fewer. I've been guilty of making pictures that didn't make a sou, and each time I've felt a certain responsibility and a deep disappointment, not only so far as I personally was concerned, but that others who wanted to do something original and new and away from the pattern would have my failure thrown up at them.

In some countries in Europe films are thought more of as an art

than they are perhaps in North America. Many Americans have long
considered that the art of film-making is further advanced in Europe
than in Britain and America. They speak and write of the whole
creative process in what some consider intellectual terms, with the
emphasis on contemporary thought and problems. Generally speaking, this may be true but why, then, do European audiences so
admire and enjoy American films? Hollywood over the years has
furnished the assembly line that provided so many thousands of
exhibitors everywhere with pictures for their "houses," and the
studios fell perhaps into traditional if not conventional procedures.
I'd say that as many good pictures, probably more, come from Hollywood auspices each year than out of any other country in the world.
One year it will seem that there's wonderful creativity in Japan, a
little renaissance there, and two or three years later, why, the centre
will have shifted to Italy. Then it's France, Poland, Sweden. Films
of quality are to be found everywhere, and I think this is a very
healthy thing, a wonderful thing. On the other hand, I think some
of the best American films have been those of social comment. I'm
afraid, though, that Hollywood is always looking for the dollar, but
it has to, it must, because by the very nature of motion picture
making in the United States, a film is required to make money.
This does create a false emphasis, it seems to me. To safeguard the
large sums of money films require for production, films must have
names that the producers reckon will bring in certain returns at
the box-office. These names have become inordinately valuable. It's
not unusual for a star to receive a million dollars for making a film.
This shifts the importance away from the subject matter, the material,
and throws it entirely on to the stars, so the picture becomes, as
they say, "a vehicle." Now there's a perverse practice that has sprung
up from this. A number of stars have their own companies, and
pictures are made according to their requirements, the requirements
of individuals who, of course, are interested in projecting their own
images. It's an unhealthy situation which is now, I'm glad to see, being
ironed out by time!

Today, more than ever before, there seems to be a marked division
in standards, in technical means, in tastes and critical acceptance.
I saw this coming for a long time. Broadly speaking, there are today
two kinds of films: there's the intimate film that can best be told
with a hand-held camera, almost with that mental approach to the
material. And then there is the big film, on the wide screen, not
necessarily spectacle. It depends on what the material is, the technique
is secondary. It's the idea that counts, and how best to tell the idea.
Some ideas require the grand screen, the colour, the money, locations

and so on—others can require a lightweight, black-and-white 16mm camera within four walls. I don't see nearly as many films as I'd like to see. I try to make sure before seeing a film that it's going to be a good one, because bad films depress me and make me not to want to make films. But I think the films are probably better today, the fine films that is, and the attendance these films get is remarkable. There's a greater audience today than ever before, but only for movies which are in someway worthwhile to the audience. I think it's altogether encouraging—profoundly.

When we decided to make *Fat City*, for example, it was with the understanding between the producer and me, and indeed the company that put up the money for it, that we wouldn't expect great commercial success. We'd be quite satisfied, delighted in fact, with the picture paying back its costs and it being well-received by a selective audience. Quite to our surprise, its acceptance has been much wider than we ever dreamed possible.

Since we have been free, comparatively speaking, of the censorship once imposed by the church and the production code, I think there is a need to make films which reflect matters of concern to society, and which people want to see at the time they exist. This has brought about the much-debated issue of sex and violence on the screen, either in combination or separately. If the subject calls for any of the elements which are part of life today, and if they were significant to me, there's nothing that, in its right context, I would flinch from shooting if it has a point and a purpose. But simply to procure, as an entrepreneur, as the proprietor of a peep-show, why, I wouldn't care to participate as a pimp, let us say! It embarrasses me somewhat when a kiss goes on too long on the screen. Why, I want to turn my face away, I shouldn't be there. That's something between them! [*laughs*]. By the same token, I'd be quite capable of making a blue film, if it were in order, although it dismays me to see sexuality introduced in masquerade. I regard most of the DeMille films as obscenities! [*laughs*]. He was using Holy Writ to arouse stark passions, carnal lusts [*laughter*]. It was absurd, obscene and hypocritical as hell. A lot of today's so-called "frankness" on the screen is of the same measure. As for violence, of course it's overdone when the story is of violence for the sake of it. But if it is true to the story, like everything else we have been speaking about, then it is justified, although how explicit it should be is according to the way the director feels it should be shown. It can be done well, or badly, and doing something well doesn't mean over-doing it!

My films have always been masculine in content, probably due to my sex [*laughs*]. I have been asked, on a number of occasions, whether I believe in themes which contain a certain derision, and division, about men's ambitions being frustrated. It never occurred to me until the question was put to me (so I'm not preaching any kind of gospel) that the pursuit of the quarry is when a man is most alive. The rewards or the benefits or the conclusion isn't all that important. Perhaps I have thought sometimes in terms of the Hemingway hero. I think Hemingway probably influenced everyone of my generation. But unconsciously. I think that essentially I am drawn towards odd assortments and gatherings of individuals and misfits, rather than other types of characters. They are more interesting. There is no such thing as the common man. I think that very phrase is rather a comment on the observer, on people who use it. I think it's the variations that are interesting, in character, in people, certainly. I guess we are all misfits in a sense. How well do we conceal it? How successful are we in seeming to be like others? Privately, we are very different, aren't we? Each of us is very different from the other, I'm sure. I also believe, like Hemingway and many other writers, that a man finds himself, discovers himself, at a time of crisis, or in an unfamiliar hostile environment. At a time of adversity, when he is cast against misfortune, I think he's in a better position to judge himself and how good a show he's putting on, that sort of thing, when things are against him rather than if everything is with him. It's how well we behave under duress. Either we disappoint ourselves, or surprise ourselves, or applaud ourselves [laughs]. Maybe it affects our behaviour the next time.

All of this discussion about adversity and character brings me to possibly the last of the many questions I've been asked throughout my career and that is, what do I consider to be the ideal background for a director. Salvador Dali said that the ideal painter's name was Salvador Dali, that he would come from Spain, that he would be whatever Dali's age was at the time he made this remark. Well, I won't go quite that far! I don't think there's an ideal background for a director. I don't think it's so largely a matter of background, but rather the relationship of the individual to his background. I mean, some people, to come into their own, need a scholastic background, and undoubtedly, some need the experience in the rather more primitive aspects of life. It all depends on the individual and what his background is. I don't think that working in television or the theatre is a necessary background. It used to be that most of the directors in the old days came from—for some reason—the cutting department, the editorial department, of studios. Then there was a change, and I was one of the first, and new directors were brought in from the writing department. Undoubtedly, theatre and television has provided and will continue to provide many talents. But I don't think that's a requirement. It's a natural source and reservoir for talent that has already displayed an interest and a bent. As for me, naturally I think my own background was best. For another person it would have been catastrophic! [*laughs*]. I think wherever talent comes from we can be thankful for it!

Appreciation

Puerto Vallarta, Mexico: December 1975

IN 1963 some three thousand people lived here, high on the mountainous coastline overlooking the Pacific Ocean. It was quiet, poor and peaceful, and very beautiful with thick, tropical vegetation, green against the reddish earth, and the blue ocean washing the white sandy beaches. Much of the coastline was inaccessible, there being no roads, and tourists were few and far between. Travellers were more like adventurers, and one such adventurer was John Huston, who in the spring of 1963, discovered Puerto Vallarta and decided it was the ideal place to film *The Night of the Iguana*.

The publicity created by the making of the film, more than by the film itself, with its glamorous, high-priced, high-living and quick-tempered cast of characters, including Richard Burton, Ava Gardner, Sue Lyon, Deborah Kerr, and the visitors, among them Elizabeth Taylor, was sufficiently compelling, ferocious and startling to keep the newspapers and magazines watching them for many weeks. The fact that a group of egocentric individuals were living together in this remote place, laughing, fighting, sulking, loving, and subject to painful illnesses, involved in the strange world of movie make-believe in the ever stranger world of Tennessee Williams's imagination, created more melodrama, or just gossip, in the minds of the journalists than actually took place.

As with all film-making in difficult locations the cast endured long hours of just waiting in the steamy, humid, mosquito-infested atmosphere, longing only to be finished and away to a more civilised place. What began as high adventure ended in dull desperation—except for John Huston, who revels in such conditions. While others fall around him, he seems to grow stronger.

Today there are more than thirty thousand people in Puerto Vallarta, and the increase is due solely to the publicity the town received as a result of the filming of *The Night of the Iguana*. Thousands, it appears, want to walk in the Burtons' footsteps, swim from Ava Gardner's beach, and enjoy, vicariously, an association with the stars who once were here. They came in their thousands to visit, many to take up residence. The buildings erected for the film, only reached by the sea while the picture was being made, now sit close to the highway. Bulldozers are everywhere tearing into the hillsides and toppling trees to make way for large homes, and tall, gleaming, 'luxury' hotels. The townspeople are as poor as ever, while speculators line their pockets with quickly-made profits. Airplanes from Mexico City, Paris, Los Angeles, pour more people into the newly-built airport and, as the years pass, the place begins to look more like the Riviera.

John Huston views this with some amusement, shakes his head in mild astonishment, and puts it down to the human comedy. The way people behave is a never-ending source of wonder, and what they do is all observed for possible use in future films. He rents a villa here, high on the coastline not far from the crumbling sets of *The Night of the Iguana*. He shows no sentiment about having been here before, and never visits the old location. Not only have tourists followed him here, but other film-makers. Out on the ocean sails Drake's "The Golden Hind," now rented to Universal and renamed for the pirate picture *The Swashbuckler,* with Robert Shaw and Genevieve Bujold on board. Faint bangs echo over the water as the ship's cannon explodes. Far down below, the surf thunders on the beach, otherwise all is peaceful in the spacious, cool and open house with its colourful tiles and plants, wide terraces and comfortable furniture.

Huston is barefooted, wearing only casual trousers and open shirt. He is reading Omar Bradley's "A Soldier's Tale," open on the table before him, "for the purpose of research on the Second World War." Gladys Hill serves coffee, and Huston lights up a new cigar. She is a helpful, pleasant and professional woman who, she says, was "left over from the days of Horizon Pictures." Originally secretary to Sam Spiegel, she stayed with John Huston after the company was dissolved. Since then, she has been invaluable to him, taking care of his business affairs and working with him on many of his screenplays. When he cannot recall names, dates and places, she is there to remember them for him. Knowledgeable about all aspects of film-making, she is an associate of tremendous ability and enduring loyalty.

Huston remains a man of incredible vitality and energy, imagination and creativity. Among film-makers in America of his generation, of which there were some fifty distinctive directors, only Hitchcock, Cukor and Preminger are still keeping up with him. The rest have retired or died. Huston is himself a character subject to endless speculation. An American who is a citizen of Ireland with a great fondness for Britain, an adventurer and traveller who speaks with the cadence and beauty of a poet, a gentleman of great charm and courtesy, he has lived out in film, as writer and director, most of the worlds of fantasy that he has created either from his own imagination or from the writings of others.

Yet, realist that he is, everything he has created for the cinema bears his strong stamp of believability. Not only does it seem convincing on the screen, it seems entirely possible in real life. Going through his thirty films in thirty-two years we see an enviable record of achievement, in which Huston has adapted or changed with the years while remaining true to his personal beliefs. He is not a rigid, unbending artist. If he believes in a film, whether he initiates it or was asked to direct another writer's screenplay, he will do it only if he feels it is important to him in one way or the other, and he is interested in filming it. He has never insisted that he be the writer, director, producer of every film he has made. But when Huston is making a film, it becomes his completely and he is always, quietly and commandingly, in charge, involved and concerned, making the picture according to his beliefs and methods. He has never made films which have no meaning to him, simply to go on working for money. For critics to write that Huston's 'golden age' is behind him, that he has lost his personal vision, outlived his creative period, and has gone into a decline, is an indication of the lack of maturity on the part of the critics. It somehow bothers them that Huston keeps on going, his standard of excellence being consistently high, and therefore, after a time, appearing ordinary. There is seemingly nothing new for them to enthuse about, so they look to others to discover, to praise, and to shortly destroy. He has never made a film that was not worth every moment of the seeing of it, even if many of them did not find large audiences. Huston is a great film-maker. He always has been and always will be. The films speak for themselves. With his remarkable achievements, he continues to be the most prolific and fascinating film-maker we have.

The ease with which his films flow, tell their stories, and make their points conceals the art which goes into them. Huston has never 'sold out' to the commercial cinema; he has always been the artist whose work is understood by all audiences, who has lived with the requirements of commercial cinema, creating only work he believes in within its difficult and demanding system. What he has said about life, people, politics, war, religion and a host of other matters, is all permanently on record in his films, the observations, beliefs and concerns of a thoughtful, learned and major director. He would not be the artist he is were he not absorbed by the challenge of something new and different: more complex or much simpler, smaller or larger, more costly or less expensive, leading to extraordinary work like *Freud*, *The Bible*, or conversely, *Independence*, to which he gives as much of himself as to *Sierra Madre* or *Beat the Devil*. He has always been a questioning, inquiring and searching individual, his work ranging widely in the thematic sense, while never straying from the tenets which he believes drama and cinematography should adhere to. During the present period of poor taste in content and treatment of films, Huston remains a pillar of decency. Gratuitous sex, violence and bad language have no place in his work.

For a person who has travelled so widely, become involved in many conflicts with individuals and companies, who has worked under self-imposed conditions of great physical hardship in the locations he has chosen for many of his films, Huston remains a gentle, sensitive person, even shy it seems, who never appears to be the hard-driving, hard-living, tough, roistering knockabout character he likes to portray in his films. He is withdrawn about himself, and at times it seems an impertinence to ask him any questions about his thoughts and feelings, for his life is very much his own, and one hesitates to ask questions which lie outside direct reference to his films. While there are tales of his drinking, gambling, card-playing, hunting, love affairs and playing of practical jokes, he never presents such an image, seeming to be a quiet man who prefers to be left alone with books rather than wasting time in conversation with other people. He reads voluminously at every opportunity. On the set, whether on location or in the studios, in a garden of Eden in Rome, in the countryside of Ireland, or the Moroccan desert, it is difficult to find him, in spite of his height, around the camera. He is always there, but never appears to be. Because he works whenever possible with the same key technicians (nine films with Oswald Morris, eight with Russell Lloyd) he knows what to expect from them and they know what he wants. He never raises his voice or grows impatient. He works out his scenes and shots with the actors and technicians and is quiet, patient, reserved. Delays, difficulties and set-backs, and adverse conditions do frustrate him, but he never loses control of himself or the situations which are irksome. He smokes and thinks constantly and devises solutions, or accepts the inevitable with a fatalistic outlook. Most of his films concern men under stress and the normality of what society calls abnormal and, to a certain extent, filming on location is a constant reminder to him of these conditions. The fact that many of his characters come to realise the fallibility of certain beliefs and ambitions, and the running out of luck at crucial moments, is also a constant reminder to Huston that his own life is subject to such risks. Partly because of this he never over-reaches himself, makes no claims whatever to any special attributes, never takes his considerable talents for granted. While he believes strongly in himself and the worth of what he is doing, he is essentially modest when it comes to talking about what he does. He enjoys telling stories about how his films were made, of the writers and actors and

various characters whom he worked with or met, but just as he has
little time for analytical and symbolic interpretations and theories,
and no time for gossip and criticism of others, nor will he talk about
why and how he made a film from the point of view of style, essence,
morality, motivation or any of the popular critical concepts which so
many European film-makers hold forth about at great length in pre-
tentious interviews. He finds it extremely difficult, if not painful, to
make statements of any kind about his work when the answers, he
believes, must be obvious to anyone of intelligence from what is on
the screen.

Huston has never had to work his way up for recognition as a
director, and this has made his career more difficult. His first film,
The Maltese Falcon, was a masterpiece, praised by the critics and
enjoyed by the public. Since that time, Huston has more or less been
judged by it and expected to live up to the achievement with every
film since. He has done this and moved successfully into more complex forms, themes and techniques, without losing the instinctive
genius which made his first picture so memorable. Many other directors
would probably have reached a tenth film and faded into obscurity,
unable to live up to critical 'expectations.' Most would have made ten
before the critics paid them much attention. This gave the film-maker
the chance to become established, or at least to become entrenched
in the system. Huston survived instant fame, and if some critics said
in the years that followed, as they often did, that he was slipping or
reaching out too far, he paid no heed, and went on with what he
believed in. He makes no excuses for work which doesn't succeed, and
declines to discuss reasons for success, wondering only at the unexplain-
able magic which draws the public into some films and not to others,
when all too often the nature of the film and who is in it would seem
to have no bearing on its wide public acceptance.

The essence of his art and philosophy is in all his work, in some
films more successfully stated than in others, and his primary theme,
the stubbornness and resourcefulness of human nature set against
difficult patterns of survival in a largely masculine world, may well
be a symbolic representation of his own life. He is the unorthodox
Hollywood professional although he has had almost nothing to do with
Hollywood in the Hollywood sense since he left there to film *The
African Queen.* He is the world's leading internationalist in the cinema.
He keeps working, creating, devising, because when he stops life will
have much less meaning for him, just as life for most of the protagonists
(or heroes) in his films is a search for paradise which turns victory into
ashes once attained. For Huston, paradise is making films: finding the
story, writing it and translating it into screen terms, being carried

away on that tide of enthusiasm necessary to start production, working with actors, creating his own world for the camera, and bringing all to life with undiminished concentration, sensitivity and perception. Should he find himself unable to continue making films, for whatever reasons, his paradise will be lost. This comes one day to all men. What is important is that, to his considerable satisfaction and enjoyment, he has enriched our lives with his remarkable work. All his films are still in circulation, still available to be seen in cinemas or on television. Not many film-makers can claim to see their life's work still around them. That this is true of Huston is one more indication that he is the extraordinary man of the cinema whose greatness cannot be denied.